Creating Meaning in Museums

Creating Meaning in Museums

Conversational Strategies for Guided Tours

Claudia E. Cornett

ROWMAN & LITTLEFIELD
Lanham • Boulder • New York • London

Published by Rowman & Littlefield
An imprint of The Rowman & Littlefield Publishing Group, Inc.
4501 Forbes Boulevard, Suite 200, Lanham, Maryland 20706
www.rowman.com

86-90 Paul Street, London EC2A 4NE

British Library Cataloguing in Publication Information Available

Library of Congress Cataloging-in-Publication Data

Names: Cornett, Claudia E., author.
Title: Creating meaning in museums: conversational strategies for guided tours / Claudia E. Cornett.
Other titles: Conversational strategies for guided tours
Description: Lanham: Rowman & Littlefield, [2024] | Includes bibliographical references and index.
Identifiers: LCCN 2024020584 (print) | LCCN 2024020585 (ebook) | ISBN 9781538193679 (cloth) | ISBN 9781538193686 (paperback) | ISBN 9781538193693 (ebook)
Subjects: LCSH: Museum docents-Training of-Handbooks, manuals, etc. | Tour guides (Persons)-Training of-Handbooks, manuals, etc. | Museums-Educational aspects-Handbooks, manuals, etc. | Museum visitors-Services for-Handbooks, manuals, etc.
Classification: LCC AM7 .C67 2024 (print) | LCC AM7 (ebook) | DDC 069/.15-dc23/eng/20240620
LC record available at https://lccn.loc.gov/2024020584
LC ebook record available at https://lccn.loc.gov/2024020585

For all the docents, guides, and interpreters who inspire museum visitors to think differently and more broadly about themselves, others, and the world.

Special thanks to Charles Cornett for his excellent research, insightful feedback, and buoyant sense of humor.

Contents

Acknowledgments

Many thanks to institutions that gave permission to use images of artworks, objects, and artifacts:

1. Dayton Art Institute, for the *Tightrope Walker*, Everett Shinn (American, 1924).
2. Dayton History, 1905 Wright Flyer III.
3. Ohio History Connection, for *Calendar Mounts*, Fort Ancient.
4. National Gallery of Art, Washington, for *Hussars*, Henri de Toulouse Lautrec, 1878.
5. Metropolitan Museum of Art, for *Moulin Rouge: La Goule*, Henri de Toulouse Lautrec, 1891.
6. Metropolitan Museum of Art, for image of *Jane Avril*, Henri De Toulouse Lautrec, 1893.
7. Museum of Art, for *At the Circus: The Spanish Walk*, Henri De Toulouse Lautrec, 1899.
8. Dayton Art Institute and Alison Saar, for *Lost and Found*, Alison Saar Wood, American.
9. Stephen Wise, curator at the Parris Island Marine Museum, Beaufort, South Carolina, for photo, the *Verdier House*, Samuel Cooley, circa 1861.
10. The Art Institute of Chicago, for *Improvisation # 30*, Wassily Kandinsky, Creative Commons (CCO).
11. High Museum of Art, for image of *Lincoln in Frogmore,*

The following individuals generously shared invaluable expertise:

- Adera Causey, curator of education, Hunter Art Museum, Chattanooga.
- Molly Flasche, docent coordinator, Columbus Museum of Art.
- Marie Gibbs, docent coordinator, Y. W. Baily Museum, Beaufort, South Carolina.
- Terry Hanes, docent, Cincinnati Art Museum.
- Helen Rindsberg, docent, Cincinnati Art Museum.
- Linda Stock, docent, Cincinnati Art Museum.
- Charles Cornett, history interpreter, Wright Brothers National Museum, Dayton, Ohio.
- Pam Hall, education specialist, Fort Ancient Museum, Ohio.
- Sally Kurtz, registrar, Dayton Art Institute.
- Laurie Kind, images and rights, High Museum of Art.
- Michael Roediger, director and president, Dayton Art Institute.
- Shannon Peck-Bartle, PhD, director of education and community engagement, Dayton Art Institute.

Special thanks to these museum guide colleagues at the Dayton Art Institute:

- Janet Estep
- Norma Landis

- Rick Hoffman
- Janine Kinnison
- Violette-Anne Onfroy-Curley
- Wayne Witherell

Note: Names of all visitors, docents, guides, and interpreters in tour "vignettes" are pseudonyms, *except* when the person is identified by *first and last name.*

Table of Key Resources

By chapter number:

ADVICE FROM MUSEUM GUIDE

ADAPTING FOR DIFFERENCES

Preface

n. an introductory statement in a book.

I started thinking about this book during a training for museum guides. A property manager sat to my left, an ordained minister was to my right, and a college student sat across the table. These people with diverse backgrounds had unique life stories, but we'd all been "called" to the profession of museum guide.

Museums tap invaluable resources when they welcome volunteers and staff from different walks of life to train as guides, docents, and interpreters. And it's not unusual for aspiring docents to have a teaching background: The inclination to teach and guide spring from the same source. Aspiring guides and docents share impulses to 1) pursue interests in fields from history, art, and science, to archaeology, architecture, and botany, and 2) serve their communities by engaging visitors in conversations, using museum objects as portals to understanding.

As with all professions, guiding requires specialized knowledge and skills—knowledge about the museum collection, and skill in coaching guests to examine objects for universal meanings that can enlighten understanding about themselves and others.

LIVE GUIDES

In the context of guide work, skills refer to *pedagogy*—knowing why and how to *teach* others to discover and create meanings from artworks, objects, and artifacts. Excellent teachers aren't born, and neither are great guides. Those called to guide need to acquire a repertoire of "strategies" to do a job that features actively engaging diverse guests in stimulating conversations that spark *personal* connections—something QR links and audio tours can't do as well as people, at least not yet. What technology does do well is synthesize facts and dates. But mini-lectures offered by machines are no better than live point-and-tell tours that leave guests with "information overload" (Peak Performance Center).

Museums at the education forefront prepare incoming guides with research that recommends engagement-oriented practices that favor inquiry conversations. Training programs can last six months to a year, followed by ongoing study to update strategies and learn content related about the museum's collection and special exhibits. The chapters ahead focus on teaching strategies and general pedagogy that catalyzes "meaning-making" during conversational live guided tours. These "best practices" emphasize coaching participants to *see* beyond surface features like colors and shapes to discover meaningful connections. Relevant information is reserved for "as needed" situations, particularly to stimulate conversation.

The most effective way for guides to learn to conduct "inquiry-based" conversational tours is to "shadow" veteran guides. Nothing substitutes for observing docents who artfully apply "tricks of the trade" and challenge visitors to weave together meanings "greater" than the objects themselves. Neither this book nor any virtual learning can replace witnessing how live guides coax visitors to unravel invisible clues that prompt meaty interpretations and *aha!* moments, which is the ultimate goal. If this sounds like teasing out implied meanings in literature, it is!

WHAT TO EXPECT

You may be training as a guide, docent, or interpreter at a museum whose mission already embraces inquiry (investigating for meaning). If so, this book can amplify what museum educators teach and demonstrate. If not, this book provides planning basics, including tour structures and a plethora of guiding strategies and troubleshooting. To provide readers with experiences close to actual tours, I have scripted *vignettes* that feature guides using strategies *in context*. Each vignette attempts to capture how guides use distinct personal styles as they interact with different visitors in unique American museums.

Choosing to train as a guide is a first step. But those inclined to guide work already possess skills, abilities, and resources that can transfer to leading tours. Each guide's personality, life, and work background are invaluable in shaping one-of-a-kind visitor experiences. Ideally, you'll be able to learn strategies and simultaneously practice them with actual objects in your museum's unique collection. Merging content (collection information) with process (teaching practices) avoids practicing fork lessons without any food! Typically novice guides ease into multiple roles, under the guidance of a mentor, tagging along as an observer, then co-guiding, and finally going solo. In these roles, guides and docents are "front-facing" representatives of the museum—ambassadors charged with helping others feel exited to learn and at home in wondrous spaces.

As a live guide, you'll eventually be scaffolding experiences that stretch people's perspectives about themselves, others, and the world. But the immediate goal is to begin acquiring professional-level teaching skills to help visitors *make* meaning versus *take* meaning from museum objects.

CHAPTER ORGANIZATION

Each chapter offers a tool kit of purpose-built strategies. Leaning hard on a three-part tour structure, you'll learn to provoke curiosity with open questions and present prompts that facilitate conversations about *seen* and *unseen* meanings in objects. To initiate inquiry, you'll learn to direct participants to *collect* ideas using different senses, and coach kids, teens, and adults to "look to *see, think, feel*, and *know*." By the end of the book, you'll have dozens of strategies at your fingertips to help guests reach deeper understanding and experience higher levels of enjoyment.

To help envision how creating meaning happens, chapter vignettes feature guides empowering guests to use the Creative Inquiry Process (CIP). Instead of giving answers, you'll see how guides encourage individuals to think for themselves and construct original interpretations based on personal connections with artworks, objects, and artifacts. Throughout example tours, you'll witness exclamations like, "I never thought of that!" and "I wouldn't have noticed that by myself!" Such expressions arise when people collaborate to make sense and discover insight—which feels joyful.

RECURRING SECTIONS

To help imagine using CIP as the backbone of tours, each chapter offers strategies to facilitate creative thinking in the tour introduction, development, and closing/wrap-up. Repeating chapter sections include:

- *Learning Goals:* An overview of "big ideas."
- *What? Why? How?;* Information about the chapter focus.
- *Word Boxes:* Related terms connected to key concepts.
- *Vignettes:* Scenarios based on actual tours that encourage readers to take roles as guide and visitor.
- *Advice from Museum Guides:* Suggestions from veterans about what to do and not to do.

- *Adapting for Diverse Audiences:* Example adjustments for visitor needs, strengths, and interests.
- *Museum Guide Tool Kit:* Multimodal strategies and scaffolds to engage guests in conversation, and a full tool kit in an appendix.
- *Recap:* A look back at key points, big ideas, and themes.
- *Up Next!:* A teaser to pique curiosity about the next chapter.
- *References:* Sources and resources for continued study.

My professional journey has taken me from classroom teacher, to professor, to author, to joining America's corps of museum guides, docents, and interpreters. The process has been intellectually stimulating, personally rewarding, and great fun. I hope yours is, too!

Best regards,
Claudia E. Cornett
ccornett@wittenberg.edu

1

The Case for Live Guides

CREATING MEANING IN MUSEUMS

- *Creating:* (v.): process of making new and useful things and ideas.
- *Meaning:* (n.): the significance of something; linked, important ideas.
- *Museum:* (n.): 1) a place where people come to learn; 2) an institution that researches, collects, conserves, interprets, and exhibits art, artifacts, and other objects.

LEARNING GOALS

By the chapter end, you should be able to . . .

1. Explain benefits of "live" museum guides engaging visitors in inquiry conversations.
2. Describe strategies to encourage guests to investigate meanings in artworks, objects, and artifacts.
3. Offer synonyms for concepts associated with creative inquiry (e.g., "investigation").
4. After considering *Advice from Museum Guides*, set personal goals as a museum guide.
5. Use the section on *Adapting for Differences* to describe common ways to customize tours for guest needs and interests.
6. Choose strategies (how-tos) from the vignette to start a personal Museum Guide Tool Kit.
7. Pose your own questions about becoming a museum guide.

LIVE GUIDES: WHO? WHAT? WHY? HOW? WHERE? WHEN?

If you're reading this book, you're probably training to be or currently are a museum guide, docent, or interpreter. You may be an inexperienced or experienced volunteer, an undergraduate student in museum education, or a staff educator charged with teaching a class on guiding tours. Whatever the circumstances, I assume you're interested in the who, what, why, when, and *how* of leading meaningful tours that feature meaningful and enjoyable conversations. And while visitors have different views of what constitutes the ideal tour, most expect to exchange ideas and make connections during intriguing conversations (Hillemann, 2016).

In today's rapidly changing reality, museums are becoming gathering places where diverse people have casual conversations to broaden understanding. Architects are on the front lines of realizing ambitions of museums to become less like "temples" and more like "playgrounds," "gardens," and living rooms—community-centered spaces that are more like "tenacled octopuses" than

1

"peacocks"—and more about creating community and connecting to nature than preserving and protecting the collection (Art Basel, 2023). Such settings call for "live" guides who can give life to museum objects by the facilitation of meaningful conversations, a skill that audio tours, pioneered in 1952 (Museum Mate), never had, and that our cornucopia of current technology—AR (augmented reality), VR, and QR codes—still struggles to achieve. And while King Tut can get guests in the door, it takes living, breathing guides to mediate understanding in ways that elude the "zoom in and zoom out" features of the Google Art and Culture Project's impressive immersive exhibits.

Visitors need live guides in the same way people want and need live theater and good conversation with live friends. And museums need feet-on-the-ground guides to sustain themselves. Skilled docents are key museum ambassadors with teaching acumen, storytelling skills, wayfaring knowledge, and the capacity to show and engender empathy that transforms how visitors think and feel about themselves, others, and the world—including the world of museums. It's understandable why guides have long been "chosen companionship in beholding" (Gilman, 1918, p. 68).

Meaningful Conversations

To describe options for tours that feature meaning-oriented conversation, it helps to first consider the unique context of spaces. Try to recall your first museum visit. I did and didn't remember much: I was five at most. I do remember being awed by grand rooms filled with huge artworks—some with naked people and strange places I couldn't imagine existed. In retrospect, my reaction was sensory—an emotional response more about place than individual objects, which were so many I didn't know where to look first.

Then, in junior high, my class toured a local landmark. A woman in high heels, identifying herself as a "docent," walked us around a house museum, pointing at ornate woodwork and doors and rolling off phrases like "dentil molding" and "rim-lock." I'd looked forward to seeing the house. But I realized we hadn't been brought there to look; we'd been brought there to hear her talk. And I had no clue why.

It's natural to want to talk about things that matter, but a degree in art history or architecture isn't necessary to express thoughts and feelings about what you're seeing (Steigelman, 2014). Conversations about museum objects can't single-handedly change the world, but museums can provide space for individuals to comfortably talk about ideas in ways that aren't possible elsewhere (Murawski, 2016). Guides begin by creating comfort and then stoking curiosity to investigate what's seen, which engages creative inquiry. If conversation is approached with genuine openness, groups bring up surprising new points, and listeners have opportunities to expand worldviews, The adage that recommends that we listen more often than talk applies.

WORD BOX 1.1

These terms are near synonyms.

- *Docent*: teacher.
- *Guide*: coach.
- *Interpreters*: explainers.

Museum Types and Purposes

The word *museum,* often connotates world-class institutions like the Smithsonian or the National Gallery of Art in Washington, D.C. But the globe is home to more than one hundred thousand museums, and over thirty-five thousand are in the United States (Institute of Museum and Library Services, 2014). It's impossible to list all varieties—from the International Towing and Recovery Museum

(Chattanooga) to New York's Whitney Museum of American Art. As for size and emphases, American museums have small and enormous collections that focus on everything from art, science, and natural history to human history and historic houses.

Museums are repositories of objects with special meanings. But museums can also . . .

- Acting as "sanctuaries" for the mind, body, and spirit.
- "Ignite imagination, curiosity, and creativity."
- "Connect us to our origins, each other, and all that is timeless."
- "Impart knowledge that . . . unlocks the mysteries of life."
- Be beacons of "hope and resilience" (American Alliance of Museums, 2024).

Live Guides: Mission and Goals

In-person guided tours reflect a museum's unique mission (goals and purposes), that usually includes variations on promoting "education" (learning) and "enjoyment or pleasure" (Ng, Ware, & Greenberg, 2017). Every guide, docent, or interpreter needs to understand the mission and grasp how tour goals fit into the big picture. For example, the mission of Cleveland's Rock & Roll Hall of Fame (RRHOF) is to "engage, teach, and inspire through the power of rock and roll" (Hanely, Nebel, & Smith, 2021, p. 73). Museum educators translated this mission into a "pedagogical philosophy" (teaching beliefs) encapsulated in "Sound-Context-Meaning" (p. 73). In practice, visitors first examine (listen closely) to musical sounds, then consider cultural and historical context, and eventually "create meaning" from coached interactions with music. This process mirrors creative inquiry: *collect* ideas (listen or look for elements like timbre, rhythm, harmony, and melody); *connect* information (e.g., context like era, geography, or social and political movements); and *conclude*—decide what the work is about and why it matters. Using creative inquiry, RRHOF audiences are coached to discover personal interpretations about songs like "The Star-Spangled Banner"—performed by Jimi Hendrix at Woodstock (1969), when bombs were literally "bursting in air in Vietnam" (p. 79).

Experiences of RRHOF educators led them to conclude that musical "meaning" depends on interpreting unique "sounds used to perform them, the cultural lens through which they are heard, and the listener's experience." In other words, like for all tours, the key is visitor engagement in understanding of the art itself (p. 76). Relationships among parts and pieces count: Understanding is synthesized from different kinds of cognitive and emotional engagement, which relies heavily on connecting past to present. Visitors are interested in "back then," but they also want to know what objects have to do with "me" and "now." To facilitate such connections docents guide guests to examine details—spotlighting and isolating images and sounds and encouraging identification of emotions and relationships. In the RRHOF example, the focus was on voices and sounds from intense guitars, the ticking of a drummer's hi-hat, followed by dramatic silence (p. 78).

Museum educators turn lofty goals like "engage" and "inspire" into tour outcomes in hopes that visitors:

1. experience insight (understanding) and pleasure from conversations about art, music, or other objects, i.e., learn and enjoy.
2. become empowered to create *personal* meaning using evidence collected from objects, i.e., understand and feel pleasure.
3. are motivated to return for repeat experiences with interesting investigations that result in shared interpretations of museum objects, i.e., education and enjoyment.

Guides and docents teach to these outcomes, aiming for guests to feel "satisfied" and "inspired" to learn more—dispositions key for museum survival.

The Holy Grail of Learning

Museum guides are unique teachers with access to visual aids that are prized objects. Unraveling meanings in such unusual objects requires knowledge (content/information) and creative inquiry skills. By definition, guiding is a "profession" that focuses on using "best practices" to engage people in constructing personal meaning or *understanding*. Understanding transcends facts and dates (Schep and Kintz, 2017), and there is no one way to accomplish this goal. There are recommended best practices that include coaching guests in the discovery of meaningful connections between objects and themselves, objects and other objects, and objects and other people and the world. Forging connections is vital to creative inquiry because it propels meaning-making forward to forming conclusions (understandings).

Understanding

Understanding is a cognitive state that goes beyond calling up memories of experiences or facts. Understanding is the product of coordinating distinct kinds of thinking to make sense—an instinctual process used by ordinary people. But guides need self-awareness of how making sense works to help visitors puzzle out museum objects or any art form (e.g., books, films). Thinking about personal, innate creative thinking opens up avenues to *purposefully* mobilize creative processes as well. As Māori teacher Sylvia Aston-Warner explained, "Before teaching others, we must teach ourselves" (1963).

WORD BOX 1.2

These synonyms are used interchangeably to refer to creating meaning.

- *Understand*: learn, comprehend, interpret, conclude, make sense.
- *Understandings*: conclusions, meanings, interpretations, big ideas, truths, themes,
- insights, discoveries, *ahas*.
- *Challenge*: problem, question, curiosity, puzzlement.
- *Inquire*: investigate, interpret, figure out, question.

TOUR VIGNETTES: WHO? WHAT? WHY? *HOW?*

The maxim, "Example is not the main thing; it's the only thing" (attributed to Albert Sweitzer), refers to understanding. As a teacher and writer, I take this pithy advice seriously. Although nothing beats observing real-life tours, each chapter in this book features a "vignette" (tour excerpt) with dialogue meant to give you a sense of "being there." As you read these vignettes, I suggest you alternatively take the viewpoint of guest and guide to gain insight into how messy, magical thinking creates sense.

This chapter's vignette features a professional volunteer guide (Nick) who's comfortable coaching visitors to coordinate thinking in the Creative Inquiry Process (CIP). He makes it seem easy, but his strategies were thoughtfully selected and are flexibly used to support visitors as they *collect* information, *connect* ideas, and derive *conclusions* (meanings or understandings).

The vignette captures about fifteen minutes of a conversational, hour-long tour with three stops. After a meet-and-greet to *welcome* visitors, Nick gives a short introduction to *orient* guests to the museum. He then coaches participants to use CIP, first during a brief encounter with a stair railing, followed by "puzzling out" an artwork.

While Nick's interactions are planned, the results are not. The goal is for guests to experience unique discoveries that lead to unpredictable meanings he could not imagine: one-of-a-kind insights about core meanings in life. This sounds heady, but it's also fun. Whatever the label, insight feels like a surprise, and it is frequently accompanied by a sense of elation that builds to a laugh-out-loud moment called the "aha! to ha-ha" response (Koestler, 1964).

After the vignette, reflect on *what* Nick did and *why*, and *how* visitors responded. (See Quick Reference on CIP.)

Quick Reference 1.3: *Creative Inquiry Process (CIP)*

The following Cs summarize thinking in the Creative Inquiry Process. Museum guides flexibly and progressively use these strategies to engage guests by:

- *Creating Context*: setting a relaxed climate.
- *Challenging* visitors to make sense.
- Coaching guests to *collect* and *connect* ideas and *conclude* what objects are about.
- Taking time to *critique* to make better.
- Offering options for communicating meanings.

Observation Cues: Tour Vignette

Imagine a group in a museum rotunda. Your challenge is to join the group, but also to stand apart and observe Nick's strategies. The following questions are meant to alert you to *how* to help guests make sense of artwork.

1. How does Nick create a comfortable context? What else might he have done?
2. What challenges does he pose to the group, and how?
3. How does he encourage conversation?
4. What is similar about his questions?
5. How does he make the tour enjoyable?
6. What events or moments show that participants are "making sense"?
7. When and why does Nick provide art and artist information (content)?

Note: Example strategies are italicized. See Museum Guide Tool Kit (Appendix A) for more.

Vignette: Creative Inquiry into Art

"Welcome! I'm Nick, your guide!" he says, scanning *name tags*. "Any first-timers today?" Spotting a hand, he makes eye contact. "*What brings you here?*"

"I'm George, here visiting family. We live on Hilton Head Island, South Carolina."

"Beaches, sunshine, and live oaks, right?"

"Nature's art off my porch."

"Lucky you!" a local responds, eliciting chuckles.

"Don't despair! We're about to see artwork that may be competition for George's porch," Nick suggests. "Sunshine definitely fits with the tour theme about how and why artists use light and dark palettes. Before going to the first gallery, what *particular interests and questions do you have?*"

"We came for the Monet," Amber says.

Nick smiles. "That's the finale. You'll see it, and hopefully with new eyes."

"New eyes?" Rachel asks.

"Yes! This is a *conversational tour*, not me talking at you. Feel free to point out discoveries, especially *personal connections*, which helps everybody, including me, see new things."

George grins. "So, you're making us do your work?"

"Yep! But I'll share 'insider secrets' about where and how to find clues, along with *relevant art and artist info.* If you ask questions, I'll talk more." He gestures toward a rack. "The tour's an hour long. You're welcome to carry *folding stools* and sit while we talk." As several grab stools, he says, "I positioned some extras upstairs. On our way, I'll point out restrooms. Anyone prefer the elevator?" With no takers, Nick ambles toward marble steps and points to an unusual railing. "*Take a purposeful look at this ironwork. There's something hidden.*"

"Hidden?" Jamie asks.

"There's more to most art than meets the eye."

"Those dots could be eyes!" Carlo says.

"Looks like the head of a snake," Rachel suggests.

"*What makes you say that?*" Nick asks. "*Look again.*"

People move closer.

"Diamond-shaped head, curved tail."

"I like it! Seems like the ironmonger had an artist's heart," Amber concludes.

Nick nods. "There're more artist's hearts ahead! And we'll be doing more *purposeful looking to see and find visible and invisible ideas.*" The group follows him upstairs into an airy gallery. "Take a few minutes to *survey* the room. Pretend you're a detective scanning for evidence. But please stay an arm's length from the art." After demonstrating, he checks his watch and waits as people roam. After three minutes, he asks, "*What stands out?*"

People gather.

"Different-sized paintings."

"Nothing abstract."

"Not totally representational, either. Some have 'suggestive' images, and bright areas," Rachel says.

"*What are you seeing that makes you say 'suggestive* and bright'?" Nick asks.

"Blurred parts and ambiguous shapes. AND lots of stark white and some yellow."

"Good spy. Light relates to the tour theme, so let's start there." Nick steps over, subtly blocking the *wall label.* He waits for guests to sit. "Here's a *challenge:* Do what you did downstairs—*look purposefully.* Start at the top and let your eyes rove around to discover *what's interesting, curious, and important.* Let's take three minutes." (View artwork: https://www.daytonartinstitute.org/exhibits/everett-shinn-tightrope-walker/.)

Quiet observation is punctuated with whispering and pointing.

"So, *what's grabbing attention?*"

"I spy a ghost on a tightrope!" George announces.

"Keep going. *What did the artist do that makes you think* there's a ghost?"

"Painted the figure translucent white," Jay says.

"It's not ALL white," Amber points out.

"Look again," Nick coaches. "*What more do you see?*"

Jay leans in. "Sprinkles of orange and blue."

"*How do the sprinkles make you feel?*"

"Uncomfortable. He looks half there."

"He's on the edge of falling and becoming a ghost," a woman points out.

"*Where do you see 'edge of falling'?*"

"His head is down, and his right toe barely touches that tiny white line. His arms are out like he's struggling to balance."

"Maybe he's concentrating," a teenager suggests.

"These are important details, and *your interpretations make sense. What about other shapes, lines, and colors?*"

Figure 1.1 The Tightrope Walker. Everett Shinn (American 1876–1953), Tightrope Walker, 1924, Oil on Canvas, 231/2x18 inches (59.7x 45.7cm), Dayton Art Institute, Museum Purchase with funds provided by the James F. Dicke Family and the E. Jeanette Myers Fund, 1998.

"The rope should bend more under his left leg, where he'd be putting his weight," the teenager adds. "Oh, I see red exit signs."

"I didn't see that red before," someone chimes in.

A man points. "That chandelier is like a beckoning light."

The teen balances on one foot. "He's about to be lifted into a sparkling afterlife or carried out through one of those exits!"

Nick smiles, watching the girl pretend. "You're right in there. *These are new perspectives for me! We could spend an hour on this painting, but before we move on, I'll share information that might give you some angles on thinking.*" He steps aside and reads "*tombstone information*" on the label (aka "didactic").

Everett Shinn (1876–1953)

American

TIGHTROPE WALKER, 1924

Oil on canvas

23½ x 18 inches

Nick holds up a screenshot. "Shinn was born in New Jersey, and here's a *fun fact*—as a kid, he loved the circus and tried tightrope walking. Eventually, he joined a twentieth-century group of urban realists, called 'Ashcan Artists,' committed to Robert Henri's credo 'art for life's sake'—versus 'art for art's sake.' They used dark palettes to capture slum conditions and harsh truths about life's seamy side—like men rooting in ashcans."

"These artists were muckrakers!" George says.

"*Key historical connection,*" Nick responds. "Shinn's Ashcan works include gray end-of-day scenes of dockworkers and a portrait of an exhausted laundress. He eventually left the group to design film sets for the likes of Samuel Goldwyn (aka Goldfish), and he painted murals in private homes and at New York's Plaza Hotel."

"This audience doesn't look like down-on-the-heel folks. They seem to be enjoying themselves," Amber says.

"This is a 1924 painting, *after* he broke with his Ashcan colleagues," Nick notes.

"An entertainment venue is part of 'real life,' recommended by Henri," Rachel says.

"It's not all light and fun," George says. "They're sitting in the dark, and there are ominous shadows. This looks dangerous."

A man who hasn't spoken raises his hand. "In 1924, many folks walked a tightrope just to survive, like some do today,"

"*What in the art made you think about that?*"

"The whiteness of the figure against the blackness of the theater suggests life's background darkness," he says. "And the figure balances on an insubstantial line that separates him from probable death. White faces in the audience look drained."

Nick wriggles. "A frisson just crossed my shoulders. *You seem to be feeling what they feel.*"

"I'm learning more than if you just told us stuff," the teenager says. "But why is there a tightrope walker in a theater?"

"Remember Shinn loved the circus and painted many circus scenes. Two of his paintings are among America's greatest theater paintings. One in the London Hippodrome looks similar to this. If you have time, I'll pull it up online after the tour, and you can do more 'purposeful looking.'"

The teen nods. "I'm in!"

"Us, too," George says.

"*So, what are your thoughts about taking time for looking?*"

"It helped me concentrate and find interesting details. Hearing everyone else's ideas helped," George adds. "Opened my ears and eyes."

"It was fun!" Judith announces.

"So far, so good. Let's continue. I have more tricks up my sleeve."

Debrief: Creative Inquiry Tour

This book focuses on guiding visitors to participate in collaborative conversation to make sense. Nick's tour offers a glimpse of how that looks, sounds, and feels. To further kick-start understanding the Creative Inquiry Process (CIP), jot down responses to these questions and talk with colleagues.

1. Which of Nick's strategies can you imagine using? Why?
2. When and what did he repeat? Why?
3. What did he do that made sense? How so?
4. When and how did Nick weave in information? Why?
5. What are you interested in learning more about after reading this vignette?

To collect more ideas about what Nick did and why, return to *Observation Cues* before the vignette. See the Tour Plan in Appendix B2 to compare it with what he actually did.

CREATING INQUIRY FOR UNDERSTANDING AND ENJOYMENT: *WHO, WHAT, WHY, AND HOW?*

While some museums refer to guides as "interpreters," others use "docents" (French for "teachers"). Labels make a difference. Museums want to distinguish themselves from schools, and there are obvious differences like architecture, and stark differences in purposes. Museums are charged with protecting and conserving special objects, selected and cared for by curators. Working alongside museum educators, curators design exhibits for visitors to learn from and enjoy. But there are no tests.

Nick's museum chose to use the term *guides*, reasoning that *docent* connotates lectures. *Guide* describes Nick's job: to lead or coach guests to collaborate on looking at and talking about objects and discovering unique connections to create understanding. The group made the most of "shared inquiry." Not only did conversational interactions provoke deeper thinking, their combined questioning and sustained looking sparked meaningful connections that triggered enjoyment, despite the serious nature of the art. Placing the creative process at the center of conversation left visitors hungry for more—something that brings visitors back. In the words of museum guide Kate Baird, "museums have an ever more important role to play in making sure we remember what it feels like to have a really good conversation" (2017).

Underpinnings of Understanding

The statement, "I don't like abstract art," can be a way of saying something that's uncomfortable to admit—that the viewer doesn't see meaning in this type of art. In other words, the viewer doesn't *understand* why this art doesn't look like a landscape or bowl of fruit. Of course, it's possible to understand something and still dislike it, but it's difficult to like what you don't understand. Since museums want diverse audiences to enjoy themselves (to like coming), it follows that guides need to help guests *understand*.

Understanding depends on openness to differing views. In the context of museums, understanding requires motivation to learn why and how objects take different forms, and how objects are considered important, even though some people don't like their looks. The work of coaching guests, with varied needs and interests, to making sense of (understanding) museum objects is important because it can actually physically change minds. Since changing minds is hard, guides often start with easy prompts. For example, participants are coached to look at familiar details like colors and shapes, which serve as entry points for examining "strange" images. Focusing on the familiar creates psychological comfort, making any art more accessible and setting the stage for thinking that can discomfit: considering alternative viewpoints.

Since the overarching goals of tours are facilitating learning (understanding) and enjoyment, guides need a repertoire of strategies to *make the unfamiliar familiar*. More time spent looking or listening (e.g., music tours) lays the foundation for *seeing* differently, making it possible for objects initially dismissed to feel more approachable and palatable.

People are drawn to interesting places that feel relaxed and comfortable, like museum galleries. But museum pieces are often invested with non-literal, sometimes ambiguous or disconcerting themes like death, violence, and poverty. Even experts don't know all possible interpretations of a work, but informed live guides can set the tone and prompt conversations that stimulate personal construction of meaning, which can feel like shade is lifted from your eyes. And even the latest AI can't deliver that—yet.

MUSEUM GUIDE TOOL KIT

Guide tool kits can be both literal and metaphoric bags of resources used for specific purposes. This book offers a tool kit of purposeful strategies and practices (knowledge and skills) meant to create *transformative* tours. Transformative tours change how guests think and feel about art and objects, which dovetails with key tour outcomes: empowering guests to . . .

1. *create personal meaning* (interpretations) from artworks and objects, and
2. *enjoy* a learning experience featuring insightful conversation.

The following chapters progressively address *how* to achieve these goals by outlining ways to plan meaningful tours that include flexible-use strategy tool kits.

Putting sense-making and pleasure at the forefront of guide work contrasts with traditional tours, which rely on giving information. Instead of casting visitors as passive listeners, each chapter explains how to use thinking in Creative Inquiry Process (CIP) to actively engage guests in making sense of objects. CIP is brought to life by strategies that coordinate intellectual, emotional, physical, and social engagement. Visitors assume investigative roles similar to medical professionals using symptoms to work out a diagnosis, only the goal is working out conclusions from clues in objects. CIP is like solving a jigsaw puzzle, only meanings in museum objects can be assembled in myriad ways.

All guides and docents have a "strategy repertoire"—a set of tools. But all guides need explicit, ongoing training about *why* and *how* to use tools to engage visitors in meaningful conversations. Without initial and continued education, it's difficult for guides to stay at the top of their game—to maintain motivation and focus to use evolving best practices that target understanding and enjoyment. Getting an "information dump" is a common visitor complaint. Across the spectrum of education, pedagogy has moved on to a focus on self-motivating approaches that support personal understanding (learning) and discovery. Lectures come up wanting to reach twenty-first century goals. That said, activity-oriented learning can also veer too much toward entertainment, providing temporary enjoyment but failing to forge thoughtful engagement. These are lost opportunities to grow guest confidence and independence with meaning-making that increases a sense of well-being.

Purposes and Guidelines

Any guide tool kit should be tied to museum goals and tour purposes, meaning it contains strategies that align with the mission. Without alignment, the vehicle (guided tours) won't get visitors to the destination (museum goals).

Assembling an effective tool kit usually begins with a modest document (handbook) supplied by museum educators, which is amplified by note taking during ongoing training. Guides and docents continue to grow their tool kits by observing tours, studying books, and watching videos, including those at museum sites and on YouTube. Most tools are honed with practice into habits or routines used during tour *introduction*, *development*, and *closing* (wrap-up). For tool kits to remain up-to-date, periodic review is needed to cull or adapt less-effective strategies and add more effective ones. In addition, labels (words) change as perspectives and values evolve around concepts like inclusivity, diversity, equity, and accessibility.

By the end of the book, you should have a trove of strategies that overtime can become "habits." To start a personal tool kit, return to Nick's tour and choose strategies he used to engage his audience with art and each other. To help organize strategies, use tour phases: introduction, development, and closing (or wrap-up). Note that Nick's vignette was one stop in a longer tour. At each stop, visitors formed conclusions about different artworks, which developed the theme "From Seen to Unseen: Life's Light and Dark." Italicized strategies in the vignette identify *some* strategies used to reach the goals for guests to experience insight (understanding) and joy from discovery.

See the Museum Guide Tool Kit in Appendix A for strategy resources.

ADVICE FROM MUSEUM GUIDES

> *"If you're excited, they'll be excited."* —Terry Hanes, docent, Cincinnati Art Museum

When asked to name best advice for new guides and docents, seasoned museum guides are quick to say, "Talk to other guides or docents about what works and doesn't work, and observe tours." Keep this in mind as you consider tips below and in subsequent chapters. Rate how important you think each recommendation is using a scale of 1=low importance *to* 5=high importance.

Guides in training should . . . Circle ideas you'd like to try first:

1. ___Check out the museum's mission to understand goal contexts for tours.
2. ___Get as much on-the-job training (OJT) as possible.
3. ___Shadow/audio-tape guides who engage visitors in conversational tours.
4. ___Find a mentor who is a practicing guide, someone flexible and good at asking open-ended questions.
5. ___Ask about museum resources and development opportunities, such as password-protected resources, mentors, docent council, team leaders, guide libraries, and training videos.
6. ___Find out if there's a blog where guides share information and ask questions.
7. ___Ask about regular meetups to share tips, ask questions, and be social.
    Before and during observations of tours:
8. ___Get to know the museum layout. Become familiar with using the map as a direction aid.
9. ___Ask about strategies guides use to help visitors reach goals that align with the museum's mission.
10. ___Ask for examples of Tour Plans. Note how tours are organized (e.g., introduction, development, closing) and strategies used in each tour phase.
11. ___During observations, notice how guides remind themselves about a few pertinent facts (e.g., note card) or use artist quotes to develop the tour theme.
12. ___Do an internet search for advice from America's corps of museum guides, docents, and interpreters. Start with the Smithsonian: https://museumonmainstreet.org/sites/default/files/tips%20for%20museum%20docents%20and%20tour%20guides.pdf.

ADAPTING FOR DIFFERENCES: *TOUR PHASES*

> *"Work with people where they are."* —Adera Causey, Curator of Education, Hunter Art Museum, Chattanooga, Tennessee

Visitors come in all colors, sizes, ages, and stages. They arrive with diverse backgrounds and beliefs, as well as different interests, needs, and expectations. We can't customize tours to meet every person's individual needs and wants. But we can assess (gather information) about these areas.

The following strategies are categorized into tour parts: introduction (beginning) and development (middle). Future chapters will have ideas for ending or wrapping up the tour.

Check off strategies that Nick used to adapt for his diverse group. Connect these ideas and strategies with recommended actions and attitudes in *Advice from Museum Guides.*

Tour Beginning: Introduction

1. Offer name tags to facilitate conversation.
2. Know the museum's full name, address, phone number, and hours of operation.
3. Use maps to orient and give guests a sense of control.
4. Assess needs and interests by observing and asking, "What should I know about you before we begin?" (e.g., non-English speakers? Special interests? Mobility challenges?)

5. Be ready to give directions to restrooms, water fountains, and seating areas.
6. Be sensitive to physical needs. Offer folding stools, mention rest areas, and rest rooms, and provide opportunities to sit.
7. Explain the conversational nature of the tour and offer options to listen and speak freely.
8. Show interest in what visitors hope to see.
9. Invite questions, repeatedly.

During the Tour: Development

1. Resist the temptation to "tell it all." Drip-feed small amounts of information that support meaningful conversation.
2. Don't feel like you have to fit everything in. Edit to essentials.
3. Monitor the group for nonverbal signs of interest, discomfort, and other unspoken needs.
4. Ask "why"? Reasons behind answers can be more interesting than the answers themselves.
5. Ask more than you tell. *Example*: "What do you see that catches your eye?"
6. Follow visitor interests when possible.
7. Show respect by listening actively (nod, paraphrase).
8. If someone hangs back, make pleasant eye contact.
9. Circulate and rotate to stand near different guests.
10. Ask for new and "different" ideas. Celebrate unique points of view. *Example*: "I've never thought of that."
11. Have a few visual aids: cards with key terms (e.g., art elements, five senses), related "touchable" items, and the artist's photo.
12. Involve chaperones in keeping groups together and engaging with tasks.
13. Offer signals to get attention, such as the ASL sign for question (bent index finger knuckle). See Quick Reference in chapter 10.

To bring these adaptations to life, get a partner, discuss what-if situations, and role-play "guide or visitor" to practice adjusting for visitor needs, strengths, and interests. *Example*: What if a visitor is reluctant to share ideas? Or hangs back? Or appears to have difficulty hearing?

RECAP

Until the 1950s, most museum tours featured docents presenting information to groups who were expected to listen, remember, and regurgitate facts (Grinder and McCoy, 1985). Today best guide practices have evolved to create participatory tours that encourage inquiry-based conversations that support meaning-making about museum objects.

This chapter focused on the overarching tour goals of helping visitors create meaning (understanding) and experience enjoyment during casual conversations. The Creative Inquiry Process (CIP) was introduced to reach these goals. The metaphor of "tool kit" was used to describe a repertoire of strategies that promote creative inquiry to make sense. The by-products of creating meaning—pleasure and delight, and sometimes awe—were emphasized as extensions of enjoyment.

In a tour vignette, Nick demonstrated *how* to coach visitors to make sense. All chapter vignettes are written to help visualize how guides engage CIP thinking in different museum contexts. For example, after creating an inviting *context* for sharing viewpoints, Nick posed tour goals as enjoyable *challenges* to uncover visible and invisible meanings. During a planned stop, he then used strategies to coax visitors to *collect* information, suggesting they look deeply and differently to see more. Once ideas were *collected*, he guided participants to *connect* details and probed for "unseen" relationships. Visitor connections set up experimentation with *conclusions* (meanings, themes, and interpretations).

Recuring features in subsequent chapters were introduced:

- *Word Boxes,*
- *Advice from Museum Guides,*
- *Museum Guide Tool Kit,* and
- *Adapting for Differences.*

To self-check your understanding, return to *Learning Goals* at the chapter start, and/or create your own meanings by writing down "takeaways" and niggling questions to discuss with others. You may also email me at ccornett@wittenberg.edu.

UP NEXT!

Chapter 2 delves into phases of the Creative Inquiry Process (CIP). Expect to join Charles's tour and witness how he owns CIP during conversations with middle schoolers.

RESOURCES AND VIDEOS

- National Gallery of Art: https://www.edx.org/learn/critical-thinking-skills/the-smithsonian -institution-teaching-critical-thinking-through-art-with-the-national-gallery-of-art. Videos feature educators explaining how to engage visitors in creating meaning. *Example*: "Creating Artful Thinkers: See/Think/Wonder."
- Art21: https://art21.org: Art21 produces documentary films, resources, and public programs, such as the PBS-broadcast series, *Art in the Twenty-First Century*. Art21's film library is free to stream online.

REFERENCES

American Alliance of Museums. (2024). https://annualmeeting.aam-us.org/callforproposals/.

Ashton-Warner, Sylvia. (1963). *Teacher*. New York: Simon and Schuster.

Bosker, Bianca. (2024, January 29). What being a museum guard taught me about looking at art. *Wall Street Journal*.

Grinder, Alison, and Sue McCoy. (1985). *The good guide: A sourcebook for interpreters, docents and tour guides*. Ironwood Publishing, Scottsdale, AZ.

Hanley, Jason, Deanna Nebel, and Smith, Mandy. (2021). A pedagogical philosophy as a guiding light for museum education departments, in *Creating meaningful museum experiences for K–12 audiences: How to connect with teachers and engage students*, edited by Tara Young. Lanham, MD: Rowman & Littlefield.

Institute of Museum and Library Services. (2014). Institute of Museum and Library Services. *Government Doubles Official Estimate: There Are 35,000 Active Museums in the U.S.* https://www.imls.gov/news/government-doubles-official-estimate-there-are-35000-active-museums-us.

Gilman, Benjamin. (1918). *Museum ideals of purpose and method*. Cambridge, MA: Riverside Press.

Koestler, Arthur. (1964). *The act of creation.* New York: Penguin Books Museum Mate. *Beginning of the History of Audioguides in Museums.* https://www.museummate.com/en/audioguidehistory/#:~:text=In%20twentiethis%20area%2C%20twentiethe%20Stedlijk,Petrie%20and%20Power%2C%202011).

Ng, Wendy, et al. (2017). Activating diversity and inclusion: A blueprint for Museum: Educators as allies and change makers, *Journal of Museum Education*, Vol. 42, no. 2, 142–54. http://dx.doi.org/10.1080/10598650.2017.1306664.

Schep, Mark, and Pauline Kintz, eds. (2017). *Guiding as a profession: The museum guide in art and history museum*. https://www.lkca.nl/wp-content/uploads/2020/02/guiding-is-a-profession.pdf.

Smithsonian Museum of Art. https://americanart.si.edu/artist/everett-shinn-4430).

2

The Backbone of Tours

CREATIVE INQUIRY PROCESS (CIP)

- *Inquiry* (n., v.): an investigative process that seeks information, solutions, answers, or truth.
- *Creative* (adj.): imaginative thinking that produces new, novel, and useful ideas or works.
- *Tour* (v., n., or adj.): 1) travel to multiple places, often led by a guide; 2) a type of guide.

LEARNING GOALS

By the chapter end, you should be able to . . .

1. Paraphrase the goal of creative inquiry using synonyms for "creating meaning."
2. Explain why and how creative inquiry elevates conversation.
3. Outline the thinking focus of each phase of the Creative Inquiry Process (CIP).
4. Describe what happens in the tour introduction, development, and closing/wrap-up.
5. Give examples of strategies (tools) and scaffolds (supports) that boost CIP thinking.
6. Using the section on *Adapting for Differences*, give examples of ways to adjust tours for visitor needs, strengths, and interests.
7. Create a poem or song to solidify understanding of CIP. See examples in chapter 9.

CREATIVE INQUIRY PROCESS (CIP): WHAT? WHY? HOW?

> *"I cannot teach anybody anything. I can only make them think."* —Socrates

Think about Thinking

Consider these "what-if" situations.

1. You're at an important business lunch, and you spill tomato sauce down your white shirt. *What are your options?*
2. You're on a long trip, and a tire on your vehicle starts making a loud, thumping noise. *What would you do first, second, third?*

These problems present different challenges. The level of confidence you have in generating alternative solutions determines what you do. If you think there's one good choice, you'll behave differently than if you believe there are many options. Expectations matter. People who think there are myriad solutions are more likely to come up with multiple possibilities. Those who lack self-confidence or know-how about devising alternatives can feel helpless, say "it's out of my hands," freeze, turn to someone else, or give up.

Guides need to be confident about how to mobilize and coordinate creative-thinking processes to empower guests to create meanings from museum objects. This chapter is a primer on what, why, and how to use creative inquiry to solve the meaning-making problem.

CIP: What? Why? How?

Creative Inquiry Process (CIP) summarizes a common protocol that goes by many names, which isn't surprising since creative process was discovered and is now used by people in different fields, from science to writing. The scientific method, artistic thinking, mathematical problem-solving, the writing process, and criminal investigation are all versions of using Creative Inquiry Process to solve problems (Cornett, 2015). The fact that a similar process is used across many disciplines testifies to CIP's usefulness. Museum educators took notice. Guides at the Columbus Museum of Art (CMA) started coaching visitors to use "inquiry" over twenty-five years ago. Called ODIP, visitors first observe, then describe, interpret, and prove (Flasche, 2023). This iteration of creative inquiry involves "long looking" to examine artworks and objects for clues to meanings that creators may or may not have intended (Center for Creativity in the Columbus Museum of Art). Whatever the label, all creative inquiry requires *collecting* evidence. See Word Box.

WORD BOX 2.1

These are CIP related words.

- *Create Context*: setting or environment.
- *Challenge*: question, problem, puzzle.
- *Collect*: gather, observe, search.
- *Connect*: relate, group, sort, categorize.
- *Conclude*: understand, interpret, make sense, appreciate.
- *Critique*: analyze, evaluate, judge, revise, and improve.
- *Communicate*: listen/read, speak/write; make/perform using art, music, drama, dance.
- *Examine*: look purposefully to *see*.

CIP Benefits

Effective use of CIP depends on understanding that . . .

- everyone is creative,
- each person possesses innate creative capacities to different degrees, and
- creativity takes different forms.

Humanity's innate, creative predispositions equip people with the intellectual power to search for and discover a panoply of new solutions and meanings. In museum contexts, this translates into coaching guests to use CIP thinking to actively *make* rather than passively *take* sense. Think of the former as "deep" thinking and the latter as "surface," or literal, thinking. It's the difference between pointing out *seen* shapes in a painting and determining *unseen* meanings suggested by shapes (deep thinking).

When embedded in collaborative conversations, CIP can change how participants think and feel about the "effects" of museum objects. As participants *make* unique personal connections, confidence grows, empathy for others deepens, and independence with problem-solving increases. In time, museum guests can become more adept at generating original ideas, a skill that can transfer to grappling with personal issues in diverse contexts. In this manner, the remarkable experience of creating meaning boosts motivation to learn and lures guests to return for more.

Curiosity-driven creative thinking is the engine that drives today's economy, particularly innovative technologies. During tours, creative inquiry is the engine that propels meaningful conversations about artworks and other objects. To make CIP a reality, guides coach everyday people to do what they instinctively do daily: use creative thinking to wrangle with challenges as small as making a meal from simple ingredients or as big as grappling with a serious illness. Fortunately, we're wired to tackle problems of varying shapes and sizes. And the more people learn about how to self-activate inborn cognitive capacities to figure things out, the better they get at skillfully using them (Rubin, 2023).

Practicing CIP feels like fun because it involves playing with novel ways to connect ideas and make sense. To experience this, consider what happens when questions are posed as jokes, which are mini-challenges to make sense from "non-sense." For example: *What do you call a museum guide whose left arm and left leg were bitten off by a shark?* Take the challenge: Use CIP to collect details from the question and devise an answer, which will probably be an improvement on mine at end of the chapter. Hint: It's two words.

TOUR VIGNETTE: CHARLES

The vignette in chapter 1 featured Nick, a museum guide who coached visitors to use different types of thinking in the Creative Inquiry Process (CIP) to construct their own understanding (Hein, 1998, p. 179). During conversations, participants jumped in with novel interpretations. The goal was not to achieve group consensus, but the conversation depended on everyone feeling respected as a contributor and feeling that meaning was being created collectively (Murawski, 2016). Meaningful conversations support overall goals museums set for guests to learn and enjoy the process.

This chapter dives into the driving force behind fruitful conversations: CIP, which relies on flexible, back-and-forth thinking (e.g., to collect ideas, connect ideas, then collect again) to make sense of historic artifacts as remarkable as the first practical airplane in the world.

To get started, join a history interpreter on a tour that engages kids in "thinking about thinking" during CIP-driven conversations. Zero in on what Charles says and does in the tour introduction, development, and closing/wrap-up. *Strategies* are what guides, docents, and history interpreters say and do (e.g., ask questions, prompt, share information) to advance meaning-making. To identify strategies in the vignette, ask yourself: What is the guide doing and saying and why?

Observation Cues: Pay attention to why and how the history interpreter . . .

1. Sets the stage (introduction).
2. Asks *open* questions (multiple answers).
3. Weaves in relevant facts.
4. Affirms students' ideas.
5. Labels aspects of creative thinking.
6. Involves students kinesthetically.
7. Makes transitions.
8. Coaches students toward insight (ahas).
9. Makes learning fun.

Vignette: 1905 Wright Flyer

Introduction

"Welcome, Tigers (school mascot)!" Charles says, passing around clipboards with blank name tags and markers. "I'm Charles, a pilot, and your history interpreter today. You're at the Wright Brothers National Memorial, which houses more Wright artifacts than anyplace else in the world! You can't touch them, but you can take photos. When everyone has on a name tag, we'll get started. What questions do you have?"

"What's an artifact?" Sara asks.

"In museums, 'artifact' means an *original* object—not a replica. Actual artifacts are stored under acrylic because they belonged to the Wright Brothers or their family members, which makes them important—that is, they hold historical significance and are a part of some good stories. Our best artifact is too big for acrylic—*this* plane." He points to a photo covering a wall. "It has its own special room."

"Whoa! You have the actual plane?"

"It's about eighty percent original, and it was assembled under the direction of the Wright brother with a moustache—."

There's a chorus of "Orville!"

"Correct. You'll see the plane. First, I understand you're studying how great inventors think, right?" Heads nod. "Thumbs up if you know one kind of thinking inventors use." As thumbs go up, he points, and kids tick off answers: *identifying problems, imagining, questioning, gathering information, experimenting, connecting ideas,* and so on.

Development

"You've already done a lot of information *collecting*, but take a look at this mural and tell me what's going on."

"That's the 1905 Wright Flyer," Rama says.

"Correct! It's a *photo* of that plane, which is a National Historic Landmark. That's why we operate under the National Park Service. What's happening in the photo?"

"Either Wilbur or Orville is flying around Kitty Hawk?"

"Yes. Look again for clues to the place."

"It looks like a field on a farm, not a beach."

"I see big trees."

"Collecting details is scientific, and you're close: It's a cow pasture, a few miles from here. And that connects to what happened between 1903 and 1905."

"Orville made the first powered flight in 1903," Terry says.

"Important fact."

"But it only lasted twelve seconds and went seven miles per hour," Mario adds.

"Keep going."

"There were many crashes," Michelle says.

"Then what?"

"They put their planes back together and tried again?"

"Why do you say that?"

"Because creative thinkers are persistent."

"Important creative trait," Charles says. "After the 1903, history-making flight at Kitty Hawk, it took the Wrights two more years to invent a 'practical plane.'"

"Meaning, it didn't crash?" Rudy asks.

"Unfortunately, all planes *can* crash, but the Wrights tackled the challenge of making a safer plane that could carry a pilot, go higher and faster, and stay up as long as it had fuel—which made it 'practical.' How do you imagine they solved these problems?"

"Asked questions about what went wrong, did experiments," Doug says.

"What else?"

"Observation," Corey adds.

"All that," Charles says. "Orville said that *'learning the secret of flight from a bird was a good deal like learning the secret of magic from a magician.'* What does this quote tell you about his thinking?"

"He pretended to be a bird?" Corey asks.

"And how would he know how to do that?"

"Watched a lot of birds," Tina says.

"Exactly. Watching and looking are important ways to collect information. And the brothers kept collecting until bits started connecting. Then they imagined possibilities and *tried them out* in a lab, which is . . ."

"Experimenting!" the students call in unison.

After several seconds of silence, Maria asks, "What motivated them to do all that?"

"Wilbur said he was inspired by a great scientist who *believed* in flying machines. Unfortunately, that guy was Otto Lillianthal, and he broke his neck in a glider accident in 1896."

"Seven years before the 1903 flight," Maria notes.

"You're quick with math! Like everyone, the Wrights lived through tough times, but they persisted. They said they couldn't wait to get up in the morning! Which suggests they were in 'flow state.'"

"What's that?"

"Everyone is born creative, but people can *choose* to use their creativity in different ways. And some use creative thinking more than others. When people get really involved in making connections and coming up with possibilities, ideas *flow* so easily that people describe losing track of time."

A boy raises his hand. "I get in trouble when I'm working on a model and forget my chores."

"Perfect example of 'flow,' Isaac," Charles says. "Let's go see how Wilbur and Orville did experiments. Then we'll go see the . . ."

"Plane!" the kids shout.

In the machine shop, Charles demonstrates how the Wrights hung airfoils (miniature wings) in a wind tunnel to record the efficiencies of various wing curvatures and lengths. He then leads them to a large propeller encased in acrylic.

"The Wrights hand-carved this propeller. Its eighty-two percent efficient. How efficient do you suppose wings are today?"

Kids call out "ninety-eight percent," "seventy-five," "one hundred!" as they follow him to a large door and stop.

"Eighty-four percent," he whispers.

"That's all?" Maria shrieks.

"No way!"

"Way. They were that good," Charles says. "And what's the museum term for something encased in acrylic?" he asks, opening the door into a large room.

"Artifact!" Maria shouts.

After high-fiving her, Charles leads them into the display. The kids enter in silence and slowly gather around the railings surrounding a well. They don't talk for looking. (View photo at: https://www.ohiomagazine.com/ohio-life/article/see-the-wright-flyer-iii-at-carillon-historical-park).

"This plane didn't fly on December 7, 1903," Charles says quietly, his voice echoing. "But this is the plane Orville *chose* to start this museum: the 1905 Wright Flyer III!"

"Because it was 'practical'?" Sara asks.

"Right. It could take off, fly around—using a control system custom-designed by the brothers—land, refuel, take off, and do figure eights, over and over. After five thousand years of trying and many people dying, Orville and Wilbur turned dreams of flight into reality."

"On fabric wings," Terry notes.

Figure 2.1   Wright Flyer III. Wright Brothers National Museum, Carillon Historical Park, Dayton, Ohio.

"Good observation! Sturdy fabric: muslin. Wilbur did the sewing for early gliders and planes."

"That probably helped with the problem of weight. But how did they finally figure out problems, like control?" Terry asks.

"After years of creative thinking and incubating, they had an 'aha!' Put your arms out like this," Charles says. "They realized the only way to create a *practical* plane was to control *all three axes of flight*: roll, pitch (up and down), and yaw (side to side)" (Crouch, 1989, p. 67). As he demonstrates, they mimic him.

"Why is he lying down?" Sara asks.

Charles points to the mannequin reclining in the plane. "Orville moved his hips to create roll. Over time, they discovered a secret—the pilot had to control yaw with the rudder at the same time as he controlled roll with his hips, and pitch—the up and down—using that rod in his left hand. Using this combination, a pilot could execute a perfectly coordinated turn."

Closing

"This wasn't magic, it was hard work!" Brent exclaims. "And the 'aha' wasn't one thing, it was putting a lot of stuff together."

"Exactly. Figuring out how to control the axes of flight—roll, pitch, and yaw—solved the final mystery. Two Ohio boys discovered this secret. And *this* plane made them famous."

A hand goes up. "Well, this Ohio boy knows why the mannequin is Wilbur and not Orville." Todd grins, waiting.

Charles frowns. "How do you know that?"

"He doesn't have a moustache."

"What!" Charles stoops down to look. "You're right!"

"Now, do you want to hear my limerick?"

"Sure!"

Todd straightens his back and recites:

"*From bicycle to plane was quite a leap,*

"For others the challenge was just too steep.
"But Wilbur and Orville never gave up,
"When people said, 'no way' they said, 'shut up.'
"And they flew into history shouting, 'What the bleep!'"

Vignette Debrief

Did you catch Brent's insight moment? His conclusion showed he'd taken a big step toward understanding how people in fields from science to math and the arts make discoveries and synthesize core meanings in similar ways. Sparked by curiosity, people—like the Wrights—use coordinated thinking that enables authors to write, scientists to discover, and artists to make visual art, music, dance, and dramas. When used by guides to coach visitors, it's called the "Creative Inquiry Process" (CIP).

CIP is backbone of planning and conducting tours that engage visitors in making meaning. To encourage diverse visitors to participate in discovery-oriented CIP conversations, guides rely on:

- Knowledge about the museum's mission and goals.
- Knowledge about the museum's collection (information about objects and their creators).
- Teaching *strategies* rooted in meaning-making driven by creative inquiry.
- Tour organization (introduction, development, and closing).
- Personal strengths—especially their passion and enthusiasm for guiding tours.

So, what does Charles's tour reveal about his mastery of each of these five bullet points? To tease out particular strategies that Charles used in his introduction, development, and closing (wrap-up), return to the *Observation Cues* before the vignette. If you're wondering why Charles paused for students to complete sentences, check out the "cloze" strategy in the Museum Guide's Tool Kit (in Appendix A).

You've probably noticed I often suggest that you *use* creative thinking, which involves *collecting* or gathering information. Visualize yourself leading a tour and list the following:

- Questions you have about doing so.
- Strategies you'd like to use in tour segments, beginning with the introduction, and
- Possible sources for content information about the object, its maker, and the time period.

CIP: FROM THINKING TO PRACTICE

The following chapters offer insider tips on how to help guests purposefully use Creative Inquiry Process (CIP). You'll also learn how to use CIP to plan tours. First, here's some background on creativity.

Creative Thinking Rewind

Investigations into "creativity" have been traced back to sages like Aristotle, who linked creativity to thinking. But in ancient Greece, China, and India, creative acts were considered "discoveries" about something already out there, like fire. During the Renaissance, the modern concept of human creativity began crystalizing (think da Vinci). By the late nineteenth and early twentieth century creatives like Einstein, Picasso, and Marie Curie were active, as was Philo Farnsworth. As a teenager, Philo read science magazines in the attic of his family's farmhouse and visualized electrons as rows in a plowed field. And through his imagination, the cathode ray tube was born, along with television.

During the twentieth century, scientists began using MRI technology to map brain activity. The scans documented widespread human capacity for "creative" thinking across cultures and time—the kind of brain activity that produced new and useful things now considered ordinary, like the humble paper clip (circa 1877); radio (late 1800s); Scotch tape (1930s); Velcro (1955); and bubble wrap (1957).

Myths about muses arriving to invest humans with creativity eventually faded, replaced with scientific evidence for survival-favoring problem solvers who imagine possibilities and take risks. And those who embrace creative thinking pass their creative traits to their descendants. By following instincts to be curious, people got more interested, learned to manage creative propensities to different degrees, and discovered that constraints of time and resources could be overcome. It may be counterintuitive, but hardship can actually boost creativity—if it doesn't kill you.

To sum up, check off what you think are confirmed "truths" about creativity:

1. ___Everyone is born with creative capacity.
2. ___Creativity is the same as talent.
3. ___Creativity is an aspect of intelligence.
4. ___Creative thinking happens in the right brain.
5. ___Creativity is teachable and learnable.
6. ___Only elite individuals use creative thinking.
7. ___Creative thinking processes are somewhat predictable.
8. ___Creativity happens magically, and people either have it or they don't.
9. ___Creative thinking is used similarly in science, engineering, writing, mathematics, art making, and daily life.
10. ___Creativity is negatively affected by limits on time and resources.
11. ___Thinking creatively demands risk-taking.
12. ___Creativity means basically "anything goes."
13. ___Creative teaching makes learning memorable.

(Answers at chapter's end.)

Museum Guides and CIP

In a nutshell, a guide's problem is how to help visitors answer basic questions like "What is this about?" and "Why should I care?" To address these questions (challenges), guides coach visitors to examine objects, collect information, and connect ideas during conversations. Using CIP strategies, guides then edge visitors toward themes (universally important ideas) suggested by artworks and objects. As groups share thoughts and listen to varying perspectives, the "two heads are better" phenomenon kicks in. Ideas get connected, understandings emerge, and people feel exhilarated and empowered.

Guides in Action

The following examples suggest how docents use interrelated CIP phases to coach guests to do flexible thinking, including backing up to collect more information. Italicized questions are prompts to think about putting CIP into practice.

Museum guides . . .

1. CONTEXT: Create a climate that's physically, psychologically, and socially comfortable. The goal is to relax visitors and put them at ease to participate in inquiry-based conversations. *What are ways to create this kind of context?* Think about Nick's strategies in chapter 1 and Charles's in this chapter.
2. CHALLENGE: Explain that the goal (challenge) is to work together to understand objects by first examining them. Invite participants to *imagine* possibilities for finding ideas (e.g., look at different angles, distances, in pairs, or sketch). *How could you make people comfortable about sharing observations?*
3. COLLECT: Explain that by looking purposefully, you *see* more. Invite conversation about discoveries. Ask: "What are you noticing?" "What's happening?" Suggest "looking again to see more."

Note: Docents at the Cincinnati Art Museum call this "fishing for facts" (Rindsberg, Mueller, and Stock, 2023). *What else could you do?*

4. CONNECT: Ask participants to categorize collected ideas and find associations and relationships. Either suggest categories in advance, like "repeated" or "emphasized" elements (closed sort), or ask them to create groupings *after* looking (open sort).

   Suggestion: Explain that *incubation time* produces more and better categories. Example: wait thirty seconds or more for everyone to take a break (e.g., stretch, take deep breaths) and then invite categories. *How can you "prime" thinking if the group struggles with coming up with categories?*

5. CONCLUDE: To help visitors synthesize important ideas, pose questions like "What was the tour/object mostly about?" "What was the big message?" Encourage guests to point out interesting ideas found by others. Or invite participants to create a headline or caption about the object. *Example:* When a student said, "I can think like Wilbur!" it showed understanding of shared human capacities. Note: At this stage, participants may experience a discovery or an "aha!" *How might you get people to work together to create a title or caption?*

6. CRITIQUE: After tentative meanings (conclusions) are shared, invite evaluation by asking, "Which conclusions make the most sense? Why? How could that interpretation be improved?" *What if you're short on time by this point?*

7. COMMUNICATE: Depending on time, invite participants to express "best" conclusions by writing, sketching, or orally sharing. Scaffold with sentence frames, "What struck me about this object /tour was _____." *What other ways could participants "show" thoughts?* (Think of daily communication forms.)

Plus One: Celebrate! Debrief by asking for highlights and insights: Use scaffolds like TOT (tell one thing) or Say Something. *Example:* "One thing I'd tell a friend about this tour is _____."

MUSEUM GUIDE TOOL KIT

There are many sources for expanding a repertoire of strategies to introduce, develop, and wrap up tours: museum educators, other guides and docents, a museum guide library. This book is another source, especially the vignettes that feature "in context" strategies that are adaptable for guest needs and interests. Examples from Charles's tour follow. Check the Museum Guide Tool Kit in Appendix A for more.

Descriptive Feedback

To reinforce useful contributions, *describe* what was said or done—which is less judgmental than praise. *Example:* "That's a new idea" (versus "good" idea!).

Personal Connections

Link to prior experiences or "known" information. Ask "What does this remind you of?"

Fast or Fun Facts

Collect and intersperse three to five relevant art or artist facts that advance conversation:

- *Example:* "Fact #1 is . . ." Then ask what the information adds to thoughts about the object.
- *Variation:* Write facts on cards and invite participants to read aloud as they see fit.

Cloze Procedure

Gestalt psychology posits that humans naturally "fill in gaps." To engage thinking, leave blanks in sentences or in writing activities for participants to complete. *Example:* "RoyGBiv is an _____ for red, orange, yellow, green, _____ indigo, violet.

Their Own Words (Quotes)

Read a quote from the artist or creator and ask what that says about the object or the thinking behind the object.

Multisensory Engagement

Invite participants to show thoughts and emotions using faces, body posture, movement, sketching, or any of the five senses.

Posing and Responding to Questions

To initiate inquiry conversations, pose questions that encourage looking, seeing, and thinking about images. Provocative questions motivate participants to . . .

- Concentrate and focus (attend).
- Become more curious and interested, which extends looking, seeing, and thinking and feeling.
- Forge important connections (relationships) that suggest interpretations and conclusions about meanings (themes, truths, big ideas). See related Quick References.

Quick Reference 2.2: *Posing Open-Ended Questions and Prompts*

Closed questions ask for "right" or "yes-no" answers, cutting off conversations. Open questions ask for multiple answers and enrich conversation.
  Open-ended questions . . .

1. Suggest inquiry is an ongoing process: "What are you seeing?" "What's happening?"
2. Encourage more and varied responses: "What makes you think . . .?" "What's a different idea about . . . ?"
3. Motivate collecting and sharing ideas by hinting at hidden meanings that can be figured out: "What's something that's invisible? Confusing?"
4. Offer choices of what to look at and talk about (shapes, colors, emotions, places, associations): "What lines are you seeing?" "What are seems curious?" *Prompts:* "Describe your feelings. Explain what's catching your eye. Explain what's going on."
5. Change up *what, why,* and *how* questions: "What are you thinking?" "How does the artist make you think that?" "What did the artist do that makes you feel like that?"
6. Ask for anchoring facts that everyone can examine: "What are you looking at that makes you say that?" *Prompt:* "Describe what you're seeing that makes you say that."
7. Suggest closer looking and deeper thinking: "What else can you find?" "What more can you see? Think? Feel?" *Note:* Repeat questions to suggest there's more to discover.
8. Connect past experiences with age- and stage-appropriate questions: "What's going on that looks interesting?" "How do the colors in the top half make you feel?" "What sounds can you imagine hearing?"
9. *Note:* Changes in phrasing affect thinking. For example, "What do you *see* in this object?" asks for listing or naming rather than finding connections. "Why?" questions invite a range of comments, but "Why do you say that?" sounds like a request for *motive,* rather than evidence (VUE, 2009).

Avoid ...

- Single-answer questions that begin with "Can you ..." or "Who can ..." set participants up for failure if they "cannot."
- Asking multiple questions at a time and run-on questions.

Quick Reference 2.3: *Responding to Answers to Questions*

1. Offer the "pass" option to give participants control. After others respond, give passers a chance to comment on what's been said.
2. Embrace silence. Use wait time to encourage processing and response.
3. Use EPR ("every person response") options such as thumbs-up to increase participation. See Museum Guide Tool Kit, chapter 9.
4. Listen actively to responses (e.g., nod, make eye contact).
5. Consider all responses as serious even if they aren't "right" answers.
6. Acknowledge all contributions to signal respect and encourage further conversation that lays groundwork for seeing beyond a single perspective.
7. Listen carefully, then rephrase without altering ideas.
8. Paraphrase answers. Clarify by saying, "Tell me more."
9. Ask follow-up questions that call for closer looking and concrete support for ideas.
10. Follow responses with, "What are different ideas?" to extend conversation.
11. Piggyback on ideas to stretch thinking and conversation.
12. Say, "Yes ... and ..." to validate responses and boost conversation.
13. Ask viewers to describe locations ("top left") to direct group investigation.
14. Accept possibilities. Treat all comments as valuable and avoid showing preference for responses that confirm your views.
15. Have confidence that the inquiry will "buoy meaning-based discoveries" (VUE, 2009, Spring).

Benefits of Paraphrasing ...

- Acknowledge that comments are heard and understood.
- Underscore efforts to understand viewpoints.
- Provide opportunity to clarify: "Are you saying that ... ?"
- Give a chance to extend thinking: "Tell us more about ..."
- Provide opportunity to investigate confusing aspects.
- Encourage conversation.
- Provide insight into speaker's thinking (Cornett, 2015).

ADVICE FROM MUSEUM GUIDES

> *"If kids lead the conversation, I don't stop them. If they bring something up, I go with it."* —Adera Causey, curator of education, Hunter Art Museum

Experienced guides, docents, and interpreters have a lot to say about do's and don'ts. For each of the "should *nots*" below, add your thoughts about "why" these practices are *not* recommended.

Museum Guides should NOT …

1. Memorize information and present or read it in a robotic fashion *because …*
2. Talk too fast or, perhaps worse, too slowly *because …*
3. Give a monologue or "information dump" (facts, dates, places, and numbers) *because …*
4. Require participation versus invite it *because …*
5. Talk too much *because …*
6. Use jargon as if everyone understands museum terminology *because …*
7. Get off track and fail to connect discoveries and information to the tour theme *because …*
8. Ask "leading" questions that call for yes-no or one-word answers (which creates a demeaning guessing game) *because …*
9. Go overtime *because …*
10. Use traditional scavenger hunts that don't engage meaning-making. (Murawski, 2011, October 22) *because …*

For advice from National Park Service interpreters, see *Meaningful Interpretation: How to Connect Hearts and Minds to Places, Objects, and other Resources*: https://www.nps.gov/parkhistory/online _books/eastern/meaningful_interpretation/mi6g.htm.

ADAPTING FOR DIFFERENCES: *NEEDS, STRENGTHS, AND INTERESTS*

Organizations have different reasons for implementing strategies that serve the needs of diverse people; "It's the right thing to do" is one of them. The 1990 Americans with Disabilities Act (ADA) accelerated efforts that coalesced around the concepts of inclusion, diversity, accessibility, and equity (DEAI), which often appear in mission and goals statements.

For museums, it's both morally right and financially important to put inclusive policies in place. At the most basic level, physical adaptations like ramps and elevators and exhibits that attract culturally diverse populations bring in larger audiences.

Museum Guides and DEAI (IDEA)

The following are examples of adaptations or actions guides can take for each DEAI principle.

Diversity

Diversity refers to understanding and respecting how people vary in age, gender, sexual orientation, race, ethnicity, nationality, religion, abilities and disability, and socioeconomic status. *To adapt:*

1. Welcome individuals with different backgrounds, identities, perspectives, and characteristics. Greet everyone personally, make eye contact, and smile.
2. Look beyond a person's appearance when making judgments about capabilities and needs.
3. Inquire about special interests and invite questions.
4. Imagine yourself as a first-time visitor who may be uncomfortable for various reasons, including previous negative experiences.
5. Create a climate that encourages risk-taking and acceptance of unexpected viewpoints.
6. Offer name tags to facilitate connections among group members and conversation.
7. Explain that voicing unusual viewpoints stretches everyone's thinking. Ask, "What's another way of looking at this?"
8. Use strategies that promote creative thinking. *Examples:* 1) Invite guests to "become" a figure in artwork and say a "one liner." 2) Ask, "Why do some faces in Toulouse Lautrec's nineteenth-century posters look distorted? How does (person) feel?"

Creating Meaning in Museums

9. Share background information that presents new viewpoints. *Example:* Consider the effect of nineteenth-century dance halls that either used gas lighting or early versions of electric lights.

Equity

Equity is more than equality. Equity is about justice and fairness, which means not treating everyone the same. Equity includes taking steps to rectify historic inequalities. *To support equity:*

1. Help individuals, regardless of background or circumstances, gain access to opportunities and resources. *Examples:* Slow the pace. Repeat key words/terms. Use a five-second wait time to allow thinking after questions. Pause to allow interpreters to translate.
2. Assume that people start from different places and need varying levels of support to achieve similar outcomes. *Example:* To adapt, 1) ask about particular needs and interests, and 2) offer alternative ways to show understanding, such as using facial expressions and body shapes to show emotions of figures. See chapter 9: "Communication Options."

Accessibility

Accessibility is about ensuring no one is excluded because of physical, sensory, cultural, cognitive, or language limitations. *Examples of adaptations include:*

1. Adapt spaces to make available services, information, and technology for all, including individuals with physical and cognitive disabilities, or other barriers. *Examples:* Offer stools, point out elevators, walk slower, talk slower and louder, and face anyone with hearing difficulty.
2. Offer options for physical access: wheelchair, ramp; digital access (websites and screen reader-friendly apps); and communication access to easy-to-understand information in multiple formats. When you use museum and educational terminology, show word cards and offer synonyms and short explanations (e.g., terms like *inquiry, curator, object*).

Inclusion

Inclusion isn't about taking photos of people with different skin colors to promote your institution. Inclusion involves fostering authentic, engaged participation in a welcoming context that communicates a sense of belonging. *Adaptations include:*

1. Creating a comfortable environment that shows respect for who people are, how they look, and what they say. *Examples:* Make eye contact, nod, and lean in (active listening) when individuals speak. Paraphrase and expand on novel ideas.
2. Using practices such as 1) encouraging unusual ideas, 2) asking clarifying questions to understand and validate unique points of view (e.g., "Are you saying that___?")
3. Eliminating unintentional personal biases by audio-recording yourself. Listen for signs of stereotyping that may offend or minimize people. Next, set personal goals to be more inclusive by not using phrases like "you guys" or "elderly guests," and avoid labels like "forefathers" and "mankind." Instead, substitute gender-neutral labels like "ancestors" or "predecessors." Chapter 5 of the style manual from the American Psychological Association provides guidelines on bias-free language: https://www.apa.org.

Diversity alone will not ensure that individual perspectives are heard, respected, and included. Equity and accessibility must work in concert to support inclusion—doing things like removing tangible and intangible barriers and providing equitable opportunities for all, regardless of backgrounds or abilities. Diversity, equity, accessibility and inclusion are interconnected. When each mutually reinforces the other, the goal of full inclusion is more likely to be achieved.

RECAP

This chapter outlined the role Creative Inquiry Process (CIP) plays in meaningful conversations, and it outlined how and why to use inquiry during tour introductions, development, and closings. The vignette featured an interpreter at a history museum coaching middle schoolers to use CIP to understand how the Wright brothers tackled the challenge of flight, solving a mystery that had bedeviled humanity for five thousand years.

Of course, challenges surround us, and each section and feature in this and every chapter address challenges of museum guides. For example . . .

- *Word Boxes* tackle terms and concepts related to CIP.
- The *Museum Guide Tool Kit* spotlights problem-solving strategies like those Charles used.
- *Advice for Museum Guides* offers recommendations for new guides.
- *Adaptations for Differences* gives examples of how to implement principles of DEAI.

Finally, as another example of how CIP is widely used in life, here's the process I used to create this book:

1. I identified a need for a particular book for guides and felt comfortable *(context)* accepting the challenge.
2. I tapped teaching and guiding experiences and gathered additional information by interviewing and observing other docents, reviewing museum publications, and doing additional research into best practices *(collecting information)*.
3. I outlined a book by sorting information into categories like advice from museum guides and guide tool kit *(connecting information)*.
4. Over time, I incubated findings and concluded that the title needed to encapsulate the themes associated with "conversations" and "creating meaning" *(conclusion)*.
5. I received suggestions from multiple reviewers *(critique)*.
6. I found a publisher willing to "make public" my work *(communication)*.

NEXT UP!

Chapter 3 drills down on the importance of creating a "context" for conversations that features the free exchange of ideas. The vignette is set in a unique context that celebrates the creative genius of America's Indigenous people. Tour planning is a special focus, so get ready for "theme-based" ideas to plan tours like that of an enthusiastic guide.

Joke Answer: "Always Right!"

Creative Truths: odd numbers.

REFERENCES

Center for Creativity in the Columbus Museum of Art: https://www.columbusmuseum.org/wpcontent/themes/cma/pdf/odipquickguide.pdf.

Cornett, Claudia. (2015). *Creating meaning through literature and the arts*, 5e. Boston: Pearson.

Crouch, Tom. (1989). *The bishop's boys*. New York: WW. Norton & Company.

Flasche, Molly. (April 7, 2023). Interview, Columbus Museum of Art, Columbus, Ohio.

Rindsberg, Helen, Terry Hanes, and Linda Stock. (March 2023). Interview, Cincinnati Art Museum: https://www.cincinnatiartmuseum.org.

Rubin, Rick. (2023). *The creative act: A way of being*. Random House/Penguin.

VUE. (2009, Spring). *Visual Thinking Strategies: Understanding the Basics, Visual Understanding in Education.* San Jose Museum of Art: https://sjmusart.org/sites/default/files/uploads/files/Understanding%20Basics.pdf.

3

Tour Introduction

CREATING A CONTEXT THAT INVITES INQUIRY

Context (n.): environment or circumstances that create the setting or atmosphere.

LEARNING GOALS

By the chapter end, you should be able to . . .

1. List reasons and strategies for creating a comfortable context that stimulates conversation during tours.
2. Describe your personal guiding "style" in a few words.
3. Match creative thinking processes (7 Cs) to these tour phases: introduction, development, closing.
4. Enhance the partial Tour Plan for Pam's tour by adding learning goals, objectives, and strategies to introduce, develop, or conclude the tour. See Museum Guide Tool Kit in Appendix A.
5. Choose a familiar object or family photo and create a web as if you were going to facilitate an inquiry conversation about the object. See basic categories for planning in this chapter and ideas in the appendix under Tour Planning.
6. List helpful categories and means of gathering information (assessing) about visitors to adapt for differences.
7. Add introductory strategies to your Museum Guide Tool Kit.

CONTEXT FOR MEANING MAKING

Context (n.): the circumstances surrounding something.

Enduring Patterns: Introduction, Development, Closing

Books, stories, trips, and projects have beginnings, middles, and ends (BME) or introductions, development, and closings (IDC)—as does life. Humans are good at discerning and using organizational patterns because such structures help us understand and communicate with each other. Creative Inquiry Process (CIP) is another useful pattern that coordinates different types of thinking to achieve understanding. CIP also has beginning/introduction, middle/development, and end or closing phases.

This chapter addresses ways to facilitate the tour introduction or beginning of creating meaning, which requires a relaxed, comfortable context. Skimping on introductions isn't wise: Successful tours begin with creating an atmosphere where people will risk working with strangers to investigate meanings in objects that may seem strange, or at least unfamiliar (Claire, 2023).

WORD BOX 3.1

- *Welcome* (v.): greet or invite in friendly manner.
- *Comfort* (n.): a relaxed state.
- *Climate* (n.): mood, feel, or atmosphere.
- *Risk* (n.): uncertainty or threat.
- *Conversation* (n.): informal back-and-forth exchange of ideas during a chat, dialogue, or discussion.

Visitor Needs, Wants, and Expectations

During a recent tour, I pointed out the artist's signature: three letters, *TLH* (Henri Toulouse Lautrec). As visitors moved closer, I stepped forward, and a guard intervened. "The curator is in the gallery, and we have to enforce the arm's length rule," he said. When I jumped back, a visitor said, "Better you than us," and we all laughed. Having embarrassed myself, I recalled an essay by psychologist Robert Coles (1992) about kids observing "guards watching over us as if they thought any second we'd pull out our knives." One boy said it made him "want to go away and not come back!" (p. 8). I totally empathized, and this was a good reminder that museums can be so intimidating that some never open the front door.

Museums are, indeed, splendiferous places, but they're also cavernous spaces where footsteps echo across marble floors and people regard objects in reverent silence, daring kids to make noise (Coles, 1992). The awesomeness of museums that hold objects imbued with the "blood, tears, and sweat of their makers" can make a person feel small and insignificant (Csikszentmihalyi, 1995, p. 74). Even when folks do make it through the door, they can panic or get disoriented—something akin to losing your bearings in an unfamiliar city. Without easy-to-read signage or a handy map, uncertain guests wander in uncertainty. But live guides know the way. Offering reassurance, docents confidently announce now and next, saying things like "We're passing the sculpture of Harriet Frishmuth, *Joy by the Waters*, and our next stop is the Blue Gallery."

Any arriving visitor could be a first- or fiftieth-timer to the museum, and people's experiences, perspectives, and expectations vary as much as their fingerprints. Like guides, guests can be also anxious about personal issues, or the unpredictability of tours that reflect docent personalities. No two tours are the same, and not just because of people. Case in point: When I arrived for the tour where I would later violate rules before a dozen guests, all six front doors were being replaced. With the entry blocked, I felt on edge, which reminded me that no one is ever in full control.

Unlike guides, visitors have less knowledge of museum spaces and zero control over key tour goals, processes, choice of objects, and guests they'll be thrown in with. *I'm getting anxious describing this!* Then there are visitors who expect to see the entire museum in an hour and are disappointed when they realize that's impossible. But as author/teacher Hiam Ginott explained, you are "the decisive element," and your mood "makes the weather" (1975). He was talking to teachers. But guides *ARE* teachers, so it's up to us to create an hour of sunshine and clear skies.

To do so, George Hein, in his now-classic *Learning in the Museum* (1998), advised museum educators to focus on a range of visitor needs (pp. 158–59), starting with an orientation to the museum space. Nearly a quarter of a century later, his recommendations, rooted in environmental psychology, remain spot-on. Imagine yourself as a first-time guest as you consider needs, wants, and expectations that underlie learning success.

Climate and Comfort

Climate refers to weather, but it also connotates atmosphere or mood. Museum guests want and need to feel safe and relaxed. Guides can help by addressing . . .

- *Physical comfort*: Concerns about basic needs negatively affect any learning experience. It's both necessary and important to point out restrooms and elevators and offer stools.
- *Psychological comfort:* People are quick to sense subtle signs of climate, such as confusing signage and guards. Guests want and need to feel genuinely welcomed and respected for who they are and what they say.
- *Social comfort:* Guests expect a relaxed tour that emphasizes enjoyment and learning, and they're more open to unfamiliar experiences when they feel comfortable expressing ideas and exploring interests without worry of embarrassment or criticism. First-name introductions and name-tags alleviate some of the anxiety and discomfort of being with strangers (like you).

Quick Reference 3.2: *Benefits of Name Tags*

(Use basic, stick-on name tags.)
First-name name tags . . .

1. Are a friendly wave, a non-threatening hello.
2. Offer a simple personal detail.
3. Comfort by shrinking psychological distance.
4. Break down barriers among strangers.
5. *Are icebreakers for conversations.*
6. Help identify commonalities and connections.
7. Facilitate courteous interactions.
8. *Remove worry over remembering names.*
9. *Help acquaintances avoid embarrassing missteps.*
10. *Hold wearers accountable, reducing issues with anonymity.*
11. Acknowledge personal identity, *humanizing the crowd.*
12. *Are preferable to "Mr.," "Ma'am," "Sir," or labels that reduce individuals to "tall guy" and "redhead."*

Check Scott Ginsberg's website: https://hellomynameisblog.com/22-reasons-why-wearing-nametags-will/.

Choice and Control

Guests want choices of places to go and what to do, see, think, and feel when they get there—in other words, control. A brief orientation that includes a map with directions allows guests to make informed decisions about where things are, how to get there, and how to access information digitally or in person.

Joining a tour is an in-person choice. But unknown tour specifics can create anxiety about loss of control. Offering choice in the introduction reduces "pushback" and shows respect for visitor autonomy and capacities to make decisions, including whether to wear a name tag or sit or stand. The role of empowerment in learning is considerable. Giving choices transfers control to visitors. Guides empower guests by describing the conversational nature of the tour and encouraging everyone to ask questions and participate as comfortable. Visitors also appreciate a heads-up on what to expect, including the conversational nature of tours that focus on sharing perspectives rather than finding the right answers.

Realizing it's impossible to see all 240 items in an exhibit in an hour is disappointing. Distress hinders interest and willingness to engage. It's up to guides to outline what's possible and persuade visitors to choose meaning-oriented conversations over a fleeting walk-through. The analogy of scanning versus reading a book can be useful. But it's the visitor's choice.

Competence and Confidence

Guests need to feel they "can do and want to do" what's expected during tours. Interest or curiosity may have brought them to the museum, but it's up to guides to get visitors to trust that you'll create bridges between their lives and unfamiliar objects. Vygotsky (1978) called this creating the ZPD (zone of proximal development). Strategies like connecting to prior experiences, giving examples, and doing "think alouds" to demonstrate thinking (see Museum Guide Tool Kit) are scaffolds to the zone.

Conversation and Connections

Casual conversation works well for creative inquiry tours. Relaxed social situations invite visitors to talk with others about connections and speculate on meanings in objects (Burnham and Kai-Keem, 2011). Name tags help everyone become comfortable and often spark unlikely personal connections as visitors chat about names, interests, places, and people (See Quick Reference: Name Tags). During informal introductory conversations, visitors also unknowingly practice types of "discovery" thinking you'll encourage later: connecting "known to new" and "familiar to unfamiliar" to find meanings in artworks and objects. Finally, as conversations buzz, guides can observe needs and interests that suggest potential adjustments, like those with hearing difficulties.

Challenge and Creative Inquiry

With a comfortable context in place, guides turn toward visitor expectations of learning during the tour. To pique innate curiosity, guides explain the challenge is to gain understanding about the importance of and meanings in works using shared inquiry. Depending on the audience, guides may explain that everyone will be using their personal knowledge to collect and connect information, which lays the groundwork for drawing unique conclusions.

Five Minutes for First Impressions

The cliché about only having one chance to meet someone for the first time comes from long experience. First impressions are important and hard to overcome. The question each guide should ask is "What impression do I want to make?" See Quick Reference: Tour Introduction.

Guide Style

Every guide has a distinct personality, which is an asset. Guides need the freedom to capitalize on their individual strengths as they acquire professional skills and knowledge necessary for serving visitors. This challenge demands self-evaluation and creative thought.

Hein suggests that guides "seduce" guests into exploring objects more deeply by enticing them with "the lure of the familiar, the comfortable, the known" (1998, p. 176). Grinder and McCoy recommend being "gracious, friendly, and warm" (1985, p. 9), which brings to mind hosting a party for guests with different needs and expectations. Both metaphors dovetail with the longtime motto of *Highlights* magazine: "fun with a purpose." Comfort and enjoyment go hand in hand to encourage visitor engagement, and coupled with shared inquiry, "fun" can motivate personal interpretation. So, what ingredients create a pleasant tour experience that's comfortable and seduces guests to engage in deep thought? A lot depends on what the guide does in the first five minutes.

The Welcome Mat!

Effective guides put out metaphorical welcome mats that suggest visitors are wanted. Greeting individuals with "enthusiasm" is at the top of the list. *Enthusiasm* has Latin and Greek origins that refer to being "possessed by divine inspiration" ("thus" relating to *theos* or "god"). Over time, "enthusiastic" got toned down, and now it describes a person's energy and passion, which can be contagious and positively affect learning (Moe, Frenzel, Au, & Taxer, 2021).

Quick Reference 3.3: *Tour Introduction Checklist*

During introductions, guides can address visitor needs, wants, and expectations by . . . (Brown, 2023).

1. Welcoming guests personally, which creates a sense of belonging (Maslow, 1987).
2. Showing enthusiasm.
3. Building rapport: "My name is _____, and I'm a guide because I enjoy having conversations about museum objects." Mentioning relevant credentials can establish credibility, but keep it short.
4. Inviting guests to share names to jump-start conversation.
5. Forecasting tour content and process: "This is a conversational tour about the theme of 'art merging with life.' Feel free to offer ideas and ask questions."
6. Offering a map and pointing out restrooms and elevators.
7. Asking what individuals expect, need, and hope for the tour.
8. Showing respect for and interest in unique perspectives.
9. Observing for signs of needs, wants, and expectations.
10. Offering stools to sit during stops for inquiry conversations.
11. Emphasizing the importance of enjoyment and feeling revitalized, refreshed, and restored.
12. Offering choices: "We'll start with general observation, but feel free to jump in with colors, lines, and shapes." *Note:* The goal is to move from looking to *seeing*, i.e., interpreting the visual alphabet (what's going on, mood, relationships, etc.).
13. Previewing challenges that pique curiosity, spark interest, and motivate investigation: "What's important?" "What's this about?" and "Why should you care?"
14. Previewing inquiry process by explaining the goal is to collect details, examine from different vantage points, make connections, and think about hidden meanings.
15. Sharing overall goals to create new understanding about objects and experience insight.

Friendliness

Whether guests are greeted with "Hello," "Bonjour," "Ciao," "Hola," or "As-Salam" isn't as important as being greeted. To create a sense of approachability and friendliness, docents look people in the eye, smile, and show genuine delight at meeting them. It's icing on the cake if the guide speaks multiple languages (National Docent Handbook, 2017).

Psychologist Rick Hanson describes *friendliness* as a "down-to-earth approach that's welcoming and positive" (2012). To help determine what makes people "friendly," notice those who come across as warm and likable. Observe how they use their faces, bodies, gestures, words, and actions to create a friendly "impression," then self-evaluate. Do you . . .

Welcome with your face and body:

- Relax your facial muscles?
- Make eye contact and soften your eyes?
- Smile sincerely? (Maybe practice in the mirror?)
- Use open body language? (Avoid looking down, slouching, and crossing your arms.)
- Answer the question posed below a mirror at the Toledo Board of Education: "How would you like to look at yourself?"

Welcome with what you say:

- Be friendly *first?* Take initiative to talk with people?
- Remember names by association and repetition?
- Use positive humor. Make fun of yourself?
- Avoid conversation stoppers, especially questions with yes and no answers?
- Include everyone in conversations?
- Give sincere compliments?
- Comment positively on small things?
- Remain polite and courteous?
- Pass on compliments?
- Use conversational threading—picking up on ideas of others?

Welcome with your behavior:

- Show interest in others?
- Remain an active listener?
- Pause and breathe before responding?
- Help people when possible?
- Remain generally positive?
- Read faces for emotions?
- Be "authentic?" (But remember friendly doesn't equal "friendship.")
- Avoid checking your phone?

Good Humor

Humor has to do with temperament. By projecting an upbeat, playful temperament, guides can persuade visitors to engage in risky creative problem-solving. Interestingly, problems are the source of humor (really), *not* happiness, so posing doable challenges primes guests to "play" with possible meanings in objects, and share "oddball" ideas. It's particularly helpful to laugh at their own missteps to show good humor, and it's easier for visitors to have fun if you're having fun. Laughter bonds groups. *FUN* is indeed a fundamental to learning.

Show Comfort with Self

I know the symptoms: racing pulse, rapid breathing, dry mouth, sweating. Although I've taught dozens of courses and given hundreds of talks, I still get "performance anxiety" before tours. I have learned it's normal to feel nervous if you care about doing a good job, but it's difficult for museum visitors to be comfortable around jittery guides. To calm yourself . . .

- Remember, you probably prepared too much! (But do prepare!)
- Rehearse key tour points, especially introductory and first stop strategies.
- Carry a small note card with key dates and facts.
- Get hydrated prior to the tour.

- Inhale and exhale five times.
- Remember, when you're comfortable, guests are more comfortable.
- Remember *why* you do what you do. Let motivation be your guide.
- Remember only you can do *your* tour.
- Think positive thoughts and avoid imagining worst-case scenarios.
- Concentrate on audience needs and interests instead of yourself.
- Get busy greeting people and stop worrying about the tour.
- Embrace mistakes. Expect that something will not go as planned and roll with it. It's not the end of the world if you break a National Historic Monument, which I did—a door on Orville Wright's mansion!
- Remember, everyone wants the tour to go well.
- Enjoy!

Museum Etiquette

Since tour guides are responsible for protecting museum objects and keeping visitors safe, museum manners are serious business. Museum behavior needs to be addressed. Here are some pointers:

- Get to a quiet area with your guests.
- Explain that that you and the security guards are responsible for protecting both objects and visitors.
- Outline museum rules: stay an arm's length away from objects, walls, and displays; no flash photography; mute all phones; and stay with the group.
- Thank guests for respecting the rules and ask for questions.

TOUR VIGNETTE

Guides strive to create museum experiences that inspire visitors to discover relationships between exhibits and their lives. A tour introduction can lay the groundwork for guests to think about extending the experience after leaving the museum (Csikszentmihalyi and Hemanson, 1995). Pam Hall, an education specialist at Fort Ancient, an outdoor museum, does this.

Outdoor museums are unique in that they are both part of the tour context and the object of investigation. On the surface, Fort Ancient is a beautiful, wooded site in southern Ohio. But right off the bat, our guide expands our perspective by explaining the site's significance in understanding the history of Indigenous people and humanity itself. The ground on which we stand evokes ancient lives, brought to life by Pam.

Pam spins our curiosity into motivation to learn by emphasizing "soulful" connections between this place and us. Pay attention to how she enlivens mounds of dirt by linking them to a "larger cosmos," forging memories that will likely endure (Csikszentmihalyi and Hemanson, 1995, p. 72).

Observation Cues

Notice how Pam . . .

1. Invites us into the world of another time.
2. Encourages us to take time to look, sense, and feel.
3. Interweaves key information.
4. Interprets details based on significance.
5. Uses pauses to encourage personal connections.
6. Extends our thinking beyond ourselves.

Vignette: Fort Ancient

Fort Ancient is wooded area with mysterious hills, a natural "exhibit" with curious features. Large mounds dot the entrance to the museum building, and larger earthworks, much bigger, surround the area and recede into the distance.

Pam bounds out of her office. "So, you want a tour," she says, smiling.

"Yes!" I say, compelled to smile back.

"Perfect timing! Fort Ancient is a National Historic Landmark about to be inscribed onto the World Heritage List—this weekend! You're invited. It will be the newest UNESCO (United Nations Educational, Scientific, and Cultural Organization) site, joining world cultural and/or natural sites considered to possess 'Outstanding Universal Value.' Let's go outside."

Following her to a broad expanse surrounded by woods, I recall World Heritage sites like the Taj Mahal, Yellowstone, and the Acropolis. When she takes a breath, I ask, "Universal value?"

"Yep." She points. "Look around." She waits for us to take a panoramic survey. "This is North America's largest ancient hilltop enclosure, started over two thousand years ago by the Hopewell culture. People came from all over what eventually became the United States and parts of Canada to build giant earthworks used as ceremonial structures. They adapted deer shoulder blades to make shovels and wove baskets to carry soil."

Arthur scans the enclosure. "These people were out front with repurposing." He points. "Was the fort on the ground where the museum building is?"

"There never was a fort here," Pam announces.

"A fort that never had a fort?"

"That's right! Our museum does have lots of artifacts that tell stories. What you're seeing here is part of the one-hundred-acre-plus enclosure, which consists of walls, moats, causeways, and mounds with eighty-four openings. See those small mounds?"

"Burials?"

"Think Stonehenge," she says.

"Ceremonial?"

"Yes."

"They planned for a big attendance," Arthur says.

Still thinking about the concept of "universal values," I ask, "Spiritual ceremonies, as in 'outside' churches?"

View the Calendar Mound online: https://commons.wikimedia.org/wiki/File:Fort_Ancient_calendar_marking_mound.jpg.

"UNESCO promotes our 'shared humanity,' and we preserve evidence of the human inclination to be spiritual. These people also had to eat, and they grew forty percent of their food, as indicated by deer shoulder blades used as spades and hoes. You'll see them inside. But they also were hunter-gatherers." She tilts her head upward. "And they looked skyward, observed, and wondered."

"Were they sun worshipers?" I ask.

"They needed to keep track of the seasons to know when to plant. How many hillocks do you see?"

She waits, so we look and count.

"Calendar mounds," she announces.

With that bit of information, we study a hill about twenty feet across and six to eight feet high.

"See at that opening—big enough to walk through—in surrounding earthworks," she says. "What do you suppose happens when the calendar mound meets up with that?"

I think about Stonehenge. "Something to do with the sun?"

"Yes. They used it to determine the winter solstice—the shortest day of the year—and the summer solstice, which is the longest. They also kept track of moon phases and counted the days."

Figure 3.1 Calendar Mound. Ohio History Connection.

"That helped them know when to plant and harvest," Arthur said. "I grew up on a farm."

"Exactly," Pam says. "You identify!"

"Shared humanity," I say. "People lived here?"

She smiles. "No. We don't live in our churches, either."

"So, they came here to celebrate, give thanks, and feast?"

"They came here to connect deeply with the natural world," she explains, "and engage in ceremonial activities."

"We came here to connect with nature, too," Arthur notes. "The Hopewell really didn't call this a 'fort'?"

"No. And the name 'Hopewell' wasn't popularized until the 1890s, when an American archaeologist explored earthworks in Ross County, Ohio. The property belonged to the family of Mordecai Hopewell—a non-Indigenous person."

"More shared humanity," I said, "but not the good kind."

"I'm assuming no one knows what the community called itself," Arthur says.

"Not that I know. Which makes it that much more important to preserve what we do know."

An hour later, we toured the museum that houses a tableaux of Indigenous people and displays of ancient artifacts made of copper that originated in the Great Lakes region. Pam points out shell hoes and ceremonial objects brought from places as far away as Wyoming.

We stop to study copper "ear loops" and then examine 1.25-to-2-inch flint arrowheads with long and narrow, serrated triangular points, traced to the Dakotas. The ear loops look decorative, like attention-getting jewelry worn today, but the arrowheads, with their high degree of workmanship, were obviously weapons, like today's lead bullets.

"How did these artifacts get here?"

"Some were brought as gifts," Pam says.

Pam's welcoming spirit, enthusiasm, use of humor, and vast storehouse knowledge had held our interest and stimulated our imaginations.

"Enjoy this weekend's UNESCO ceremony," I say, still thinking about shared humanity. "Looks like you have room for thousands."

"We're hoping for hundreds," she says.

After we left, we marveled at the geometric precision in Fort Ancient's earthworks. (Website: https://stateparks.com/fort_ancient_state_memorial_in_ohio.html.)

"These mounds weren't 'discovered' in the traditional sense," Art says. "They were built by ingenious people who lived during the time of the Roman Caesars—long before Europeans set foot on this continent."

NOTE: The 1990 National American Graves and Protection Act details the process Federal agencies use to address discoveries of Native American human remains and cultural property intentionally excavated or inadvertently discovered on Federal or Tribal lands (Bureau of Land Management, United States Department of the Interior).

Vignette Debrief

Check *Observation Cues*, before the vignette, and consider the strategies Pam used during the tour to finish these sentences:

1. Pam's guiding style includes _____.
2. In the first few minutes, she _____.
3. She introduced and developed the theme of "shared humanity" by _____.
4. The outdoor "context" set a tone of _____.
5. Pam set up understanding about time periods and what's available at the site by_____
   _____.
6. She transported visitors to another time and place by _____.

PLANNING TOURS

Tour planning is a challenge that involves collecting ideas about what to look for, where, and how. Docents at the Cincinnati Art Museum (CAM) select focus artworks, choose themes, do research, determine the order of art stops, and choose strategies. At other museums, educators may choose the objects and themes and even write the tour plan, including teaching strategies (Vatsky, 2023).

The *who* question is important: "Is the tour for adults? Mixed ages? A public tour? A school tour for children, middle schoolers, teens? Information about groups affect most aspects of planning, but overarching goals remain the same: to have guests discover personal connections that inform understanding and experience enjoyment from inquiry conversations.

Planning: Challenge-Collect-Connect-Conclude

Planning involves collecting and connecting information in these categories:

Tour goals (visitor outcomes): Specific content and process objectives? For school tours: target standards (objectives).

Tour theme(s) or "common threads" (big ideas)? See Quick Reference 4.4: Themes.

- *Content Sources*: Information about artist or creator, key concepts, facts about objects, timelines, etc. Note: CAM docents use a "five facts" rule of thumb for each art stop to prevent "information overload."
- *Sources for Strategies*: Focus on teaching practices that fit tour goals, objectives, and visitor needs.

Tour Structure: Determine priorities and organize content and strategies into IDC tour phases and stops.

- *Introduction*: In the first five minutes, what will you do? Why? How?
- *Development*: Sequence tour stops (stations) from easy, familiar, simple, and concrete ideas to more complex, abstract, and ambiguous objects.

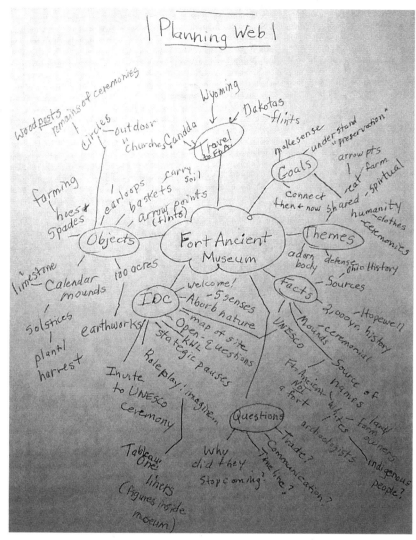

Figure 3.2 Planning Web. Author created.

- *Transitions* between tour stops: What can you say or ask to link the current stop with the next and continue the common thread or theme?
- *Closing*: Plan strategies that bring the tour back to the goals and themes.

One way to organize *collected* information is to "web," or brainstorm, on paper. Examine the planning webs in figure 3.2 (above) and 4.1 (next chapter) to see how ideas are connected with tour outlines (see Appendix B2).

Webbing is brainstorming on paper. The web's center might be an object's title or tour theme. Categories that radiate can include:

- features of the object (style, materials),
- information about the creator (background, materials used, process), and
- teaching strategies.

As other connections are found, more lines (legs) are drawn to show links.

Webbing releases and connects ideas that are then prioritized and organized into an IDC tour outline. The final step is timing stops for the schedule.

By using CIP to plan tours, you eventually arrive at conclusions, which take the form of tour outlines like the partial plan in the Quick Reference 3.4.

Quick Reference 3.4: *Tour Planning Template*

Date/Time: 1 hour
Audience Information: 15 adults
Tour themes: Shared Humanity, Universal Values
Learning Goals: Participants will ...

1. make personal connections that lead to understandings about outdoor earthworks and indoor objects that offer insight into "shared humanity."
2. enjoy being in outdoor spaces and investigating objects inside the museum.
3. OTHER:

Performance Objectives (content and process): Participants will be able to ...

1. Explain factors that motivated Hopewell people to build calendar mounds and surrounding earthworks.
2. Give examples of how the Hopewell had needs and wants like people today.
3. Explain ways archaeologists use the Creative Inquiry Process (CIP).
4. OTHER:

Materials: (map, laser pointer)
Strategies to reach goals and objectives ...
Introduction (beginning)

1. Offer enthusiastic welcome. Ask about special interests and needs. Offer name tags and map. Explain goals and the tour's conversational nature.

Development (during tour)
Stop #1: Survey site.

1. Purposeful looking: What are you seeing? Why might ancient people construct these enormous earthworks?
2. Interweave information about UNESCO and two thousand years of history.
3. Encourage speculation after looking at outdoor site.
4. Introduce theme of "shared humanity." Solicit personal connections.
5. Ask about shared needs and wants of people.

Stop #2: Objects in museum. See Quick Reference 6.2: *Examining Artifacts*.

1. Purposeful looking: Shoulder blade (used as spade). What are you noticing? Possible uses?
2. Baskets: Possible uses? Connections to mound construction?
3. Ear loops: Connections (e.g., ceremonial, decorate body)?
4. After giving information about diet (maize, squash, beans, and game), invite "one-liners" from woman and child in cooking tableau.

Closing (wrap-up)
1. Ask for thoughts about theme of "shared humanity."
2. Ask about: Surprises? Most interesting? Remaining questions?
3. Invite to return for UNESCO event.

Transitions: Before going inside, suggest looking for objects made by the Hopewell for *practical* and *ceremonial* purposes.
Adaptations: Offer a map to independently explore mounds.
Note: The basic tour template stays the same, but selected objects and accompanying information change, as do adjustments for visitor needs and interests.

Pre-Tour Information

As a part of scheduling the tour, a museum coordinator requests and shares the following with guides:

- Nature of experience (e.g., curriculum related? highlights tour? thematic tour?)
- Number and age range of participants
- Audience interests, needs, accommodations? (e.g., wheelchair?)
- Date, day, length, start and end time
- Order of objects to be investigated
- School Tours: Number of teachers and chaperones. Note: Some museums set a ratio of adults to students for supervisory purposes.
- Museum expectations for teachers and chaperones for group management

Pre-tour packets of information should be sent to the contact for groups, along with the suggestion that information be shared with families and accompanying adults. Packets often include information about the museum and exhibits, a map, expectations for "museum etiquette," and supervisory recommendations for teachers and chaperones.

At some museums, guides follow up with a letter or email that solicits more detail about needs and interests. If it's a school group, it helps to get advice from teachers about pre-tour study, behavior management, and post-tour activities.

MUSEUM GUIDE TOOL KIT

To grow your personal tool kit, pull strategies from Pam's tour and consider the following strategies Pam also could've used, described in the Museum Guide Tool Kit (Appendix A).

- Know, Want to Know, Learn (KWL): to assess and set goals (Ogle, 2022).
- Two Words: to describe.
- Sign Language: for attention.
- Every Person Responds (EPR): to increase participation.
- Inventory: to gather information.
- Open Questions: to extend conversation.
- Piggybacking: to continue conversation thread.
- One Liners: to say something in role.

ADVICE FROM MUSEUM GUIDES

"I like being in a group that . . . inspires me to keep learning." —Linda Stock, docent, Cincinnati Art Museum (CAM)

CAM docents suggest the following strategies to create a context that encourages visitors to take risks. Check the ones you're likely to use.

Tour Introduction

1. ___Don't assume visitors are familiar with museums and types of art.
2. ___Be a good host: Make visitors feel welcome. Give your name and ask theirs.
3. ___Show enthusiasm by varying your voice (volume, rate, tone, pitch, pause) and facial expressions. Use body language to convey excitement and interest—i.e., lean in.
4. ___Poke fun at yourself.
5. ___Show interest in guests.
6. ___Build trust by listening and making eye contact.
7. ___Ask, "What brings you here today?"
8. ___Engage by asking about background, interests, and needs.
9. ___Piggyback on visitors' ideas, or paraphrase ideas and respond with follow-up questions.
10. ___Show respect by listening and paraphrasing.
11. ___Preview tour theme(s), goals, length, number of stops (focus works), and participation options (e.g., listen, ask questions, offer ideas).
12. ___Emphasize the special nature of museum tours.
13. ___Offer folding stools, even for middle and high schoolers, to increase comfort.
14. ___Create a cue to bring group together (e.g., raised hand).

ADAPTING FOR DIFFERENCES: *READ THE ROOM ASSESSMENT*

When guides have little or no information about a group, a quick "read the room" assessment of numbers and ages helps. It's like reading between the lines in a book to identify signals about general mood, characteristics of individuals, needs, and so on (Brown, 2022; NDS Handbook 2, Vatsky, 2023).

Group Arrival

- Observe physical needs and plan adjustments for those in wheelchairs, pushing babies in strollers, handling toddlers, and so on.
- Scan for clues to unease, concern, and puzzlement.
- Circulate, greet, and chat, noting comments about anything special, like how far people traveled and mode, and particular needs and expectations.
- Observe for needs that may require slowing down, speaking louder, simplifying directions, repeating, giving more examples, shortening stops, or completing fewer.
- Notice facial expressions and body language: smiles, raised eyebrows, frowns, crossed arms, avoidance of eye contact. Assume facial and body language are hints. Remain open to interpretations. People mask feelings and can be reticent among strangers and in unfamiliar environments.
- Don't take negative verbal and nonverbal indicators personally. Remain pleasant and polite and continue to collect information.
- Ask what you should know about the group.
- Inquire about expectations and interests. Ask, "What do you hope to see today?" and "What questions do you have?"
- Invite guests to share and compare previous museum experiences.

- If there are "leaders" (teachers, chaperones, caregivers), recruit help in keeping the group focused and together.
- Listen closely to guests without thinking about responses. Note what's said and how (tone).
- Note reactions, including unspoken cues (e.g., facial expressions, posture).
- Paraphrase or repeat questions and pause before responding.
- Step away to observe what's happening within the whole group. Inventory relationships, including how people group together and who stands alone.
- Don't overtalk!

During the Tour

- Continue to take the group's temperature. Note who talks, who's quiet, who seems reluctant, who looks tired, and who seems interested.
- Be flexible. Make changes as needed: Pick up the pace, speak louder, stand next to different people.
- After asking questions, wait a three to five seconds for thinking. During pauses, continue to assess who's participating.
- Note shifts in attention—checking watches, drifting off. Change your pace; show more enthusiasm and energy. Use Curiosity Hooks (chapter 4) to draw attention to an object or stimulate a personal connection: "How is this like something you've seen before?"
- Do progress checks: List a couple of key points and ask, "What else have we talked about?" Ask, "What's interesting so far? What stands out?"
- Think on your feet. Switch from asking questions to giving key information.
- Lighten the mood with humor. Laugh at yourself. Throw in punny riddles like "What do you call a guy who hangs on the wall?" (Art). "What did Vincent say when his minibus stopped? (Van Go!).

RECAP

This chapter focused on creating a comfortable context for creative inquiry conversations. Recommendations emphasized ways to relax and motivate visitors during the tour introduction. The featured vignette was set in an outdoor museum, where the guide used strategies to "transport" visitors to another time and promoted the theme of "shared humanity." An example tour plan showed common elements, along with planning tools and a checklist.

The Museum Guide Tool Kit focused on strategies for a personal tool kit. *Advice from Museum Guides* and *Adapting for Differences* reinforced and expanded the chapter theme of setting the stage for shared inquiry conversations in the first five minutes. Consider returning to the opening *Learning Goals* to self-evaluate.

UP NEXT!

Chapter 4 tackles the overall challenge of prompting guests to make sense of objects by evoking interest, curiosity, and the motivation to learn.

REFERENCES

Brown, Clair. (October 12, 2023). Help! My group doesn't want to participate . . . *Thinking Museum* podcast, https://thinkingmuseum.com/captivate-podcast/help-my-group-doesnt-want -to-participate/.

Coles, Robert. (1992). Whose Museums? *American Art*, Winter (pp. 6–11).

Csikszentmihalyi, Mihaly, and Kim Hemanson. (1995). *Intrinsic motivation in museums: Why does one want to learn?* https://arts.berkeley.edu/wpcontent/uploads/2016/01/Csikszentmihalyi Herma nson-1995_Intrinsic-Motivation-in-Museums.pdf (pp. 67–75).

Haim, G. Ginott. (1975). *Teacher and child: A book for parents and teachers.* New York, NY: Macmillan.

Hanson, Rick. (2012, November 7). Be Friendly. *Psychology Today*: https://www.psychologytoday .com/us/blog/your-wise-brain/201211/be-friendly.

Levi, Daniel, and David Askay. (2021). *Group dynamics for teams*, 6e. Thousand Oaks, CA: SAGE.

Maslow, Abraham. (1987). *Motivation and Personality*, 3e. Boston: Pearson Publishing.

Moe, A., A. Frenzel, Au, L. and J. Taxer. (2021). Displayed enthusiasm attracts attention and improves recall. *British Journal of Educational Psychology*, 91(3), 911–27.

NDS: National Docent Symposium Council. (2017). *The Docent Handbook 2.* www.nationaldocents .org.

Ogle, Donna. (2022). KWL and KWL+: What We Know, What We Want to Know, What We Learn/ Still Need to Learn. New York: Routledge, https://doi.org/10.4324/9781138609877-REE176-1.

4

Tour Development

USING CHALLENGE TO SPARK CURIOSITY, INTEREST AND MOTIVATION

Challenge (n.) a question or problem that stimulates interest, curiosity, and motivation to investigate.

LEARNING GOALS

By the end of the chapter you should be able to . . .

1. Explain challenges in becoming an effective guide.
2. Use synonyms to clarify the concept of "challenge," in the context of conversational tours that seek meaning.
3. Describe group-dynamics issues that guides need to consider.
4. Compare the roles of challenge in life to understanding museum objects.
5. Give examples of strategies that tap attention, curiosity, interest, and motivation to engage guests in the challenge of creating meaning.
6. Use the example tour planning "web" (Photo 4.1) to practice brainstorming ideas about a theme. Consider web "legs" in categories like people, places, things, needs, and wants.

THE CHALLENGE OF BECOMING A GUIDE

Before taking on the challenge of guiding tours, it's important to get the "big picture" of what's considered "effective" guide dispositions and practices. Although museum guides are routinely acknowledged for their contributions as educators, ambassadors, mediators, and choreographers (Weiler and Black, 2015), few studies focus on specific traits and practices of effective guides (Bajrami, 2022; Butler, 2009; Schep & Kintz, 2017). The following self-assessment tool, based on available studies and advice from veteran museum educators, outlines the scope of desirable guide traits and practices.

Effective Museum Guides and Docents

Rate your comfort levels with the traits and practices below, using a scale of 1=low to 5=high. After self-assessing, circle the priorities you want to develop.

1. Management of Groups and Individuals: *Guides should …*
___Show enthusiasm, openness, and flexibility.
___Create a comfortable, relaxed climate.
___Build rapport with visitors.
___Assess needs and interests and make reasonable adjustments.
___Show interest in ideas, questions, and backgrounds of visitors.
___Engage and supervise groups while protecting museum objects.
___Adjust tours according to time constraints.
___Monitor group dynamics.

2. Communication: *Guides should …*
___Demonstrate effective verbal and nonverbal skills.
___Speak clearly and listen actively.
___Solicit and use visitor questions and interests to initiate and develop conversations.
___Use a repertoire of strategies to facilitate meaningful conversations.
___Observe and respond to group relationships (dynamics).
___Be prepared to troubleshoot situations, like resistance to unfamiliar ideas.

3. Knowledge: *Guides need …*
___Knowledge and understanding about the museum's mission and goals.
___General information about the museum's collection.
___Accurate artistic, historical, and cultural information about objects selected for tours.

4. Pedagogy: *Guides need …*
___Knowledge about "best" practices that align with respected learning theories.
___Strategies to facilitate conversations, tell stories, ask and respond to questions about artworks, objects, and artifacts, and ability to appropriately convey information,
___A repertoire of strategies that meaningfully and flexibly engage visitors in inquiry, including tools that motivate purposeful examination of objects to gain insight.
___To collaborate with colleagues and educators to plan, conduct, and revise tours.

5. Professionalism: *Guides should …*
___Be reliable.
___Positively represent the museum.
___Reflect on personal performance and set goals for improvement.
___Be open to giving and receiving feedback.
___Show interest in developing as a guide.

Quick Reference 4.1: *Tips on Group Dynamics* (Levi and Askay, 2021)

Group dynamics refers to interactions that affect relationships and ability to reach goals. In any group, guides can *expect …*

1. People will assume roles as leaders, followers, and/or mediators.
2. Norms (expectations) for working together will be assumed.
3. Members will communicate thoughts and feelings verbally and nonverbally (facial expressions, body language).
4. Leadership styles will influence the group's ability to work together (e.g., autocratic leaders often repel members).
5. Social influences (e.g., perceived status/peer pressure) will affect attitudes and behaviors.

Creating Meaning in Museums

6. Diverse backgrounds will produce broader perspectives, but stark differences may create challenges.
7. Conflict may impact cohesiveness and create obstacles to achieving goals.
8. Cohesion (connections among members) will influence commitment to reaching goals and cooperating.
9. Groupthink can hinder creative thinking if members prioritize agreement over candid sharing of ideas and objective evaluation.
10. Decision-making may take different forms, from informal consensus to majority vote.

CHALLENGE: WHAT? WHY? HOW?

At the gym this morning, I watched a video of abstract expressionist Helen Frankenthaler talking through the challenge of setting up a gallery exhibit—a process she compared with artistic (creative) process she called a "kind of magic" (CBS Morning, 1984). While pedaling off calories, I connected her thoughts to the challenge of staying fit, which requires finding creative ways to motivate myself to do boring bicycling. Videos about artists work their own magic: thirty minutes pass like five.

This chapter explores reciprocal relationships between challenge and motivation in the context of museum tours, where guides work their own magic to empower visitors to create personal meaning.

WORD BOX 4.2

- *Attention*: sensory (visual, auditory, etc.) awareness.
- *Curiosity*: urge to investigate.
- *Interest*: disposition to learn.
- *Motivation*: need and desire to learn or act.
- *Imagine*: visualize, image, conjure, picture.
- *Possibilities*: options, potentialities.

The Meaning-Making Challenge

Challenges take many forms: questions, problems, issues—some imposed, others self-imposed. Central to the challenge of becoming an effective museum guide is figuring out how to translate theory and research into engaging practices that help visitors make sense of objects.

Guests choose to visit museums, and most expect to participate in object-based learning (McLean, 2011; Weiler and Black, 2015; DePrizio, 2016). Passive listening doesn't generate the kinds of personal connections or yield the benefits of discovery that museums hope guests experience. But when visitors expect a traditional lecture, guides face the tricky challenge of getting people to choose "discomfort with the unknown," which is a core feature of investigative conversations. This challenge which calls for creative inquiry, first requires collecting information.

Elements of Challenge

Knowing what to expect is an essential substrate for understanding. When you expect a book, piece of music, or work of art to possess important "unseen" meanings, you're more likely to find them. Possibility is driven by expectations, which guides need to make clear.

Clear Goals

"I don't know what to do or where to go," is a common visitor complaint. Anxiety is the enemy of curiosity: Anxious visitors are less likely to take risks, which obstructs creative inquiry. Offering a guided tour gives comfort and choice, and choice bolsters openness to participation.

Guests also want to know what the tour is about (subject and themes) and what they'll be expected to do (process and goals). Forecasting opportunities to *do* creative thinking and not just view creative work provides an advanced organizer. Mentioning *casual* conversations about discoveries in objects introduces something that sounds nonthreatening and familiar, and familiarity comforts.

Once the tour gets started, providing feedback on progress toward the challenge of making sense sustains interest. For example, during a tour about "transformations" featuring Washi paper, I asked, "What ideas so far make sense about *why* and *how* these Japanese artists 'transformed' thoughts using paper?": A spirited five-minute conversation got into recycling, climate change, art making as meditation, and embedding paper with messages about ancestry.

Guests need, want, and deserve to know the tour's "big picture" theme. Frontloading goals and suggesting upcoming opportunities to figure out hidden meanings in objects helps. To further lure reticent guests to investigate, Hein suggests combining the familiar and the *curious* (1998, p. 76). Words like *hidden* or *unexplained* are curiosity hooks.

Curiosity, Interest, and Motivation

People are familiar with curiosity—the persistent urge that ignites interest. Museums have long tapped innate curiosity to motivate people to visit, at least since 530 BCE, when the Ennigaldi-Nanna's museum became famous for curious Mesopotamian artifacts. By the mid-sixteenth century, "cabinets of curiosities" dotted Europe (Tishman, 2017, pp. 69–77). These "wonder rooms" were precursors to modern museums that display exotic natural specimens and human-made objects that mix science with superstition in depictions of artificial worlds (MOMA). The world's fifty-five thousand museums scattered across more than two hundred countries testify to humanity's continued curiosity.

How Curiosity Works

Curiosity ignites when people spot something missing, mysterious, or nonsensical to them, like abstract art or huge mounds of dirt in the middle of nowhere. Curiosity provokes mental investment in creating "wholes" (gestalt) from parts and pieces—a phenomenon that intrigues cognitive psychologists (Sternberg & Sternberg, 2012). While widely regarded as positive, mechanisms of curiosity themselves remain mysterious. So far, brain science has yielded mere glimpses into "neural aspects" of exploratory mindsets typical of curiosity. Observable effects of aroused curiosity are found in levels of dopamine flooding the brain, producing excitement and energy that motivate the urge to "figure things out" (a key tour process). And after the challenge is resolved, people experience pleasant states, like happiness (Costa et al., 2014).

It's good news that guides can positively alter brain chemistry by triggering the strong inclination to seek completeness, which sits alongside the urge to make sense.

Benefits of Curiosity

Humans aren't the only curious creatures. But the degree to which we are curious outstrips other species, even cats. Without curiosity, creativity shrivels, and without curiosity, we'd still be living in caves (Baumgarten, 2001).

It's understandable why curiosity advantages humanity: Curiosity assists basic needs for food (eating anything once) and shelter (any port in a storm), as well as "high-level" needs for a meaningful life (Maslow, 1987). And while curiosity can't explain the meaning of existence, it does engage creative thought about big questions (Baumgarten, 2001). Curiosity persuades us to explore ambiguous things outside ourselves, like intriguing situations, odd objects, and puzzling artworks. This takes time and energy. But curiosity also staves off boredom and indifference, which is consequential given the fact that negative emotions obstruct satisfaction with life (Baumgarten, p. 9).

Quick Reference 4.3: *Curiosity Is ...*

- A desire to know that prompts investigation.
- A first fleeting feeling or state of arousal, like a mental itch.
- A sense of uncertainty and need for completeness and meaning.
- A choice to investigate something interesting.
- A combination of mental and emotional engagement.
- A mental state that prepares the brain to learn and makes learning enjoyable.
- A capacity for asking questions and seeking answers.
- Distinct from interest, attentiveness, and openness.
- A key to friendship because it intersects with care and concern.
- Essential for survival.

References: Baumgarten, 2001; Costa et al., 2014; Fastrich et al., 2021.

Combining Curiosity and Interest

Curiosity is the oil for the engine of creativity that powers human advancement (Rubin, 2023). By stimulating curiosity, guides catalyze interest in inquiring into objects. Curiosity and interest work hand in hand—curiosity propels short-term inclination to take risks, try new experiences, and seek knowledge—i.e., investigate. In contrast, interest is a milder, but grounded, sustainable feeling that can produce long-term engagement that propels effort and action (Fastich et al., 2021). As a friend explained, "I see curiosity as more fleeting and serendipitous, [as in] 'What's going on at that house?' [while] interest is deeper and wider, [as in] 'What kind of architecture is that? When was it popular? Who liked it?' ... a lot of questions overlap ... and often spring from a different place" (Schuller, 2024).

So, curiosity and interest inhabit the same space: Both are positive emotions that motivate information-seeking, especially collecting ideas by looking, reading, listening—all essentials for learning. They also complement one another: Curiosity prompts discovery, and interest facilitates ongoing collection and consolidation of information, preparing the brain to construct interpretations and conclusions. It makes sense to use curiosity and interest in tandem to propel creative inquiry forward, beginning with raising curiosity in the challenge (see Curiosity Hooks), then appealing to current interests and capitalizing on curiosity-induced new ones.

Mobilizing Curiosity and Interest

Curiosity activates desires, motivations, and appetites, emotion-laden "states" that excite exploratory behavior to search, gather, and collect. When we get hungry, we look for something to eat. When we get curious, we seek for "food" for thought. Driven to make sense of the strange, the incomplete, and the hidden, we collect information. But once the strange becomes familiar, missing pieces are found, and "what's behind the curtain is revealed," curiosity subsides.

By rearranging the letters in "motivate," you get "move at it," which defines *motivation*. Curiosity motivates interest, which moves people to investigate objects. To stimulate curiosity, guides suggest collaborative conversations to discover "unseen" things in artworks. Words like *unseen* provoke investigation, as do mentions of mysteries and secrets. Curiosity then motivates interest in uncovering *clues* and *possibilities*—other words that excite imagination and interest in thinking deeper to create understanding.

Note: In practice, guides first coach visitors to look for familiar, interesting, and easy-to-understand see-able things like colors and shapes—part of the art alphabet. After warm-ups, guests become more comfortable with wrestling with complicated ideas, like Toulouse Lautrec's curious habit of "radically" cropping off body parts in artwork.

Curiosity Cons

Curiosity isn't always a virtue. While it's tempting to share sordid details about lives of artists like Toulouse Lautrec, such information can distract from serious investigation into remarkable artwork. Emphasizing details about an artist's private life is a form of voyeurism, or "pure nosiness." As the sixteenth-century proverb warns, too much curiosity killed the cat.

THEMES AND BIG IDEAS

Effective tours are usually structured around themes, suggesting objects have universal messages often revealed though hidden stories with a beginning, middle, and end. Guides challenge visitors to find and connect these "common threads" that imply "deep meanings" greater than the objects themselves (Shep and Kintz, 2017). This can be tricky: Embedded meanings are usually "betrayed" not "paraded" in art forms from literature to music, art, dance, and theater (Gilman, 1918). Think of themes as a work's "soul." For example, in essence, *To Kill a Mockingbird* is about injustices done to those who are vulnerable.

Chapter 7 suggests techniques for turning thematic concepts like "injustice" into full statements of understanding, or *conclusions*. Listing all variations on themes about people, life, and our world, is impossible, but Quick Reference 4.4 lists examples to prompt thinking about "big ideas" that underlie life messages in artwork, objects, and cultural artifacts.

Identifying potential themes and big ideas starts during tour planning. For example, themes about success and courage emerged from webbing Toulouse Lautrec's life and artworks (figure 4.1). To discover themes, ask, "What is this art, object, music, or book *really* about?" or "What's the most important message of the whole work?" Multiple themes can be pulled from any given object or text, so you might plan to focus on "resilience," but guests may see "persistence," which is an opportunity to validate other viewpoints and deepen investigation by asking, "What are you seeing that suggests persistence?" Encouraging guests to put forth alternative themes supports creating conclusions that reflect how the object holds significance "greater than itself."

Quick Reference 4.4: *Themes and Big Ideas*

To stretch a theme into a universal statement, ask, "What's important about ___?"

Arrogance	Choice
Balance	Communication
Beauty	Consequences
Betrayal	Courage
Birth	Creativity
Change	Danger
Chaos	Death

Desire
Division
Doubt
Dreams
Empowerment
Emptiness
Evil
Evolution
Failure
Faith
Family
Fate
Fear
Gender roles
Good versus bad
Greed
Growing up
Heartbreak
Heroism
Hierarchy
Honor
Hopelessness
Hypocrisy
Identity
Ignorance
Injustice
Innocence
Inspiration
Isolation
Inspiration
Judgment
Justice
Knowledge
Loneliness
Loss
Love
Manipulation
Materialism
Names
Nature
Needs
Obstacles

Oppression
Optimism
Patriotism
Persistence
Pessimism
Pleasure
Power
Pride
Progress
Quest
Racism
Reality
Rebellion
Rebirth
Resilience
Revenge
Roles
Rule breaking
Sacrifice
Salvation
Self-awareness
Self-reliance
Shared humanity
Simplicity
Social mobility
Spirit
Stereotyping
Success
Technology
Temptation
Tradition
Tragedy
Truth
Unity
Vanity
Vulnerability
War
Wealth
Will
Wisdom
Youth

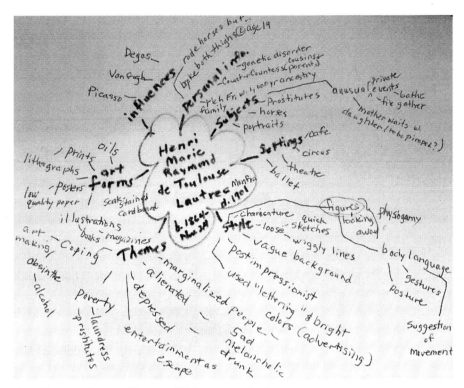

Figure 4.1 Toulouse Lautrec Planning Web. Source: Author.

TOUR VIGNETTE

Theme: When Art Merges with Life

Observation Cues

During Clara's tour, think about why and how she . . .

- Assesses and taps student background.
- Gets attention.
- Provokes curiosity.
- Follows interests.
- Poses and returns to the challenge (question).
- Piggybacks on student ideas.
- Uses partial sentences (Cloze).
- Integrates relevant facts and quotes.
- Prompts "looking" by suggesting categories and ways to look.
- Probes for themes or "messages."
- Asks questions that prompt investigation.
- Pairs students to write captions that recast conclusions.

Vignette: Toulouse Lautrec

Note: Clara's full introduction isn't included in the following tour excerpt.

After welcoming the high school French class with *bonjour*, Clara asks what they know about the artist Monsieur Henri Marie Raymond de Toulouse Lautrec.

"He was a short guy who made cool posters," Frank says.

Figure 4.2 Hussars. Courtesy of National Gallery of Art, Washington.

"What made the posters 'cool'?"

"Bright colors and action stuff, like ads at movie theaters."

"Where else have you seen these kinds of posters?"

Constance throws up her hands. "Everywhere! Zoos, pharmacies, billboards, car lots!"

"Today's advertisements owe a lot to Monsieur Toulouse Lautrec," Clara explains. "What else do you know about him?" Clara waits.

"He spoke both French and English," Kay says.

"Which suggests . . ."

"He was educated," Josh finishes the sentence.

"And died young," Tara says.

Clara nods. "Yes, but he produced 6,459 pieces of art, which means . . ."

"He worked triple time?" Frank suggests.

Everyone laughs.

"Seriously," Frank says, "that's a lot of pictures! Was he the 'father of posters' or something? If so, what did he do that was special?"

Clara cocks her head. "That's what I want you to figure out. I don't have all the answers, so I'm interested in what you find in his art. Your question about what makes his work so special is our challenge. Let's start with finding clues in his art that may explain his lifetime success and lasting fame. Follow me!"

She leads them to a gallery, where stools are arranged before artworks.

"Have a seat, but feel free to move around. Take a few minutes to examine these four artworks, beginning with the one on the left, painted when Lautrec was about your age. The one on the far right was made before his death at the age of thirty-six. Find what's curious or interesting—anything that surprises you or seems odd." After a minute, she softly invites them to look closer. "But stay an arm's length from the art, or Chuck will come over here." When she indicates the security guard, students

Figure 4.3   Moulin Rouge: La Goule. Metropolitan Museum of Art, Public Domain.

turn, and he salutes. "Try squinting to blur details, or make fist telescopes to isolate details," she says, demonstrating.

Josh moves to study the horse painting on the far left. Others gradually approach different artworks.

"What ideas are you finding?"

"Horse art bookends his life," Liza says. "The soldier on a horse is an oil painting, unlike his famous posters. If he painted it as a teenager, he was either a born artist or had a super teacher!"

"Both!" Clara says. "How else are the 1878 and 1899 artworks different?"

"The 1899 horse has more movement, like it's performing, which he must be because the title is *At the Circus*."

"It looks like bright lights are making weird shadows!"

"I'm seeing leg movements in the horse art and the posters of dancers."

"The two posters and the circus horse have unusual viewpoints."

Clara smiles. "You're on a roll. Keep trying different perspectives."

Figure 4.4 Jane Avril. Metropolitan Museum of Art, Public Domain.

"I'm seeing the backside of the horse from a ringside seat, and I'm seeing the dancers from behind, too."

Clara turns toward the snickering students. "If it's about the art, please share!"

Frank looks over his brows. "It is. Lautrec seems to invite us to look up her skirt."

"So, it's provocative. What's the message, and for whom?"

"Maybe, 'Hey guys, come and look at this.'"

"Can you read the lettering on the poster?"

"*Moulin Rouge*. It was a big Paris dance hall."

"La Goulle must be her name, but that translates into something like 'greedy guts.'"

"She had a reputation for downing customers' drinks," Clara explains.

"The dancer in the other poster isn't having much fun."

"What in her face and body imply that?"

Liza steps closer. "In a couple of lines, he shows it's hard for her to hold her leg up."

"Let's get off the leg thing and talk about the neck of a bass coming out of nowhere. And how about that big hand with tiny hairs sticking up?"

"Looks like he's really jamming!" Josh says.

"Try to connect these ideas to the question about what made Lautrec's art special," Clara suggests.

"Posters like this enticed people to attend, so cabarets made money, as did Lautrec."

"How do they 'entice?'"

Figure 4.5   At The Circus: The Spanish Walk. Metropolitan Museum of Art, Public Domain.

"Bright colors. Lots of movement. Leg."

"Stop with the leg thing," Constance says. "Look at the weird angles that must have broken art rules."

"Look again at the oldest painting—the soldier on a horse. What rules did it break?"

There's a whole minute of silence. Then Kay raises her hand. "It's a nice, traditional painting with an impressionist background that recedes in the distance."

"So, how are the posters and the 1899 sketch of the circus horse different?"

"The posters have cartoon and comic-book colors and lettering and curious things, like yellow balloons."

"Lautrec said, 'I paint things as they are.' What does his quote suggest?"

"He didn't see the women as pretty," Jennifer says. "But maybe they're caricatures."

"We know the names of most of his subjects, especially dancers and singers. Some didn't like the exaggerated features and movements," Clara explains.

"But he sounds honest," Josh says.

"He's known for capturing intimate moments, like a dancer adjusting her garter. He'd make quick sketches to catch feelings of everyday people and everyday movements."

Matt raises his hand. "The dancing circus horse looks like a sketch."

"By the time he painted these circus sketches, he was very sick. They were based on his memory. So far, which ideas seem like clues to the secrets of his success?"

"He tried things that surprised people. Made them curious. They wanted to look?"

"What would have been new and surprising in the late 1800s?"

"Pasteurized milk, paper clips, electricity!" Frank says.

"Paper clips, huh! I didn't know that! How would early electric lighting have made dancers look?"

"Ghoulish! Like when you shine a flashlight on a face."

"Is that what the strange yellow balls are, electric lights?"

"You figured it out!"

"What made Lautrec sick?"

"He had a genetic issue that affected his legs. He broke one femur falling off a horse at the age of thirteen and the other the following year. Then his leg bones stopped growing. He had lifelong pain."

"That's why he was so short. And that explains his obsession with legs. If he couldn't dance himself, he could make his paintbrush dance."

Clara smiles.

"Was he ridiculed?"

"Maybe, she says, "but he used self-deprecating humor to make friends. He told his mother she was 'definitely the hen who hatched a famous duck.'"

"That's sweet," Jennifer says.

"Did he use painkillers?" Terry asks.

"Unfortunately, he got addicted to alcohol."

"At least he lived in Paris!"

"Yes, in the Montmartre area, where working people, craftsman, artists, and immigrants lived because it was cheap."

"On a mount or a hill?"

"Your French is right-on! We have about five minutes. Pair up and create a French phrase that captures important ideas behind Lautrec's impact. To get started, here's a final quote: 'Ugliness has its beautiful aspects.'" She hands out large Post It notes to write out "captions."

Post Tour

Clara posted student captions on a "Response to Exhibition" board. Here are two examples: "L'honnetete faite meilleur talent artistique." (Honesty makes the best artistry.), and "He took 'break a leg' seriously and created drama with color and line."

Tour Debrief

- What stands out about Clara's tour?
- To what extent did she accomplish the goal of getting students to accept the challenge to "create meaning"?
- Which of her strategies would you add to your tool kit?
- How does she "customize" the tour?
- What other strategies could she have used?
- Check the *Observation Cues* prior to the vignette to stretch your thinking.
- How would you rate Clara on "effective" guide traits and practices?

Note: Students periodically referred to museum labels during the tour. Some museum educators think "didactics" put "factual communication at the center of the text" (Bowers, Nov. 23, 2017), implying "right answers," and sending the message that "facts on plaques" are more important than creating personal interpretations (Bosker, 2024).

Quick Reference 4.5: *Museum Wall Information*

Museum labels (aka "didactics") are short information texts placed near objects. These labels, or tags, contain "tombstone" information:

1. *Artist facts*: birth/death, country of origin, or artistic activity.
2. *Title of the object*, date created, and media.
3. *Accession number*: usually catalogued by date/year the object became part of the collection, followed by number that shows its position in the year's acquisitions. *Example*: 1931.511.
4. *Credit line*: identifies donor, fund, or institution that made it possible to show the object as part a museum collection or exhibition.

Example:
Vasily Kandinsky, 1866–1944
Improvisation No. 30 (Cannons)
Germany, 1913
Oil on canvas
Signed, l.l: "Kandsky i9i3"
111 x 111.3 cm (43 11/16 x 43 13/16 in.)
Arthur Jerome Eddy Memorial Collection
1931.511

Historians, museum professionals, and educators debate the usefulness and placement of labels. To find examples of what's considered "great," check out MuseumNext: https://www.museumnext.com/article/what-makes-a-great-museum-label/.

MUSEUM GUIDE TOOL KIT

Attention correlates with the ability to focus on stimuli, especially anything new or surprising. Guides create "attentiveness" by inviting visitors to look, see, name, list, and describe. But attentiveness is not the end point; the goal is to "go beyond" (Baumgarten, p. 4). By challenging visitors to direct their attention to objects, guides can extend the experience, spark curiosity (questions, discoveries), and motivate long-term interest in inquiry. Chapter 5 includes ideas for moving guests from "attentiveness" to *seeing* (understanding).

Of course, objects, situations, or ideas can be judged unworthy of curiosity by reason of being trivial or uninteresting—like counting the splats in a Pollock painting (Baumgarten, 2001, p. 8). The challenge is to avoid inane activities and direct attention to curious and interesting things with genuine potential to forward meaning-making.

During her tour, Clara used several strategies to capture attention, ignite curiosity, and pique interest in investigating tour questions/challenges. Here are more tools:

Hooks for Curiosity and Interest

Novelty: anything new or different.
Surprise:—anything unexpected, incongruous, or odd (e.g., details like names and numbers).
Dissonance:—anything that unsettles emotions, or provokes feelings of . . .

- Uncertainty—being unsure.
- Incompleteness—gaps, something missing.

- Unfinished stories, art, images, or sentences.
- Hidden or ambiguous things.
- Conflict—a mystery, problem, question, or challenge that needs solving.
- Complexity—something not easily understood or complicated.
- Unknown or secret information.
- Incongruity—things that shouldn't go together; impossible feats (e.g., how did a man in such pain [Toulouse Lautrec] make 6,459 pieces of art in such a short life?).

Questions (open ended)

What if . . .
What would it be like if . . .
How might we . . .
What would you do if . . .

Sentence Starters

I wonder . . .
Suppose that . . .
Imagine if . . .

ADVICE FROM MUSEUM GUIDES

"Curiosity is one of the best things!" —Janine Kinnison, museum guide, Dayton Art Institute

Docents at the Cincinnati Art Museum and Molly Flasche at the Columbus Museum of Art offer the following tips:

1. Don't be afraid to *not* know!
2. Start small: Volunteer to work alongside another docent on a tour. Phase in by leading at one art stop, then two, and so on.
3. Volunteer for short assignments. Example: CMA features "10 minutes on the dot" days that are open to the public. Docents arrive in front of a "dotted" artwork (plastic circle on the floor) at a posted time and guide visitors to investigate.
4. Ask about "Roving Docent" opportunities to hang out in galleries to answer questions and help with wayfinding.
5. Volunteer to research artworks or objects for which little information is available.
6. Find out if your museum has "touring tools" or "art carts" with supplemental items for tours. Examples: cultural textiles, clipboards, and pencils to record responses; magnifying glasses, and tubes for "seeing differently"; paintbrushes to use as pointers or to show brushstrokes; low-wattage laser pointer (under 5mW) to direct attention to specific areas; art cards (notecards with art elements).

ADAPTING FOR DIFFERENCES: *DISABILITY ETIQUETTE*

After Henri de Toulouse Lautrec broke both femurs, he limped and used a cane for the rest of his short life (he died at the age of thirty-six). It seems appropriate in this chapter to address ways to interact with people with disabilities. Here are suggestions:

1. Respect individual privacy by not asking about a person's disability.
2. Speak directly to any person with a disability, not a companion, aide, or interpreter.
3. Don't assume someone needs help. Respect independence. Many people with disabilities are capable of independently navigating accessible spaces.
4. Make small talk with people with disabilities as you would with anyone else.
5. Don't exclude anyone because of presumed limitations.
6. If a person appears to need assistance, ask to help before jumping in—unless the person is falling. Unsolicited physical intervention can imbalance those who rely on their arms for balance.
7. Avoid touching the following types of equipment, which people with disabilities consider part of their personal space: wheelchairs, scooters, and walkers.
8. Don't ask someone using a wheelchair to hold things for you.
9. When someone asks for an accommodation, make the adjustment if possible. Ask, "What can I do to help?"
10. Keep accessible paths of travel clear.
11. If someone has a vision disability and needs to be guided, offer your arm.
12. Give more specific directions to people with vision disabilities.
13. Face people with hearing loss when you speak.
14. If you have trouble understanding someone, ask the person to repeat.
15. Service animals are on the job. Don't touch them without permission.
16. Service animals are usually well behaved. If one isn't, ask the owner to bring the animal under control or explain it will be removed.

Intellectual Disabilities

People with intellectual or developmental disabilities have degrees of difficulty with reasoning, learning, problem-solving, and adaptive behavior. Adaptive limitations impact daily events like travel, shopping, following directions, and understanding environmental and social cues. Suggested adjustments include:

- Use respectful language, including the word *person* before identity (e.g., "person *with* autism"). Don't use "high" versus "low functioning" to describe anyone.
- Speak to adults like adults. No baby talk!
- Use clear, concise sentences and simple language.
- Give one direction at a time.
- Repeat or rephrase if someone doesn't respond.
- Be patient and allow time for people to process information.
- If someone seems anxious to please you, emphasize that everyone can refuse to do or say anything that doesn't make sense.

Sources

United Spinal Association: http://unitedspinal.org/pdf/.
> Practical advice on basics, helping, physical contact, making assumptions, requests, terminology, and more. The site includes sections on adjustments for people with disabilities that affect learning, mobility, vision, hearing, stature, speech, and more.

Art Education for the Blind (AEB): Artbeyondsight.org/sidebar/aboutaeb.shtml.
> AEB's mission is to make art, art history, and visual culture accessible to people with visual impairments. AEB provides and promotes the tangible benefits of art education, museum visits, and art making for children and adults with sight loss.

Metropolitan Museum of Art Accessibility Programs: https://www.moma.org/visit/accessibility/.

RECAP

This chapter explored the second *C* in *Creative Inquiry Process* (CIP): *challenge*. Innate human inclinations to pursue the curious and interesting were examined for their potential to spur motivation to create meaning. Research on traits and behaviors of "effective" guides was offered to self-asses and to examine Clara's themed tour based on four artworks. Themes were emphasized as core aspects of meaning-making because "big ideas" lead to conclusions about self, others, and the world. Hooks for curiosity and interest were suggested in the Museum Guide Tool Kit, and *Advice from Museum Guides* featured recommendations from docents. The section on *Adapting for Differences* described "Disability Etiquette."

To do a self-check, return to the Learning Goals in the chapter opening.

UP NEXT!

Chapter 5 explores "collecting information," which initiates the "development" stage of conversational tours structured around CIP. Since you've "seen" vignette guides coach visitors to "collect" ideas from objects, the challenge is to prepare for the next chapter by looking at an object in your environment for one minute. Collect as much visual information as you can, then list, web, or sketch what you see. Go for quantity first.

REFERENCES

Bajrami, Dunja Demirović, Nikola Vuksanovic, Marko Petrovic, and Tatyana Tretyakova. (2022, June). Competencies of a Museum Guide as Predictors of Visitors' Learning Outcomes: A Case from Canada. *Journal of Museum Education* 47(2): 251–62; DOI: 10.1080/10598650.2022.2062542.

Baumgarten, Elias. (2001). Curiosity as a Moral Virtue. *International Journal of Applied Philosophy*, Volume 15, Number 2 (Fall).

Bosker, Bianca. (2024, January 29). "What being a museum guard taught me about looking at art." *Wall Street Journal*.

Butler, Sharisse. (2009, November 4). Docent teaching practices: An implementation evaluation. Dallas Museum of Art.

CBS Sunday Morning. https://www.youtube.com/watch?v=pBKNifpTSFk.

Costa, V. D., V. L. Tran, J. Turchi, and B. B. Averbeck. (2014). Dopamine modulates novelty seeking behavior during decision making. *Behavioral Neuroscience, 128*(5), 556–66. https://doi.org/10.1037/a0037128.

DePrizio, Jennifer. (2016). Making the case for transforming training. *Journal of Museum Education Reader Guide*, 8, 3–9.

Fastrich, Aslan, Donnellan Jones, and K. Murayama. (2021). People's naïve belief about curiosity and interest: A qualitative study, *PLoS ONE* 16(9): e0256632. https://doi.org/10.1371/journal.pone.0256632.

Flasche, Molly. (2023, April 7). Interview with docent program coordinator. Columbus Museum of Art, Columbus, Ohio.

Gilman, Benjamin. (1918). *Museum ideals of purpose and method*. Cambridge, MA: Riverside Press.

Levi, Daniel, and David Askay. (2021). Group dynamics for teams, 6e. Thousand Oaks, CA: SAGE.

McLean, Kathleen. (2011). Whose Questions, Whose Conversation? in *Letting Go: Sharing Historical Authority in a User Generated World*, edited by Bill Adair, Benjamin Filene, and Laura Koloski, 70–79. Philadelphia, PA: The Pew Center for Arts & Heritage, 2011.

MOMA. https://www.moma.org/calendar/exhibitions/272.

Schep, Mark and Pauline Kintz, eds. (2017). *Guiding as a profession: The museum guide in art and history museum*. https://www.lkca.nl/wp-content/uploads/2020/02/guiding-is-a-profession.pdf.

Schuller, Constance. (2024). Personal conversation.

Weiler, Betty, and Rosemary Black. (2015). The changing face of the tour guide: One-way communicator to choreographer to co-creator of the tourist experience. https://www.tandfonline.com/doi/full/10.1080/02508281.2015.1083742.

5

Tour Development

COLLECTING IDEAS THAT FEED THOUGHT

Collect (verb): research, pool, or gather evidence to answer a question or resolve a challenge.

LEARNING GOALS

By the end of the chapter, you should be able to . . .

1. Explain why collecting ideas follows "challenge" in the Creative Inquiry Process (CIP).
2. List ways people collect information (receive ideas and emotions) and use options to express thoughts and feelings.
3. Describe strategies to engage guests in collecting visual information from museum objects.
4. Explain differences among looking, seeing, observing, noticing, and examining objects.
5. Explain how strategic/purposeful looking promotes meaningful conversations.
6. Describe how to *flexibly* use strategic looking.
7. Explain ways to debrief guests after strategic looking.
8. Give examples of useful categories to direct looking to *see* details.
9. Choose art elements "categories" to create a web. Put the name of a familiar object in the center and record visible details on legs. See examples of webs in chapter 4 and the appendix.

MUSEUMS ARE FOR LOOKING

Changing how we notice, changes what we notice. Claudia Cornett, museum guide

Museums collect and preserve objects for varied reasons, most related to "contributing to the common good" (Tishman, pp. 72–77). Opportunities for guests to investigate objects for personal enlightenment can develop a broader sense of self, others, and the world. To make that happen, inquiry into object meanings needs to be purposeful.

In everyday life, people continuously *look* for various reasons: to find car keys, monitor traffic, and scan for obstacles. A stand of cannas at the interchange can distract, until a speed limit sign is spotted, prompting a speedometer check. These instinctual kinds of looking are essential for survival. But people can *learn* to control observational skills, as scientists, law enforcement agents, and medical professionals do. Training in strategic looking aligns how you look with purpose. For example, to make sense, people need to look systematically for important details and try different perspectives (Choi et al., 2022).

Strategic looking is essential in gathering data that supports scientific discoveries, diagnosing diseases, and solving crimes. Strategic looking is also a powerful tool for advancing CIP. Of course, seeing something beautiful or surprising can be pleasurable and worthy in its own right.

REVIEW AND ADD TO

This and the following chapters progressively build on each other, and each chapter addresses a different thinking process in creative inquiry. The *collect* phase of CIP relies on thinking that comes before and thinking that follows. Previous thinking involved . . .

- *Creating Context* that establishes a welcoming environment and makes people comfortable and willing to take risks. The goal is for guests to feel respected and free to voice unique ideas and experiment with viewpoints.
- *Challenging* guests to tackle intriguing problems and questions by provoking curiosity and interest in clarifying the challenge, partly by reminding visitors of similar circumstances. What-if thinking triggers "best guesses" (called "hypotheses" by researchers), which suggest sources of what to look for and where.
- *Collecting* (this chapter) focuses on gathering information from sources to address the challenge. Observation is a mainstay of "collecting" and involves looking to *see* more and *see* differently. Guides suggest participants scan like criminologists to identify small details that could be clues to big meanings. Note: We use all five senses to collect information, but it says something that visual regions of the brain occupy the most real estate.
- *Connecting* (the next chapter) involves tying together collected information by exploring associations and relationships with past experiences, including unseen (implied) connections. But since minds don't wait, collected ideas typically stir quick connections that may or may not be relevant—like my own misinformed views in the next section. Since leaping to conclusions is problematic, this chapter offers strategies that slow things down and focus on purposefully thinking about meaning (e.g., overall tour themes) while collecting information.

COLLECTING INFORMATION: WHY? WHAT? HOW?

This chapter explains the why, what, and how of collecting information using our senses, particularly sight.

WHY COLLECT INFORMATION?

When I was eight, my grandmother heard me call a neighbor "ugly and mean." Quickly taking me aside, she said, "You need to think before you talk." She turned the moment into an object lesson about rash judgment with a sad ending: I learned the neighbor had been in pain from cancer. She died a month later.

Learning to delay interpretation until sufficient evidence is collected is an important life lesson. Withholding judgment is equally important in the context of tours. Purposeful, prolonged examinations of objects results in seeing more, seeing accurately, and seeing differently, which creates more meaningful connections with integrity (Hailey, Miller, and Yenawine, 2015; Tishman, 2017; Yenawine, 2013). Various protocols have emerged from studies about looking at museum objects that outline benefits of purposeful, prolonged collecting of visual information. Most include being more thoughtful about jumping to conclusions.

Professor Jennifer Roberts explains important relationships among art, vision, and time that extend beyond art history. She suggests we focus on "the value of critical attention, patient investigation, and skepticism about immediate surface appearances" (2013). To put Roberts's advice into practice, guides coach guests to look openly at surface features and then look differently to see beyond for *deep meanings*.

To discern what's significant in objects, visitors need to move into the role of *active* listeners (and viewers) and out of passive postures (Brown, May 2022). Strategic looking and other types of purposeful active engagement are important ways to actively collect "food for thought." This happens when guides suggest using visual strategies—what's seen by the eye—while keeping an "interior eye" on insight. And while "sudden understanding" appears to come out of nowhere, it actually doesn't. Most *eureka* experiences emerge from basic collecting of information using one or more senses over some period of time—sometimes years.

Guided tours usually last about an hour with three to four stops to investigate select objects, with a spare twelve to fifteen minutes per stop. Fortunately, researchers have discovered strategies that maximize observation. Brown reports that children as young as six can look intently at museum objects and art for fifteen to twenty minutes (November 2020), which is out of range for most tours. But three to five minutes spent collecting visual clues can significantly enrich inquiry that seeks thoughtful conclusions.

To understand how collecting visual information contributes to making sense of museum objects, think about the act of reading, which also begins with *looking*: What do you *see* when you look at the word *pule*? Four letters comprised of different lines. Two consonants and two vowels. What else? Is there a pattern? Can you recall another word with an e on the end that's spelled similarly? Yes! *Mule*. Maybe *pule* rhymes with *mule*? Okay. But what does *pule* mean?

Surface features like letters, colors, and shapes can't by themselves have meaning. Patterns help in that letters form spelling patterns that *suggest* sounds. But pronouncing (sounding out) isn't "reading," and looking isn't seeing. Reading is comprehending (creating meaning), which requires thinking beyond the word's (or object's) surface appearance. Context clues are vital. Try explaining the meaning of "run" without context. Context is also key to finding "unseen" connections that reveal meaning-laden relationships—which is the subject of chapter 6.

The point is, if you spot a stranger holding a bag of white powder, instinct kicks in. But you can tell yourself to look more carefully, consider the context, and your control impulses to suspect the worst, which can have disastrous consequences. Gathering more information is the wise thing to do in life, and it's highly productive in museums. For that reason, coaching guests to take a few minutes to do strategic looking—or listening, in music museums—is time well spent. With practice, visitors grasp the value of purposeful looking, including increased enjoyment and motivation to do further inquiry into objects.

Five Senses

We are fortunate to have multiple means to collect information for thought: We look to see and hear to listen. We also smell and taste, and receive, and perceive tactile sensations from touch, which triggers emotional responses. Of course, eyes don't see, ears don't listen, noses don't smell, and tongues don't taste. Eyes, ears, noses, tongues, and skin receive and then send signals to the brain. Only a brain can make connections and transform raw material (disparate ideas and emotions) into meaning. Chapter 6 address "connections."

WHAT AND HOW TO COLLECT IDEAS

Museum guide Janet Estep tells a story about asking students, "What's the first thing you do when you approach art?" Once a fifth grader replied, "Stand and soak up colors!"' That student had a plan for what and how to collect ideas. "Soak up" is a great way to receive information, which is essential to communication. But there's more to it.

Receptive versus Expressive Communication

Communication is a loop. After we *receive* sensory information, the brain processes this stimuli and makes connections, which Jean Piaget theorized happens by *assimilation*—adding to preexisting mental categories—or *accommodating* by creating new categories (Scott and Cogburn, 2023). People are then able to *express* thoughts and feelings by retrieving and sharing them in a multitude of ways: speaking, singing, writing, miming, and creating artwork, plays, music, dance, architecture, technology, and so on. Using expressive communication, we essentially convert *invisible* thoughts and feelings into visible, audible, smellable, hearable, touchable and feelable forms. Chapter 9 focuses on "communication options" for guests to receive and express thoughts and emotions using different vehicles, particularly art forms.

WORD BOX 5.1

These are key communication concepts.

Types of Looking

- *Strategic*: purposeful.
- *Slow:* low speed.
- *Prolonged*: extended time.
- *Careful*: thoughtful.
- *Close*: near distance.
- *Survey, inventory, scan*: do overall observation.

Receive Visible Ideas and Feelings

- *Looking*: taking in visual information (sense of sight).
- *Seeing*: process of brain making sense of visual information.
- *Noticing*: paying attention.
- Observing: looking with purpose.
- *Examining*: inspecting in detail to make sense.

Express Ideas and Feelings

- *Naming*: labeling concepts.
- *Listing*: compiling or recording ideas.
- *Describing*: noting salient details.
- *Transforming and showing or performing*: writing, miming, singing, dancing, etc.

Visual Communication

Since half our brains deals directly or indirectly with vision, "understanding the process of vision provides clues to understanding fundamental operations in the brain" (Sur, 1996). And the most fundamental mental operation of this abundance of gray matter is creating meaning. To facilitate meaning-making, guides coach visitors to view, observe, notice, scan, watch and stare at objects, which signals eyes to relay visual images to the brain for meaning processing.

Strategic Looking

Interest in how and why to use visual sensing in museums continues to grow. Multiple studies on looking at objects have now yielded practical advice on ways of looking to *see* (Broudy, 1987;

Brown, 2020; Chaparro, 2022; Feldman, 1992; Housen, 1988–2003; ODIP, n.d.; Tishman, 2017; VUE, 2009; Yenawine, 2013). Since frameworks for looking at museum objects—from "aesthetic scanning" to close looking—are purpose-oriented, the labels *purposeful* or *strategic* are used henceforth.

Strategic/purposeful looking involves collecting information by observing, noticing, or examining an object to reach the two-part goal of creating meaning and experiencing enjoyment. Both the quantity and quality of looking change thinking. *Usually* the longer you look purposefully, the more you see, and the more you see, the more you know.

Here are flexible guidelines to coach strategic looking:

- Focus visitors' attention on purposes (understanding and enjoyment).
- Encourage concentration (staying in the moment).
- Start with surveying the whole work. When looking at three-dimensional objects, suggest walking around, and looking from above and below (stoop or sit).
- Recommend several minutes of observation, using both whole-to-part and part-to-whole looking.
- Advise resisting the urge to see what you expect to be there and focus on what *is* there (Bosker, 2024).
- Experiment with distances (close/far) and angles (above, below, sideways). See Quick Reference.
- Suggest resting, if desired: Close your eyes or look away and look back.
- Look silently or talk softly.
- Work alone or with a partner.
- Debrief about discoveries and the observation process.

Categories for Collecting Visual Information

Some observational frameworks start with open-ended "looking." At some point, most recommend categories, often beginning with *easy-to-see* features. For example . . .

1. Sensory Aspects: Visual, or "seen," elements include things like color, line, shape, and texture, and subcategories of dark and light, straight and crooked, regular and irregular, large and small, and rough and smooth. *Example prompts and questions*: List or name colors you're seeing. How might this area feel if touched?

- Other senses: What might you hear? Smell? How might ___ taste? If you could touch ___,What might it feel like?
- Emotions/feelings: List ways the object makes you feel (e.g., confused, happy, curious).
- Adjectives: Add words that describe the look, feeling or emotions like "blood red."
- Opposites: Look for contrasting images (large/small, dark/light).

See Quick Reference 5.2: Art Elements and Composition Principles.

2. Form Aspects: Form aspects include organization or design of objects, created with repeated elements, perspective, emphasis, contrast, balance, rhythm, variety, unity, repetition, contrast, perspective, etc. *Example questions*:

- What's repeated?
- What stands out?

3. Expressive Aspects: These are ways to convey ideas and emotions. *Example questions*:

- What's the overall mood or feeling? What makes you say that?
- What relationships are suggested among the figures?
- What is the artist's message?

4. Technical Aspects: The technical aspects include materials (found items, oil paint), tools (torch, brush, camera), and methods (mold, paint, print) used to create the work. *Example questions*:

- How was this made?
- What kind of materials and tools were used?

5. Other Categories:

- Nouns: people, places, things.
- Verbs: actions and movements.

Quick Reference 5.2: *Visual Art Elements*

Use the following categories to prompt thinking about visual images. *Example:* "What are your ideas about *[category]* in this object?"

Art Elements

1. COLOR: *reflection of light off a surface.* Hues and pure pigment; endless tints, tones, and shades.
2. LINE: *a dot that continues on* (e.g., straight). *Note: Most basic element.*
3. SHAPE: *organic or geometric images* (e.g., triangle).
4. TEXTURE: *feel of an object.*
5. SPACE: *areas around objects* (e.g., background).
6. FORM: *2D "flat" object (LxW)* (e.g., painting) or *3D object (HxWxD)* (e.g., sculpture).

Composition/Design Principles

1. VARIETY: *using art elements in unique ways to create interest. Example:* infuse bits of old paper in painting.
2. EMPHASIS: *making one area stand out or look important. Example:* an element that takes up space.
3. CONTRAST: *using elements to highlight differences. Example:* put opposites like shadow and light together.
4. PATTERN: *repeating elements. Example:* parallel lines.
5. RHYTHM: *using elements that suggest movement. Example:* using "beats" of color.
6. UNITY: *when disparate elements feel like a whole.*
7. BALANCE: *harmonious arrangement of elements.*

Example: Strategic Looking for Two to Three Minutes

Invite guests to ...

1. Remember the goal is to create sense and enjoy discoveries.
2. Relax. Get comfortable. Focus on the immediate environment.
3. Start with silence or quiet (Vatsky, 2023, p. 92).
4. Let the art soak in: Survey the whole object and absorb details.
5. Think quantity first: Collect many ideas.
6. Take a few minutes to look to see/think/feel.
7. Let ideas and questions flow.

After a minute or so, coach visitors to ...

1. Go beyond first impressions. Look deeper. Think about what you're seeing and what's going on.
2. Suggest specific categories (e.g., art elements).
3. Look away for a few seconds or close your eyes.
4. Look again, but change position: zoom in and zoom out (move away).
5. Examine: Look to discover new features and details (Clothier, 2012).

Debrief: Use pairs or small groups to boost conversation.

- Ask: What ideas do you have so far? What are you seeing? What details are you noticing? What are you seeing that makes you say that? What else can you find?
- Invite to list (jot down) or name five things or happenings.
- Encourage guests to share observations. *Example:* Pass around and add onto: "I see _____. What do you see?" or "You saw ___. I see ___."
- Invite questions: What questions are you thinking about?
- Offer sentence starters: "I'm wondering ..."
- Encourage divergent ideas. "Tell me more about ..."
- Paraphrase comments to validate speakers and help participants remember what was said.
- Clarify observations: "Are you saying that ..."
- Ask for evidence: "What do you see that shows nervousness?" "What do you see that makes you say that?" or "Describe where you see ___."
- Prompt describing: "If you were talking to me by phone, what would you say about this object?" Or, "Describe this as if you are a reporter and I can't see the object."
- Extend descriptions by soliciting adjectives: "What kinds of browns do you see on the horse?" "Describe lines that show movement."
- Ask, "What are your thoughts about using looking to investigate objects?"

Before-and-After Observation

"Name it," "describe it," and "explain it" call for different levels of thinking. These "directives" can be used before looking to orient thinking and after looking to stretch thinking. To make guests comfortable, start with lower-level thinking (recall), which often is easier.

Naming: This involves giving labels (remembering and matching) for persons (tightrope walker), animals (horses), places (dance hall), or things (colors). Guides can say, "Look at the object and name what you're seeing," or after looking, ask guests to "Name things you saw."

Describing: Describing is more than retrieving from memory; it requires capturing key features by enumerating, comparing, and distilling details. Without specific instructions, description can funnel impressions that feature personal perspectives with unique emphases and omissions, as in "The Blind Men and the Elephant" fable. Trained observers like scientists, detectives, and journalists demonstrate that people can learn to objectively see and describe *observable* phenomena—"what's knowable" (Tishman, 2017, p. 54).

Explaining: Explanation builds on description but addresses how and why questions, as in "Explain how and why the artist created this sculpture."

Strategic/Purposeful Looking Tips

1. Start small (one to two minutes), and be flexible.
2. Set purpose. *Example:* "Take time to look carefully to see what's important."
3. Think aloud to demonstrate: "I'm letting my eyes travel over the whole sculpture—top to bottom, side to side. I'm examining details for clues to meaning. Next, I'll step back to see the whole work and squint for a different take."
4. Think "quantity first": Explain that longer looking sends more images to the brain, which enriches potential connections and promotes synthesis of concepts into meanings.
5. Offer choices like partnering, quiet talking, and viewing tools. See Quick Reference 5.2: Visual Art Elements.
6. After initial observations, look again to find more details. Suggest categories: shapes, colors, lines, texture, and "meaning-oriented" categories (chapter 6).
7. Acknowledge thoughtful connections. *Examples:* "Let's all take a look at the curious shape Joe pointed out." Or, "Your mention of artwork in the previous gallery is interesting."
8. To sustain attention, allow sketching and listing.
9. Follow up with questions that seek evidence-based interpretations. *Example:* "What do you see that makes you think that?" Or, "Describe where you're seeing that." See previous section on "Debriefing."
10. Ask open-ended questions for which you don't have answers. Avoid questions with yes-no or one-word answers. Use a three-to-five-second wait time after questions and ask for "every person response" (EPR) signals (e.g., raise number of fingers to indicate details noticed).
11. If visitors seem confused, restate ideas, give additional examples, or ask, "What might clear up confusion?"
12. Use sentence starters to invite conversation: "This _____ makes me think _____."
    a. "If you think . . . then . . . " or "What I notice is ___, and it makes me feel _____."

POVs: Points of View

It's impossible to process all incoming visual stimuli from objects while keeping an eye on insight. Inattention can be a problem. And *intentions* can cause us to "miss the forest" by focusing on trees. To prevent blindness to what's before our eyes, guides can suggest looking with "fresh eyes" to see more (Tishman, 2017, p. 37). It also helps to try out strategies beforehand. For example, sit on the floor to see what you don't see when standing. See Quick Reference 5.3 for more suggestions.

Quick Reference 5.3: *Point of View (POV) Strategies*

To change points of view

- Focus on collecting "whats," and save "why "and "how" questions for later.
- Do more than glimpse and glance.

- Alternate between considering the impact of the whole and examining details.
- Zero in or parts and pieces: Examine halves, quarters, or sections of objects.
- Explore new POVs by stooping or tiptoeing.
- Change distance: Move closer or farther away.
- Notice what stands out: Squint to blur details.
- Spatter vision: Do a full scan, then alternate between fixed gaze and scanning. Note: The Secret Service does this to identify movement in crowds, and Indigenous people use this to track game (Day and Schoemaker, 2006).
- Assume different roles (drama) to view (e.g., thief, nurse).

Viewfinders

- Use cardboard tubes, fist tubes, "finger framing" to narrow vision, direct looking, and discover surprises.
- Use a magnifier to find missed details.
- Use mirrors, sit, or tiptoe to see from different angles.
- Use a flashlight to highlight details.
- Use colored glasses or lenses to change appearances of objects.
- Hold up paint chips to compare colors.
- Offer textures to stimulate tactile sensations.

TOUR VIGNETTE: *LOST AND FOUND*

Since Miguel is a sculptor, he's particularly suited to guide a tour about "off the wall art." The group is at the last stop—a sculpture by Alison Saar entitled *Lost and Found*. View online at: https://www.ohiotraveler.com/lost-and-found-sculpture/.

Observation Cues

Looking leads to observation, and observations start conversations that propel collective investigations. The casualness of everyone sharing random ideas about seeing different things enhances conversation. As more ideas emerge, the potential for insight increases, uplifting everyone's understanding (Evans-Palmer, 2013).

Figure 5.1   Lost And Found. Alison Saar (American, born 1956), Lost and Found, 2003, Wood, tin, wire, 281/2 x 125 x 33 inches (72.4 x 317.5 x 83.8 cm), Dayton Art Institute, Museum purchase with funds provided by the 2004 Medici Society, 2004.16 copyright Alison Saaar, Courtesy of L.A. Louver, Venice CA.

Notice how Miguel primes the group for strategic looking by coaching students to . . .

1.   Understand and enjoy themselves.
2.   Concentrate on staying in the moment.
3.   Survey the whole sculpture and then its parts.
4.   Slow the pace and use observation options.
5.   Experiment with different points of view.
6.   Reflect on personal connections and meanings related to the theme of "shared humanity."
7.   Give feedback about the discovery process (strategic looking).

Be alert to how Miguel uses many strategies, including variations on these examples from the Museum Guide Tool Kit (Appendix A):

- *Short and Silent:*
- *Round About:*
- *Speed Viewing:*
- *Shifty Eyed:*
- *Find Five Flip:*

Vignette

After Mr. Hartje's American History class catches up, Miguel says, "Our last stop is the American Gallery. You're looking at modern art—twenty- and twenty-first-century paintings and sculpture. So, which sculpture catches attention?"

"That weird one with all the hair," Doug says.

Miguel waits as others look.

"The car door looks interesting," Constance says, "but Doug's right. That hair is curious."

"Curious rules. Space out and choose a spot around this sculpture. Take a minute to quietly look to see as much as you can. Get ready. Go!" Miguel checks his watch, then watches students stare and crane necks. When Georgia squats down, he catches her eye and smiles. "Ten seconds," he says. "Now turn around backward and call out what you were seeing."

Students tick off: "Two red chairs, lots of hair, brown bodies, arms and legs, wire, carving, tattoos, wavy lines," and more.

When they run dry, Miguel says, "Turn around. What are you seeing that makes you think that's hair?"

"The figures have people parts and wiry stuff coming out of their heads, only I don't see any heads," Todd explains.

"This isn't real," Lisa points out. "The same hair is growing out both heads."

"What do you mean, 'this isn't real'?"

"Unless they're Siamese twins, real people don't share body parts," Porter states.

"Before everyone jumps to conclusions, let's collect more information," Miguel says. "This time, slowly move around the sculpture for two minutes and do what Georgia did—try different angles to see more details. Any questions?"

"Can we sit?"

"Sure. And experiment with looking at different areas. Look for clues to what this sculpture is about." After a few seconds, he says, "Go!"

Mr. Hartje moves to the other side of the sculpture.

Miguel circulates around the perimeter. With one minute to go, he says, "Focus on details you didn't see before—textures, colors, lines, shapes." At two minutes, he calls, "Stop!"

"That was amazing," Georgia says. "I'm seeing a lot I didn't see before!"

"Like what?"

"That chair has the word 'LOST' and the other says 'FOUND.'"

"Who else sees that?" Miguel asks and hands go up. "Give me a finger count of how many new details you discovered." When a forest of hands go up, he says, "Get into small groups and share a couple of top finds."

After they rearrange themselves, Mr. Hartje joins the smallest group. As conversation buzzes, Miguel checks with groups.

"As a group, decide on your top-three ideas. When you're ready, give me five in the air." Shortly, hands wave like animated starfish.

Miguel smiles. "Choose a reporter to tell one idea from your group. We'll go around with each reporter repeating the other group's idea and adding on. Got it?"

"We're good," Mr. Hartje says.

"Okay! Have a brief confab to choose a reporter and give me a V sign if you're it." He looks around. "Okay. Georgia, you're on."

"The figures are metal."

"Good spy." Miguel points to the next group.

"The metal figures could be male or female."

Miguel points to the next group.

"The metal figures could be any gender, but the only colors we see are red and brown."

"This is getting to be a long sentence!" Miguel says, pointing to the next group.

"The crouched metal figures are androgenous, and everything is either red, brownish, or blackish."

"*Androgenous*! Impressive word. Mr. Hartje's group?"

Mateo hesitates. "Can I change the sentence?"

"Sure!" Miguel says.

"Well, Mr. Hartje's always telling us the word 'history' contains 'story,' and that's what history is about. So, we decided this could be a story of ways people are connected. Some have wiry hair, some are brown—those kinds of things."

The room goes silent.

"It reminded us of *The End of the Trail* sculpture, where we talked about people being resilient," Mateo adds.

"If you want to go with the shared humanity theme," Miguel says, "how might the red chairs fit?"

Camille's hand goes up. "Everyone feels lost or found sometimes."

"The figures might be mirror images of the same person," Doug says.

"How so?"

"They're almost identical on the outside, but maybe the words are about what's inside?"

"Look closer. Are they identical?" Miguel asks.

Students creep closer. After several seconds, Doug says, "There's raised, tattoo-like images."

"It looks like the pieces of tin on my grandma's kitchen ceiling."

"That's what it is, Porter, ceiling tin. The artist finds materials and recycles them into art."

"Is this sculpture an assemblage?"

"It is! But the artist also used molding, and carving." Miguel waits while they look. "So, how might those materials relate to history and story?"

"Maybe the beat-up tin belonged to someone, and it kind of absorbed things about the owner," Constance says.

"Things like what?"

"Hurtful things that left scars?"

"Hmm. The artist, Alison Saar, explains that in Africa, scarification is used to mark group identify. Her art explores themes about uniqueness that creates individuality. She thinks of the tin as skin, which protects us. She also thinks art helps us think about where the real-world ends and dream worlds begin, which connects to what Lisa said."

"Is she African?" Porter asks.

"Multicultural: American, African, and Caribbean ancestry. So, Mr. Hartje, how did we do with eking out story from this sculpture?"

"Amazing!" he says. "We'll continue making connections back at school."

"Can we sing the song about being lost and then found?" Georgia asks.

"That's an amazing connection!" Miguel says. "And you've been an amazing group!"

At that, the students applaud and sing "Amazing Grace" as they file out.

Debrief

Use the *Observation Cues* before the vignette to identify strategies Miguel used to coach students to collect information.

- What questions do you have about how he adapted strategies?
- What other strategies could he have used? (Review section on guiding strategic looking.)

MUSEUM GUIDE TOOL KIT

In Appendix A, the "Collecting" section describes these and other strategies:

Before and After Poem (Baird, 2017)

Write down three to five words that describe immediate reactions to an object. Then do purposeful looking, share thoughts, and make connections. Then write down three to five more words that express thoughts and feelings and compare.

Example: *Lost and Found*
Before: dumb, weird, silly
After: interesting, helpful, deeper, connected

Half and Half

Assign two groups to each look at half an artwork (Left, right, top-bottom, quadrants, etc.). Debrief using Turn and Talk. Compare observations.

Look, Sketch, Web

Use clipboards. Take five minutes to simultaneously look and sketch or web. Focus on a small area (e.g., one figure) or a couple of elements (color or shape). *Variation*: Free-write phrases.

Puzzle Pieces (National Portrait Gallery: https://www.npg.si.edu/)

Take a photo of the object. Cut into pieces that show something significant. Give each group one piece and challenge them to 1) study the piece, 2) describe what is seen, and 3) explain how the piece relates to the whole work. Invite them to assemble the puzzle on the floor.

ADVICE FROM MUSEUM GUIDES

"The best part is the light in their eyes." —Helen Rindsberg, docent, Cincinnati Art Museum

Check all recommended strategies that you might use:

1. ___Invite visitors to stand in the middle of the gallery and slowly rotate. After a minute, ask for general impressions.
2. ___To create a sense of calm, suggest picturing a serene landscape.
3. ___To think on your feet, make a Go Bag of alternative strategies.
4. ___Make tours more conversational—more about "doing" creative thinking than "viewing" creative work (Murawski, 2012).
5. ___Remember, wall labels make it harder to see what's in front of you (Bosker, 2024).
6. ___Refer back to the object and repeat ideas discovered by guests.
7. ___Use visitor interests to shape the tour, but note this makes tours less predictable.
8. ___Stimulate curiosity and conversation with scaffolds that direct attention to details. *Example:* "Find an area that's confusing or intriguing."
9. ___To boost participation, partner guests to share ideas.
10. ___Create a "cheat card" with open-ended questions: "What are you noticing? What else?" "What do you see that makes you think that?"
11. ___Explain that you ask questions because no one has all the answers!
12. ___Use three to five second wait time for everyone to process questions and directions.
13. ___Drip-feed information. Give a little *often* (e.g., three bits at each stop) and refer back. *Example:* "How was the previous sculpture different?"

ADAPTING FOR DIFFERENCES: *ADULTS*

Lackluster lectures deter guests from actively participating in their own learning. The following adaptations can engage all ages but are particularly important for adults (age eighteen and above). After perusing, choose three pieces of advice you want to use.

1. Be humble: Presume you know less about visitors than you think. Ask about interests, unique experiences, expectations, and needs. *Examples:* What's something else someone noticed about . . . ? How about a different idea? What's another way of looking at this?
2. Instead of thinking of guests as "blank slates," think of them "curious companions" who want to collaborate to make sense (DePrizio, 2016).
3. To encourage conversation about how artworks connect to personal experiences and emotions, emphasize there are no "wrong" things to say (Baird, 2017).
4. Ask open questions that guests can customize for themselves. *For example:* KWL: What do you *know* about . . . ? What do you *want* to know? What have you *learned* so far? Or what interests you about . . . ? (Ogle, 2022).
5. For younger adults, prompt connections to contemporary technology, culture, and current events.
6. Use tablets, phones, and other technology to enhance points.
7. Tailor adult tours to adults' wants: to feel at ease, have social interaction, participate intellectually, and feel challenged by experiences that expand perspectives and create worthwhile learning (Hood, 1983).
8. Show empathy for visitors who seem disappointed or distracted by issues like sore feet, fatigue, hunger, bladder pressure, crowds, noise, or hovering guards (Csikszentmihalyi and Hemanson, 1995, p. 72).

9.   Since visitors expect to hear from experts and actively engage in museum experiences, coach them to connect to objects with personally relevant themes (e.g., loneliness), and share pertinent information about *why* objects are considered "important" or valued over others.
10. Remember, most visitors don't want "expert" monologues and *do* want to participate in the conversations (McLean, 2011).
11. Insert background information to stimulate conversation and encourage purposeful looking, thinking differently, and processing from unique perspectives.

Mature Adults

Opportunities to share personal experiences benefits adults, engages listeners, and can generate valuable information for future tours. *Guides should ...*

1.   Invite perspectives on current events and past experiences using "remember when" and "compare and contrast" moments that comfort and spur participation.
2.   At history and art museums, invite guests to contribute perspectives from experiences that connect to exhibits from time periods during their lives.
3.   At science museums, ask for thoughts about technologies invented during their lifetimes.

RECAP

This chapter went into detail about what, why, and how to collect information, especially visual clues to object meanings. To self-assess, return to Learning Goals at the beginning and probe Miguel's vignette for ideas about putting "strategic looking" into practice. Use the Museum Guide Tool Kit as a resource for collecting strategies, along with recommendations in *Advice for Museum Guides* and ideas for adjusting for adults in *Adapting for Differences*.

UP NEXT!

The vignette in chapter 6 takes place in a house museum oozing with complex Southern history. It's a special challenge to engage guests in conversation at the site where the Union set up headquarters after invading Beaufort, South Carolina, on November 7, 1861.

REFERENCES

Baird, Kate. (2017). https://museumquestions.com/2017/02/13/how-can-museums-help-us-relearn-the-art-of-conversation/.

Bosker, Bianca. (2024, January 29). What being a museum guard taught me about looking at art. *Wall Street Journal.*

Brown, Claire. (Jan. 19, 2023). *How to Make Space and Time for Slow Looking.* Thinking Museum Podcast: https://thinkingmuseum.com/2023/01/19/how-to-make-space-and-time-for-slow-looking/.

Brown, Claire. (Nov. 19, 2020). *What Is Slow Looking? (and How Can I Get Started?).* Thinking Museum. https://thinkingmuseum.com/2020/11/19/what-is-slow-looking-and-how-can-i-get-started/.

Choi, Ji Yeon et al. (2022). Integration of visual thinking strategies to undergraduate health assessment course: A mixed-method feasibility study. *Nurse Education Today,* https://doi.org/10.1016/j.nedt.2022.105374.

Clothier, Peter. (2018). One Hour, One painting video. https://peterclothier.com/one-hour-one-painting/video-demonstration/.

Clothier, Peter. (2012). *Slow Looking: The Art of Looking at Art,* CreateSpace Independent Publishing Platform.

Elkins, James. (2000). *How to Use your Eyes.* New York: Routledge.

Horowitz, Alexandra. (2013). *On Looking: Eleven Walks with Expert Eyes.* New York: Scribner.

Murawski, Mike. (August 6, 2012). Doing, not just viewing: Working towards a more participatory practice. *Art Museum Teaching: A Forum for Reflecting on Practice*, https://artmuseumteaching.com/2012/04/06/doing-not-just-viewing-working-towards-a-more-participatory-practice/#comments.

ODIP: Columbus Museum of Art: ODIP: Columbus Museum of Art: https://www.columbusmuseum.org/wp-content/themes/cma/pdf/odipquickguide.pdf.

Roberts, Jennifer. (2013). The Power of Patience: Teaching students the value of deceleration and immersive attention, https://harvardmagazine.com/2013/11/the-power-of-patience.

Sur, Mriganka. (December 1996). Brain Processing of Visual Information, *MIT News*, Department of Brain and Cognitive Sciences, https://news.mit.edu/1996/visualprocessing.

Tishman. Shari. (2017). *Slow looking: The art and practice of learning though observation.* New York and London: Routledge, Taylor, and Francis Group.

VUE. (2009, Spring). Visual Thinking Strategies: Understanding the Basics. *Visual Understanding in Education*, San Jose Museum of Art, https://sjmusart.org/sites/default/files/uploads/files/Understanding%20Basics.pdf.

6

Tour Development

CONNECTING IDEAS TO CREATE MEANING

Connect (v): link, form, sort, group or classify to discover meaningful relationships.

LEARNING GOALS

By the end of the chapter, you should be able to . . .

1. Give examples and meaningful connections.
2. Explain how meaningful connections expedite creative inquiry (CIP).
3. Describe how categorizing, and finding patterns, associations, and relationships, supports meaningful connections.
4. Describe strategies (questions and prompts) that help guests make meaningful connections.
5. Explain why museums preserve historic artifacts and how these objects connect to expanded human perspectives.
6. Choose a personal artifact and use "Entry Points" for artifacts to explain what the artifact might tell archaeologists about you.

CONNECTING: WHAT? WHY? HOW?

> *"Everyone makes connections, it happens naturally."* —Adera Causey, Curator of Education at the Hunter Art Museum

Saying "I put two and two together" acknowledges that making meaning involves connecting disconnected ideas. The ability to connect discrete pieces of information is essential to creating sense, as demonstrated in a study of patients with amnesia. Asked to describe being at a museum with many exhibits, those who'd lost the "capacity to connect things to one another and find meaning" limited their responses to "big doors" and "people" (Greene, 2010, p. 2). Unable to get beyond names and labels, patients were left with isolated details.

From Collecting to Connecting

To connect the dots, chapter 5 focused on using purposeful or strategic looking to *collect* information, particularly visible details on the surface of objects. Since people possess an innate impulse to look, especially if there's something missing, hidden, or curious, strategic looking is a self-motivating strategy that lures visitors to puzzle out mysteries. Collecting visible clues is a start. But to make sense, clues have to be connected to one another. The search for links helpfully triggers dopamine, activating the brain's reward system and producing sensations of joy and fun (Greene, 2010; Tishman, 2017).

This chapter picks up where the previous chapter left off and addresses how to tie together the seen and *unseen* in objects—like symbolic meanings attached to artifacts as historic as the Liberty Bell. Collecting ideas continues throughout Creative Inquiry Process (CIP), but this chapter goes beyond collecting *more* ideas to *meaningful* connections among ideas.

Collecting can be open-ended, as in "pick any artwork and tell me what you're seeing," but guides and docents may also direct visitors to examine categories like colors and lines or more thought-provoking categories like "interesting," "curious," or "important." Whatever the categories, grouped "bits" of information have to be connected further to make sense (Tishman, 2017). Meaningful connections aren't end points, but they're a step toward creating interpretations that can produce insight into the larger human story.

From Seeing to Thinking to Knowing

The more we look, the more we see, and the more we see, the more curious and interested we become in investigating objects. Motivated to explore, we look for meaning. But seeing isn't knowing. If it was, young children wouldn't make stick drawings of adults with inaccurately disproportionate large heads. Kids don't draw what they see; they draw what they *know*—and they know heads are the most important part of people (Lowenfeld, 1987). They come to "know" this by looking: scrutinizing details, noticing patterns, grouping ideas, discerning relationships, and interpreting signs—mentally manipulating and combining sensory information. By connecting myriad clues, young children *conclude* heads are important. And they draw what they know.

If kindergarteners can turn visible clues into invisible conclusions like "size matters," so can museum visitors.

Connections and Brainy Processes

The ability to create meaningful connections can't be overstated. Without finding relationships among past, present, future, and persons, places, and things, each thought is "fleeting and unrelated, each precept without relevance, each person a stranger, every event unexpected" (Greene, 2010, p. 2).

Memory is dispersed across brain regions responsible for language, vision, hearing, emotions, and other functions, and neurons make and break astonishing numbers of connections, called synapses. To connect bits of information, the brain's nerve cells (neurons) have to find each other and communicate. While brain structures and processes like dendrites, axons, and synapses are beyond the scope of this book, it's important to know that the brain continues to develop well past middle age. And it's important for guides to know what can be done with this information.

Implications for Guide Practices

Knowing that memory is all about connections has "revolutionary implications" for education, "that suggest 'connecting' should be center stage in tours." Since "memory springs from the connections" (Greene, 2010, p. 3), and not the other way around, integrating connection strategies is vital to meaning-making. In addition, the brain's ability to strengthen or weaken synapses depends on plasticity, creating a "use it or lose it" situation (Dance & McAllister, 2020), which further justifies time spent connecting previously collected ideas.

Connections anchor and organize complicated bodies of information in the world, and in the world of museums. Coaching guests to connect unrelated ideas collected from museum objects establishes the foundation for understanding and comprehension (Greene, 2010).

MEANINGFUL CONNECTIONS

Thanks to brain research, we know humans are wired to recognize and organize coherent connections that create understanding. Meaningful connections are the opposite of mnemonics (memory tricks) like "Every good boy does fine"—a crutch for recalling lines of the treble clef (EGBDF). In contrast, meaningful connections arise from discovering sensical relationships among disconnected ideas—sometimes unexpected associations. Case in point, the *New York Times* "Connections" puzzle challenges players to *sort* sixteen unrelated words into four unknown categories. Today I spotted five words related to "foot parts": arch, ball, sole, toe, and heel. But each category can only have four words, so I randomly chose "heel" and dropped "sole." Bad choice. It took two more tries to discover the "right" combination, leaving one chance to figure out the final category. I stared at the words "dog," "heel," "jerk," and "snake," and pulled the trigger. Lacking background in slang, I failed. Fortunately I gained insight into humility, persistence, chance, and word connotations, which led to connections between this game Creative Inquiry Process.

Understanding Is Complex

Wall labels hovering beside art send the message that art is a riddle with a right answer (Bosker, 2024). That idea vastly underestimates the power of museum objects to provoke new perspectives. This happens when complicated images are viewed as treasure troves of *invisible* connections that can't unify parts into meaningful wholes. Guides can give visitors open-mindedness and patience, but they can offer "finding" tools and direct visitors to dig in places that are likely to produce conclusions. One of these places is relationships among collected details from observations.

Museum "wall cruisers," who grab glances at objects, miss all that comes with guided inquiry tours that focus on looking purposefully and making connections and having meaningful conversations. When visitors join such tours, they give themselves gifts of potential insight. As one visitor said, "It's like finding another world."

Personal Connections

Nothing is learned in isolation. Understanding depends on connections: *relating or associating* new ideas with past knowledge and remembered experiences. Even a small memory can reactivate a network of neurons, re-animating the past. As Anthony Greene, professor of neuroscience, explains, "Remembering is reliving" (2010, p. 22). Remembering is also connecting.

Connecting to prior knowledge isn't "taking" meanings *from* objects (or texts like books or music), it's "making" sense by linking to new to known. Art forms have meaning when a person creates it by connecting *objects to self, objects to other objects, and objects to the world* (Cornett, 2010). When connections are personally relevant, new learning becomes part of our brains and our being (Greene, 2010).

During tours, connecting begins with observing features like lines in paintings and finding simple relationships, perhaps how angles lead to a focal point. Over time, viewers not only learn that size matters, but so does positioning, as in being "center stage." Eventually connections form substrates for synthesizing big ideas that interact with beliefs that guide life. Those who take time to really examine *drop* the "baggage of prejudice and expectation," which frees them to untangle complex relationships (Clothier, 2012).

Categorizing

Humans take in vast amounts of sensory stimuli and categorize it like a well-oiled machine. Compelled to make sense, we automatically try to connect disconnected information by sorting. This starts early: Children notice objects with similar colors, shapes, and sizes and group them using cultural contexts. Throughout life, we continue gravitating toward figuring out similarities and differences and organizing disorganized information. We group, sort, and rearrange until the furniture looks right or the essay "comes together." Known categories are also used to *direct* information collection: Doctors examine skin for *signs* of cancer, detectives look for *patterns* in footprints, and teachers checks faces for signs of interest—same collection process, different categories suited to purpose.

Survival has depended on categorizing huge quantities of information into perceived groups, which are vital in situations in which discerning snake from stick can mean life or death (De Langhe and Fernback, 2019).

WORD BOX 6.1

These terms are used synonymously.

- *Connect, Relate, Associate*: link, join, group, or couple.
- *Categorize*: group, sort, or assemble.

CONNECTING: ROUND UP

To create museum experiences that go beyond naming, listing, and describing, guides ask *process-oriented* questions and engage visitors in conversations that focus on:

- *Creating* meaningful categories from collected ideas.
- *Connecting* collected information to prior knowledge and experiences.
- *Associating* objects with other objects, ideas, people, places, and things.
- *Finding relationships* within, between, and outside objects (e.g., pattern, variety, rhythm, contrast, balance, unity).
- *Using common thinking frameworks*.

   Connecting is messy thinking, but meaningful connections predicably connect . . .

- The object to self.
- The object to another object.
- The object to people or the world.

   As associations and relationships entangle and overlap, meaning unravels.

Guides help visitors meaningfully connect by . . .

1. Asking process-oriented questions

Process questions call for pulling together ideas. *Question:* "What's happening? What's going on? What's the story?" (VUE, (2009).

2. Focusing on meaningful categories

These categories stretch beyond identifying *seen* colors, lines, figures, etc. to . . .

- *Unseen* relationships and associations that imply mood, a narrative, and so on. *Question:* "What's the mood? What are you sensing that creates atmosphere?"

- *Signs and symbols* are seen things that stand for something else, like an idea (freedom), emotion (fear), traits (bravery), or states (importance). *Question:* "What are you seeing that suggests _____?"
- *Meaning-invested categories. Questions:* "What are you seeing that's curious? Interesting? Important?"
- *Patterns or repeated elements. Questions:* "What might *repeated* colors suggest?" "What's going on with the horizonal bands of colors?" "What kinds of feelings does soak staining stir?"

3. Linking to personal background

Associate something unfamiliar or "new" with something known to provide a foothold in meaning. *Example*: if a guest dismisses abstract art as "weird," make the strange familiar by asking, "What's something you recognize, perhaps colors or shapes? How is this like something you've seen before?"

- Offer scaffolds: "This object reminds me of_____," or "This object looks like _____. Follow with "How so?"
- Think aloud to demonstrate: "*This reminds me* of (sitting in a theatre, watching *Phantom of the Opera) because of* (the chandelier and phantom figure) (Shinn's *Tightrope Walker*).
- Refer to previous learning and solicit connections. *Question:* "What do you know about life in urban areas in the early twentieth century that might help us understand Ashcan artists?"

4. Probing associations and relationships

Cobbled-together observations can create inferences that lead to insightful moments about life "truths."

- *Present if-thens.* For example, "*If* we accept Robert Henri's idea that 'art is for life's sake,' *then* how does this exhibit contribute to life?" This if-then prompted conversation about how Washi paper benefits life by being meditative, repurposing, and preserving the past.
- *Combine parts and pieces.* Encourage guests to think beyond isolated surface features (colors, shapes, lines, and so on). *Question:* "What do all different lines and shapes suggest?"
- *Associate emotions, smells, music, and so on. Question:* "If you were in the audience of the *Tightrope Walker* painting, what music would you be hearing?"
- *Examine relationships within a whole composition. Questions:* "What are you seeing that connects the foreground, midground, and background?" Or "What seems important about the relationship between these two figures?"
- *Relate details that suggest context* (place and time). *Question:* "What are you seeing that creates the mood or atmosphere?"

5. Offering thinking frames

These common structures are used for thinking and writing:
Compare and contrast. Compare like things, and "also disparate things, such as what do we like more, a new shirt or a candy bar?" (Schapiro, 2022, p. 39).

- Ask how the object is *like* and *different* from other objects in terms of subject matter, composition/design, style, etc. *Example from a house museum tour:* "What does this house and its artifacts show about how life in the early nineteenth century was different from today?"
- Ask guests to compare/contrast human experiences. "How does nineteenth-century life contrast with yours?" or "What do you have in common with this family?" or "What's a big idea here about people and life?"

- Invite *similes* that call for comparisons using "like" or "as." *Example:* "This nineteenth-century house is as remarkable as _____." Or "This artifact is today's version of a _____."
- Represent one thing as another. *Metaphoric* comparisons without "like"/"as." *Example:* This house is a (frozen moment in time).
- Probe opposites. *Question:* "How do light versus dark colors make you feel?"

Cause-effect. Ask what happened *before* the moment in the image and what might happen *after*. Ask for clues to "causes" and "effects" (consequences). *Example from a house museum:* Guide says, "This house was bought with money from cotton and harvested by enslaved people. What so far suggests causes and effects of these decisions?"

Sequences or orders. Coach visitors to examine objects for signs of a beginning, middle, or end, or sequences of first, second, third; before, before/after; today, yesterday. *Question:* "What are you seeing that shows time passing? Or "Look at these photos and figure out the order in which they were taken." To probe narrative sequences overtime (Tishman, 2017, p. 49), ask:

1. What are you seeing? What's going on or happening?
2. What's the story?
3. What's suggesting "beginning," "middle," or "end"?
4. What's implying "before" and "after"?
5. What's this all about?

Problem-solution. Ask, "What's puzzling or doesn't make sense?" Suggest assembling parts and pieces to resolve the meaning problems (Tishmman, 2017).

6. Other Options

- *Change points of view (POV). Question:* "Thinking about Frankenthaler's interest in nature, what's another way to look at her 'abstraction' of reality?"
- *Connect to diverse human experiences* across time, culture, and place. Take the role of a figure, object, or place in an artwork or object: "Pretend you are _____ and think about how you feel." Pause. "Say a one-liner that expresses your thoughts or emotions."

ARTIFACTS: OBJECTS THAT REVIVE HISTORY

The upcoming vignette is set in a house museum full of artifacts. Artifacts are a distinct category of museum objects made by humans for specific purposes. To understand why museums preserve artifacts, consider the "tangible force" of an artifact like Abraham Lincoln's top hat and what it symbolizes. As "concentrated bits of history," artifacts directly connect people with the full spectrum of humanity's problems, values, successes, and failures. Artifacts are unmatchable tools for exploring the past. But coming facet-to-face with objects that represent views and norms that conflict with current thoughts and beliefs can be disconcerting.

Since artifacts carry the force of past reality, they require ongoing review. To help save humanity from itself, museums invite new interpretations that expand understanding about the human story, including our complicated history of repeating mistakes. When guests look purposely at artifacts and consider their use in particular contexts (setting and time period), they join curators, historians, and archaeologists who dedicate their lives to learning about and from the past. In sum, artifacts . . .

1. Make history real.
2. Reflect and shape history.
3. Are complex objects that contain multiple meanings and stories.

Entry Points for Artifacts

Connect visitors with artifacts by inviting them to ...

1. Think like archaeologists, historians, and curators who use artifacts to explain, connect to, and understand the past and present (Lubar and Kendrick, n.d.; Material Culture).
2. Imagine the artifact in the context of people, time, places, and events.

To connect to a narrative and explore history as the story of change ask ...

*   What were important events of the era?
*   Who would have been living here at the time?
*   Who may have handled the artifact or owned it, used it?
*   What roles did the object play? (Useful? Ceremonial?)
*   What knowledge and values of the time does the artifact reflect?
*   How do artifacts and artworks reflect change?
*   How can artifacts help us understand why society and culture change?
*   How can artifacts cause change? Example: Bicycles freed women to make life-changing choices.

To explore multiple meanings ...

Explain that artifacts are material things and communication vehicles that hold ideas, stir emotions, and symbolize values.

Ask ...

*   What could this artifact have meant to different people and communities in that time? (e.g., the confederate flag).
*   How was the artifact part of a web of relationships? (e.g., passed on).
*   How have meanings associated with the artifact changed over time?

To explore artifacts as time capsules ...

Explain that artifacts capture needs, wants, values, and behaviors of an era, holding clues about past life.

Ask ...

What do stylish shoulder pads worn by women in early film noire suggest about tastes? What roles did "candlestick" telephones play in technological evolution?

*   Why do objects from different times look different?

VIGNETTE: *VERDIER HOUSE MUSEUM*

Creating meaning relies on connecting existing knowledge to new information within particular contexts.

Science museums are rich contexts with objects that provoke natural curiosity to figure out how things work.

Art museums preserve artworks that invite us to connect with the creative thoughts of artists and their creating, inviting us to see and understand people in different times and places.

History museums hold objects that link us to the collective memory of our species and connect us to past, present, and future civilizations.

House museums are usually history-soaked old homes that guests visit to collect and connect with information about the past, compare ways of living with the present, and understand how to change the future. Visiting an historic home is also an opportunity to interact with someone's personal belongings.

Deriving meaning and insight from historic artifacts requires looking at surface features (outlined in chapter 5) and making personal connections by thinking about patterns, associations, relationships, and symbolic meanings.

Observation Cues

Historic houses contain artifacts, but they're also artifacts themselves. Guests typically want to know:

- What's the history of this house? (provenance)
- Who lived here? What were they like? (social and culturally influenced beliefs and behaviors)
- What did the owners do? (work)
- How was living back then different from and the same as today? (needs and wants)
- What happened to them? What's the backstory?
- How was the house and its artifacts made? (materials and tools)
- How has the environment affected the house and its artifacts?
- What do this house and its artifacts represent? (symbolize)
- What makes this house and its artifacts significant enough to be preserved? (meanings)

To keep from turning the tour into a "tell it all," the docent at the John Mark Verdier House uses prompts and questions, like those in Quick Reference 6.2, to help visitors make connections. Notice how he parcels out facts at strategic moments to transform the tour into something more than looking at an old house full of old objects.

Quick Reference 6.2: *Examining an Artifact*

Artifacts reveal what people valued, how they lived, and what they ate, wore, and used. Artifacts also unveil cultural views and behaviors. Use the following questions and prompts to coach visitors to collect-connect-and conclude.

Look Purposefully: Collect Visual (Seen) Information

1. What is it? Name or label it.
2. What does it look like? (Describe size, shape, and materials it's made of.)
3. What catches your eye? What stands out? What makes you say that?
4. Describe images, symbols, or writing on object.
5. Describe signs of use, age, or damage.

Create Meaningful Connections

What does the artifact suggest about the past? (e.g., "unseen" relationships and associations).

1. How is the artifact different or like familiar objects?
2. For what purpose was the artifact made? How was it used? (fulfilled needs or wants).
3. What familiar objects have similar purposes?
4. Who might have owned the artifact? Why do you think that?
5. What does the artifact suggest about customs: the ways people lived, behaved, dressed?
6. What does it suggest about how people thought, worked, and traveled?

VIGNETTE: JOHN MARK VERDIER HOUSE

"Y'all can come up either set of steps," Brantley says from the portico. "Hold the rail." Rolling up his sleeves, he waits for a mixed-age group of nine to ascend. "Welcome to the John Mark Verdier House, circa 1804. John Mark was the only son of French Huguenots—emigrants who fled persecution by Catholics in the eighteenth century. He built this town house with money from his plantations, including one over on Lady's Island." He points toward a bridge across the Beaufort River. "Like other plantation owners, he bought and sold hundreds of slaves, who did backbreaking work—planting and picking Sea Island Cotton." He holds up a faded photograph. "Here's the house sixty years after it was built. What are you noticing?"

"Soldiers. Probably Federals," a lanky man says.

"African people," Mary points out. "If those are Union soldiers, this man and woman are now free!"

"The steps got moved back," Tony notes.

"Why do you think?" Brantley asks.

"Probably to widen the street, like today."

"Exactly. Old houses are artifacts—big ones—that link past and present. What else looks interesting or curious?"

"Missing shutters, broken spindles in that arch. Houses are maintenance nightmares in any time period!" Barry says.

Brantley chuckles. "Well, this is a 'back to the future' tour. I'll give you some information, but keep an eye out for how artifacts connect us with yesterday and forecast tomorrow. Questions?"

"Who took the photo?" a young woman asks.

"Samuel Cooley. He worked for the Union Army. He shot this after November 7, 1861,when Beaufort was invaded. You probably have ideas about what happened between 1804 and 1861, but this house and its artifacts tell a story from American history from the viewpoint point of one family: the Verdiers. This front door is a replica of the original mahogany one, which we keep downstairs. Mahogany was expensive imported wood."

"So, Verdier strutted his stuff!"

Brantley laughs. "Let's go with Bill's conclusion and look for more evidence in the surrounding area." He indicates molding along the door and the pediment across the top.

"Lot of work to carve all this," Marion observes.

"You're right. This didn't come from Home Depot. Here's where it was recently repaired."

Everyone moves closer to examine a rosette.

"More deteriorating decorations," Barry says.

"It's beautiful," Marion responds. "And cool rope molding that goes on and on."

"You have a keen eye. It continues inside the house. Verdier was an exporter, so how might rope molding connect?"

Figure 6.1 John Mark Verdier House: Circa 1861. Courtesy Paris Island Museum.

"Ships have lots of ropes," Tony says.

"Ropes tie things together. Maybe Verdier was obsessed with holding his fortune together?"

"What makes you say that, Mary?"

"George Washington signed the Slave Trade Act in 1794, and the British banned transporting slaves from Africa in 1807. Verdier and fellow slave owners had to see smoke on the horizon," she explains. "I teach American history."

"Facts count," Brantley says. "Let's go inside and investigate more *art*ifacts." He opens the door and gestures. "Please stay on the floorcloth. No photography inside."

He waits while the group surveys an ample foyer with a large, ornamented arch supported by Corinthian columns. Beyond it, a stairway divides at a landing with a full story window.

"What's a floorcloth?" Amanda asks.

"It looks like a rug," Marion says.

"Handpainted and varnished canvas were *used* as rugs in the early nineteenth century. Mr. Verdier got rich by working his way up from merchant. He inherited five hundred acres from his father, who died when John was seven, but he purchased most of the three thousand acres he eventually owned. He must have been prudent with money—at least early on. Floorcloths were beautiful, durable, and cheaper than Orientals. This one's a replica from a Charleston house but it's 'period correct'—meaning it fits the time."

"The checkerboard pattern looks like marble," Mary observes.

"People knew how to fake then like now," Barry says.

"Keep your eyes peeled for more artifacts that suggest how people thought and behaved," Brantley says. "This is called a 'Federal style' house because it was built in the wake of the Revolutionary War and reflects views about democracy and the new government. The United States looked to Roman and Greek philosophy for perspectives on being a republic and a democracy. Keep an eye out for architecture that features balance and proportion."

"There's a central front door and equal numbers and sizes of windows," Barry says.

"What other architectural elements stand out?"

"The arch is stunning, and the support columns are the highest order, right?"

"Yes, Doric is 'dull,' Ionic has ram horns, and Corinthian is ornate. These columns separate the public space from private areas."

"Nothing but the best for Mr. Verdier," Marion comments.

"That centered window on the landing is something! What do you know about that?" Terry asks.

"Andre Palladio's sixteenth-century books on architecture included a three-part design, now called a Palladian window. He was Italian, but his designs were influenced by a Greek named Vitruvius."

"The past does influence the future," Barry notes.

During the next fifteen minutes, Brantley leads the group through a parlor with creamy paneled walls, and a dining room with a table set for guests. Each room has bespoke moldings, including fingerling and dentil molding. In the dining room, they investigate a case full of monogrammed silver that belonged to the Verdiers, and a pair of English knife urns (circa 1790) made of satinwood with walnut inlay. Tops are lifted to reveal circular mounts fitted to hold cutlery.

"We use slots in drawers for knives," Barry says.

"Keep the personal associations coming. You have anything like this?" Brantley points to a hand-blown bottle on a sideboard.

"A decanter?" Tony asks.

"It holds something. But it first captures something. What annoys you while dining al fresco?"

Bill chuckles. "You couldn't capture traffic noise in that."

"A bug holder?" Tony asks.

Mary throws up her hands. "It's a flycatcher. The Verdiers had flies like everybody else! And no screens."

"They also got hot in the summer and cold in the winter," Bill says. "Fancy fireplaces in every room."

"And no A/C," Brantley says. "They opened front and back doors and windows to catch breezes. Let's take this pass-through to what may have been a warming kitchen."

"It's not that now," Mary says, homing in on an artifact identified as Robert Smalls's desk. A wall label explains Smalls was an enslaved man who heroically piloted a ship called the *Planter* into Federal hands. Everyone quietly reads his bio, which details his service in the U.S. Congress from 1875–1886—five terms.

"Wow! This is 'in your face, Mr. Verdier,'" Tony says.

"Smalls also recorded slave life and reported seeing one slave wearing 'an iron collar with two prongs sticking out like cow's horns The owner was John Mark Verdier'" (Miller, 1995, p. 8).

"That's unconscionable," Marion says.

"There's more. Mr. Smalls was owned by the McKees—the family whom John Mark's son eventually married into. I'll tell more upstairs in the ballroom."

The group pauses on the landing to look across rooftops.

"Verdier owned land back to Craven Street, where the 'dependencies' were—kitchen house, stable, garden, living quarters for slaves. Gone now."

"House slaves, too?"

"Yes. You'll see their names outside the ballroom."

They go up, pause to read names, and enter the ballroom. Brantley allows time for them to scan elaborate architraves above each door, cornice moldings, picture rail molding, and abundant matchstick moldings. They gradually congregate in front of an ornamented fireplace.

"What's the story behind this scene on the mantel?" Amanda asks.

"It's a mythical depiction of Servius Tullius, the sixth king of Rome, head ablaze as a symbol of goodness and greatness. Mr. Verdier was drawn to classicism and ancient history. But things didn't go as planned. Around 1811, he ran up debt funding a lavish wedding for a daughter and college for a son and ended up in debtors' prison. Forced to liquidate property, he managed to transfer this house to John Junior, who eventually married Caroline *McKee*—remember that surname? They had five children. John Mark Senior died in 1827, and John Junior in 1857. Come over to this jib window and imagine it's November 7, 1861. Caroline Verdier was living here, but she couldn't have seen the great armada attacking Fort Beauregard."

"Not if that pink building was here," Tony says.

"It was, but she could have heard cannon booms. Along with most White folk, she skedaddled, went to Florida taking the family silver that could be converted into cash. The Union used the abandoned house as headquarters during six years of occupation."

"Then what?" Mary asks.

"The government had a tax sale to pay for the War and many Beaufort homes were bought by Union officers. Caroline paid her one-hundred-fifty-dollar tax bill—maybe sold silver—but never again lived here. The first floor was rented to a tavern and a barbershop, and this ballroom became the telephone exchange. Over the years, it deteriorated. In 1942, a committee used public subscriptions to buy it. Eventually it was renovated in the sixties by the Historic Beaufort Foundation and became a house museum."

"That's quite a story," Bill says.

"John Mark seemed like a smart man with questionable morals. And he worried too much about appearances," Mary says softly.

"Thanks, Mary. Let's check out the bedrooms and then go downstairs. I want to hear everyone's take on this."

Five minutes later, they're back in the foyer.

Brantley again holds up the Sam Cooley photo "John Mark Verdier knew firsthand about discrimination: He was the son of a man who fled religious persecution. He became a successful businessman who rose to the planter class and enslaved other people. So, what are your thoughts about three questions: First, What does the Verdier House teach us? Second, How is this house important? And finally, Why should we care about it?"

After ten minutes of spirited conversation, Brantley says, "Our time together is up. But I have one last request: If you could say one thing to John Mark Verdier, what would it be?"

Debrief

Return to *Observation Cues* to pull out strategies Brantley used to engage guests in "connecting" with history via an 1804 house and its artifacts. What's your opinion of the degree to which he shared information? What other strategies could he use to make the tour more interactive and conversational?

MUSEUM GUIDE TOOL KIT: MEANINGFUL CATEGORIES

To challenge visitors to find unseen or invisible relationships, suggest these categories:

- Subtleties: tiny details or ideas "in between" or "just beyond."
- Implied emotions and processes.
- Associations among colors, figures, places, etc.
- Mood, feel, or atmosphere.
- Symbols (stand ins) for ideas, values, emotions, people, places.
- Grouping pieces and parts that fit together.
- Interesting, curious, disturbing, confusing, surprising, important.
- Compositional elements: emphasis, variety, pattern/repetition, balance.

Check the appendix for more connecting strategies such as . . .

Closed sorts: Start with collecting in given categories (color, shapes, etc.), then find personal associations and relationships among what's seen (Tishman, 2017, pp. 10–12).

1. Open sorts (discovery): Observe and note feelings, then group into meaningful categories like most important, surprising, puzzling.
2. Multisensory inventory: Do an open survey of objects using all senses and emotions and then sort into groups.
3. Thinking Frame: Use a cause-effect frame to respond: I felt _____ because _____; I heard _____ because _____, and so on.

ADVICE FROM MUSEUM GUIDES: *CONVERSATIONAL TOURS*

"I love when they make a connection—learn something—and we're all excited." —Janine Kinnison, museum guide, Dayton Art Institute

Check priorities for engaging visitors in meaningful conversations:

1. ___Explain the conversational nature of the tour in advance.
2. ___Create a relaxed climate that invites unfettered sharing of viewpoints.
3. ___Explain the goal is creating personal meaning through inquiry: looking to see, making connections, and finding relationships.
4. ___Avoid relying on wall labels that imply meaning is in the work not the viewer.
5. ___Ask process-oriented questions that emphasize doing things: looking, seeing, thinking, feeling, relating, connecting, and associating.
6. ___Encourage thinking about implied or disguised ideas and emotions.
7. ___Use pauses and let ideas emerge naturally during conversations.
8. ___Encourage conversations about common features, links, categories, connections, associations, and exceptions.
9. ___Emphasize the importance of supporting opinions with evidence in the object. Ask visitors to describe evidence using directional words. *Example:* center right of painting.
10. ___Paraphrase what viewers say.
11. ___Clarify observations by asking, "What are you seeing that makes you say that?"
12. ___Link differing opinions by saying, "One person saw ___ because ___, and another viewer saw _____ because ____."

ADAPTING FOR DIFFERENCES: *CONNECTING TO MAKE MEANING*

Circle adaptations that you consider most important:

1. Reiterate the importance of listening to *all* ideas as the group works together to make sense.
2. Give advance notice that most questions have multiple answers.
3. Invite guests to share personal histories that address diversity themes like "shared humanity."
4. Adjust questions to meet needs: Repeat, speak slower, explain there are multiple answers.
5. For concrete thinkers, be specific: Instead of "What do you notice?" ask, "What do you notice at the center of the painting?" or "What shapes stand out?"
6. Use active listening, paraphrase comments, and ask individuals to repeat ideas for clarification.

To encourage adults and others to delay interpretation:

1. Explain that "strategic looking" is purposeful looking to collect ideas.
2. Explain that understanding is built on evidence collected by examining visual details in objects, describing what is seen, and having conversations about personal connections.
3. Instead of starting with, "Tell me what you *think*," say, "What is everyone seeing?"

4. Explain that to increase brain processing time, it helps to observe and then describe. This also enriches interpretations and impedes "rash" conclusions.
5. Suggest that it is worthwhile to examine the entire image before deciding what it is all about.
6. To help visitors report details, suggest taking objective roles (e.g., detective, nurse).
7. To promote objectivity, suggest naming, listing, or describing what you see as if you're talking to someone on the phone.
8. To encourage diverse perspectives, ask about variations on themes: "What's another way of looking at how the past affects the present?"

RECAP

This chapter explored what, why, and how to connect ideas collected during observations. Strategies featured ways to categorize and create personal associations. A special section on "artifacts" provided an advanced organizer for the vignette set in an historic house. The Museum Guide Tool Kit offered ideas for developing a Guide Tool Kit. Recommendations in *Advice from Museum Guides* focused on engaging conversations, and *Adapting for Differences* suggested adjustments to improve audience participation.

UP NEXT!

Get ready to learn how to inspire *eureka* moments!

REFERENCES

Clothier, Peter. (2012). *Slow looking: the art of looking at art*. CreateSpace Independent Publishing Platform.

Cornett, Claudia. (2010). *Comprehension first: Inquiry into big ideas using important questions*. Scottsdale, AZ: Holcomb Hathaway.

Dance, Amber, and Kimberly McAllister. (August 18, 2020). "Making and breaking connections in the brain." *Knowable*. https://knowablemagazine.org/article/health-disease/2020/what-does-a-synapse-do; https://neuroscience.ucdavis.edu/news/making-and-breaking-connections-brain.

De Langhe, Bart, and Philip Fernback. (2019, September). The dangers of categorical thinking. *Harvard Business Review Magazine*.

Greene, Anthony. (2010, July 1). "Making connections: The essence of memory is linking one thought to another." *Scientific American Mind and Brain*. https://www.scientificamerican.com/article/making-connections/.

Lowenfeld, Viktor, and Lambert Brittain. (1987). *Creative and mental growth*. Macmillan.

Lubar, Stephen, and Kathleen Kendrick. Looking at Artifacts, Thinking about History. Smithsonian Institution. https://smithsonianeducation.org/idealabs/ap/essays/looking3.htm.

Material Culture. (n.d.). Nine modes of interpretation. Marianna Kistler Beach Museum of Art. https://beach.k-state.edu/documents/photo-curriculum/material-culture.pdf.

Miller, Edward. (1995). *Gullah Statesman: Robert Smalls from Slavery to Congress*. (Columbia: University of South Carolina.

Tishman. Shari. (2017). *Slow looking: The art and practice of learning though observation*. New York and London: Routledge, Taylor, and Francis Group.

7

Tour Development

CONCLUSIONS THAT CREATE SENSE

Conclusion (n.) a judgment, understanding, or decision. synthesized from evidence using reasoning.

LEARNING GOALS

By the end of this chapter you should be able to . . .

1. List synonyms for *conclude* and *conclusions*.
2. Explain how Creative Inquiry Process (CIP) advances conclusions.
3. Explain the nature and importance of grounded conclusions and why unfounded conclusions can be harmful.
4. Connect the concepts of inspiration, insight, and conclusions to creative inquiry.
5. Distinguish among conclusions, interpretations, and inferences.
6. Describe ways to inspire people that produce insight.
7. Outline strategies to help visitors expand themes into conclusions.
8. Explain ways to create meaningful conversations that facilitate conclusions.

CONCLUSIONS: WHAT? WHY? HOW?

> *"The best thing is when someone has an 'aha' moment."* —Violette-Anne Onfroy-Curley, museum guide, Dayton Art Institute

---

WORD BOX 7.1

- *Conclusion* (n.): meaning, understanding, interpretation, big idea, insight.
- *Conclude* (v.): understand, interpret, synthesize.
- *Theme*: truth or concept.
- *Theme Statement*: proposition.
- *Text*: object that holds meaning.
- *Universal*: widespread, general.
- *Synthesize*: Pull together.

Creative Inquiry Process (CIP)

This chapter marks the point in tours when guests synthesize meaning. To review, tour introductions focus on creating a *context* for meaningful conversation and clarifying the *challenge.* Tour development involves *collecting* and *connecting* information to generate *conclusions.* Conclusions result when guests organize ideas into statements that express significant meanings about core "content"—what the artwork or object is about in a larger sense. Unlike a work's "form"—what's see-able" that motivates inquiry—content *"betrays but does not parade"* (Panofsky, 1955, p. 14; Tullio, n.d.).

Conclusions lift us above the work itself to underlying universal messages marked by "themes." For example, the film *The Shawshank Redemption* is about an unlikely friendship (theme), and the story exposes corruption (theme) in prisons. But the *overarching* or *unifying* theme comes from a comment from an inmate: "Some birds aren't meant to be caged," referring to effects of institutionalization on human beings. And as Picasso explained, "Art is a lie that makes us realize truth" (1923, p. 316).

From Themes to Conclusions

Themes are stepping-stones to conclusions. For example, the theme "freedom" is an abstract universal idea (concept)—as are intangibles like love, courage, and evil, which can be "sensed" from seen clues. Conclusions grow from themes: "Some birds aren't meant to be caged" is a poetic way of stating the conclusion, "Freedom is more important to some than others."

To turn one- or two-word themes into universal understandings (conclusions), you have to read the whole book, watch the entire movie, or fully investigate (look/see, think/feel) an entire artwork. Book jackets and museum labels offer teasers, but it takes the full experience of art forms to create meaningful theme *statements*: big-picture "truths" about humanity and the world. For example, a blurb about *The Hunger Games* can't provide what's needed to grasp the greater message about love. Is it . . .

- Love taken to extremes can be dangerous?
- Loving yourself makes a happier life?
- Love can make you care more about others than yourself?

The answer has to be personally "figured out" by reading or listening to the book or viewing the film.

Conclusions: Universal Meanings

To help visitors grasp themes, universal messages, and truths . . .
Connect to the known:

1. Ask about meaningful personal experiences (events, memories, and dreams) and what makes them "meaningful."
2. Ask for examples of powerful intangibles like fear, safety, hope, greed, and isolation. Connect universal concepts with themes, then ask, "What about (theme)?"
3. Explain that linking ideas to universal concepts adds relevance and power to messages. *Example:* A history interpreter might associate the Wright brothers with advances in aviation, but connections to human creativity and persistence reaches a wider audience by piquing innate curiosity and interest in universal intangibles (www.nps.gov/parkhistory/online_books/eastern/meaningful_interpretation/mi6j.htm).

Scaffold: Co-create meaning by stretching concepts into theme statements or conclusions using Quick Reference 7.2.

Generating Conclusions

Conclusions are theme-based statements about overall understandings derived from objects and experiences that communicate thoughts and emotions. Listing what's visible, like colors and shapes, isn't enough. Conclusions are *anchored* in collected ideas, but you can't simply "take" meaning; you have to "make" it. Generating conclusions requires *synthesizing* invisible messages that are more than summaries of parts, pieces, points, and subpoints.

Invisible meanings are built by connecting thoughts and feelings and expecting them to coalesce around important truths communicated by works. To fashion conclusions, think about themes (big concepts) and construct overall generalizations by asking questions and using sentence frames in Quick Reference 7.2.

Quick Reference 7.2: *Strategies for Generating Conclusions*

To prime synthesis

1. Unite parts and pieces to understand underlying idea: *"What is going on in this art? (object)?"*
2. Speculate on significance behind what you're seeing (e.g., motives and relationships): *"What's happening and why?"*
3. Determine importance: *"What's this really about?"*
4. Connect using metaphors or symbolic thinking: *"This reminds me of____."*
5. Offer evidence: *"What do you see that shows that?" "How you know_____?"*
6. Continue searching: *"What more can you find about _____?"*
7. Forecast insight: *"What new ideas are there?"*
8. Extend motivation: *"What do you want to know more about?"*

Questions

- What's the greater meaning?
- What messages are you left with?
- What's this mostly about?
- So what? Why should I care? What does it matter?
- What's most important?
- How is this work important beyond itself?
- What's most interesting or surprising?

Sentence Starters (Frames)

- In the final analysis, this is about _____.
- The overall message is _____.
- The important thing about this work is _____.
- My big takeaway is _____.
- The hidden meaning is _____.
- What's important but invisible is ____.
- A question this object asks is _____.
- My insight or *aha* is ____.
- The main things I noticed were _____, so I suspected____, and concluded_____.

References: Brown, 2022; Cornett, 2010; VUE, 2009.

Example Conclusions/Theme Statements

Conclusions are ultimate meanings or understandings about how and why people and events interact with one another. Conclusions explain and interpret important guidelines for living and often take the form of aphorisms, like "Don't hide your lamp under a bush"—a conclusion that advises capitalizing on one's talents. The following conclusions were generated from museum objects investigated in tour vignettes:

- *Risk* is necessary to achieve your dreams.
- Everyone wears a *mask* to present a desired image.
- *Power* takes constructive and destructive forms.
- Knowing history helps prevent repeating *bad decisions*.
- *Evil* deeds are their own punishment.
- *Identity* grows with life experiences.
- *Trust* is hard to achieve and easily broken.
- You can feel *alone* in a crowd.

WORD BOX 7.3

- *Eureka*: "I found it!"
- *Insight*: Moment of discovery.
- *Aha*: Expression of sudden understanding.
- *Ha-ha*: Laughter after an *aha!*
- *Inspiration*: Urge to create.

Magic Moments

Conclusions arise from reflection on connections (associations and relationships) among ideas that are then synthesized into threads of "greater" meaning that can appear as insight. The potential for insight is innate, as demonstrated in a series of experiments: Boxes were positioned near the chimps with fruit hung nearby. When chimps observed they couldn't reach the fruit, they stopped, looked around, and seemed to think. After some time, they stacked the boxes, climbed up, and got the fruit. This moment of realizing the solution was interpreted as "insight" (Kohler, 2019).

Instances when conclusions suddenly materialize are also called "light bulb" moments. But such eruptions of clarity have nothing to do with electricity: Most insight extends from the *intentional* collection of ideas, followed by the brain experimenting with connections. A famous insight moment, from the second century BCE, occurred when King Hero wanted to know if his crown was pure gold. He posed the challenge to Archimedes, a Greek polymath, explaining the crown couldn't be harmed, and Archimedes accepted. The polymath started collecting and connecting ideas, and at some point, he prepared to take a bath (a good way to incubate ideas). Lowering himself into the tub, he noticed his body displaced water, did quick calculations involving volume and density, and reached a conclusion so wonderful he jumped out and shouted, "Eureka!" Fourteen centuries later, Isaac Newton (fully clothed) had a weighty "aha" moment after watching an apple fall from a tree (Newman, 2022).

Eureka! moments are insight experiences that follow collecting, arranging (connecting), and rearranging information to uncover clues related to a challenge. Insight can appear after a few minutes, or after decades. Insights—fully formed conclusions—feel exhilarating, like a gift of understanding.

Inspiration Matters

Inspiration also stems from unexpected connections between known and new information (Scott, 2011). Unfortunately being inspired *by* something doesn't guarantee *acting on* inspiration (Thrash and Elliot, 2003). In the context of guided tours, the goal is to inspire individuals to *act* by coaching them to use CIP to generate conclusions that rise to insight.

To inspire visitors, encourage them to . . .

1. Engage in inquiry by accepting challenges, which is mental preparation for inspiration.
2. Put forth effort (e.g., do purposeful looking).
3. Remain open to experiences, including subtle signs ("feelings") of being on the right path.
4. Persist in searching for larger meanings.
5. Savor small discoveries (connections) that energize creative inquiry.
6. Remain optimistic and confident in the inquiry process.
7. Expect intrinsic versus external rewards, like praise or medals.

Inspiration "favors the prepared mind." Mastery of work, absorption, creativity, perceived competence, and optimism are also *consequences* of inspiration, suggesting that inspiration produces positive psychological states (Scott, 2011).

Coaching Inspiration

After museum educator Jason Pallas (2021) noticed a pattern of insight following student interactions with someone or something that sparked new thinking, he developed an inventory to determine which conditions nurture insight. Here are examples:

1. Spend more time on a *few* objects.
2. Emphasize that "inspirational" moments stem from *unusual* connections.
3. Use arts-based communication as response options. See chapter 9.
4. Facilitate conversations that focus on "important" ideas.
5. Offer "provocations" that yield the "most inspiration" (Scott, 2011, pp. 171–75).

Provocative objects stir awe, suggesting there's something "greater than the object itself." Inspiring objects are perceived to have intrinsic value, as opposed to extrinsic (e.g., monetary) value (Scott, p. 173).

To inspire visitors:

1. Select objects and activities that trigger wonder. Challenge guests to *"Find a work you can't stop looking at."* Or, *"Stare at the painting until you feel immersed. Feel the emotions."*
2. Share personal "captivation": *"I stood in front of Michelangelo's sculpture of David and couldn't stop looking!"*
3. Share examples of awe: *"The art gave me chills because stars from the chandelier are falling onto a figure doing something both breathtaking and beautiful."*
4. Explain the "art attack" phenomenon: a psychosomatic condition sparked by encounters with beauty. Symptoms include rapid heartbeat, vertigo, confusion, and hallucinations (Marinho et al., 2021).

WORD BOX 7.4

- *Draw Conclusions*: figure out, interpret, make judgments.
- *Reason*: use evidence to form conclusions, make predictions, explain.

Conclusions versus Inferences

Conclusions and inferences are similar, but not the same. Both tap collected information and personal frames of reference. However, inferences are guesses based on limited information. For example, I can *infer* that mud on my kitchen floor came from my husband's shoes, but this is an *assumption*, meaning I didn't see him do it, and we have a dog. Connecting past behavior, I could *infer* he made the mess. But it's unreasonable to use one instance to form a solid conclusion. Without further evidence, I can only speculate (make a *tentative conclusion*).

Inferences *are* associated with cause-effect and other relationships, but the information base is thin. Valid conclusions require more, like evidence that establishes patterns. For example, if Spouse X *repeatedly* makes messes that he doesn't clean up, Spouse Y might reasonably conclude that "persistent disregard for another person damages a relationship."

We learn by connecting ideas, images, events, and outcomes. Connecting new with known produces strong conclusions when judgment, interpretation, and decision-making are used to unite *bodies* of information. Over millennia, humans have created uncountable conclusions about profound experiences, especially love: Love is a reason for living; it's better to have loved and lost than never loved at all; and so on.

Inferences based on limited information feed speculations that can eventually rise to conclusions about why something is important, how one event influences another, and how one thing provokes another. But as with reading books, collecting facts about objects is not enough to generate full-bodied conclusions. Grounded conclusions are the goal, and they require cogitating on what facts *mean* in life.

Conclusions about museum objects can seem like solutions to mysteries. Think back to Shinn's *Tightrope Walker* (chapter 1). Using inductive thinking, visitors collected visual evidence, made connections, and inferred—from collected evidence—that the figure was a performer because there's an obvious audience. But so what? Conclusions answer meaning questions like, "What's this painting all about?" and "What message does it communicate that's important enough for the painting to be preserved in a museum?"

STRATEGY ROUND-UP: GENERATING CONCLUSIONS

To facilitate conclusions, guides ...

1. Establish comfort with ambiguity and complexity.
   - Explain that no one knows everything, but everyone can *wonder.* Ask, *"What do you wonder about this painting?"* Or use the frame: *"I'm wondering _____ because _____."*
   - Share perspectives about ambiguous or complex objects: *"We can't always know what the artist intended."* Or, *"Some people think the figure was meant to look see-through, but no one knows."*
   - Model comfort with complexity: *"Kandinsky's art is complicated, but that makes it more fun to investigate."*
2. Pursue additional investigation and evaluation.
   - Suggest that objects look different from other perspectives: *"Let's try sitting down and looking up at Kandinsky's work."*
   - Respond to questions about alternative meanings by inviting continuing search: *"Look again and find something you didn't see before."*
   - Pose curiosities: *"What is in this work makes you curious?"* or *"If you could ask anything, what would you ask about this artwork?"*
3. Collect-Connect-Conclude.
   - Review collected information to "connect dots": Coach guests to search for patterns, groupings (categories), associations, and relationships.

- Suggest thinking about hidden or unseen meanings. *"For example, the color red draws attention and can imply heat or intense emotions, like rage and passion. But how do these associations relate to this object?"*
- Suggest finding unusual connections by pulling together ideas and looking for common threads (themes and big ideas).
- Incubate: Disconnected ideas can make sense after reflection and incubation. Social psychologist and educator Graham Wallas proposed that "breaks" advance creative thinking (Wallas, 1926). After guests collect and connect ideas, suggest a recess: *"Take a thirty second vacation from inquiry. Breathe in and out and give the brain time to process connections into discoveries."*

4. Coach for Conclusions.
- Think aloud to model "speculation" (whys, how might, and maybes). *Example: "I'm still wondering about the figure's relationship to the audience. Maybe he's worried about falling on them!"*
- Suggest personal connections to speculate about meanings. *Example: "All the short, wiggly lines feel like being in motion is exciting."*
- Explain: *"Objects hold visible and invisible clues. Look carefully and think about the overall composition. What are possible messages?"* or *"What does this [object] say about people, places, things, or processes?"*
- Provoke curiosity: *"What is hidden? Confusing? Missing? Intriguing?"*
- Explain how to interpret: *"Try to get beyond what you're seeing and 'read between the lines.' On the surface, 'Three Little Pigs' is about silly pigs and a wily wolf. But the deeper message is about building a solid foundation for life."*
- Ask for interpretations: *"What does the work say about life?"* or *"What else could this be about?"* or *"What questions does this object raise?"*
- Invite groups to create headlines, captions, or alternate titles. Explain that titles often refer to big ideas (e.g., *To Kill a Mockingbird* is about the mindlessness of abusing vulnerable living things).
- Ask, *"What will you remember most about this object?"* *"What's the artist's main message?"*
- Prioritize "best" ideas that unite bodies of information. Tie together what's most important to form a conclusion that answers: *"What's this all about?"* *"What's the big idea, truth, or meaning?"*

Facilitating Meaningful Conversations

Think of tours as casual conversations among "curious companions" (DePrizi, 2016) who cooperate to make discoveries and share insight. Guides facilitate these conversations by . . .

- Encouraging the free exchange of ideas.
- Posing issues and raising confusions.
- Asking open-ended questions.
- Asking for evidence: "What makes you say that?"
- Listening attentively and connecting comments: *"So, Sue said ___, Mary thinks ___, and Todd thinks ___."*
- Encouraging empathy.

Conversations cultivate empathy when people "think they are talking about a portrait, and it turns out they are reflecting on how we treat one another," or they're "talking about colors and shapes, and it turns out they are struggling to make sense of the past" (Baird, 2017). Quick References 7.5 and 7.6 have more conversation pointers.

Quick Reference 7.5: *Inquiry Conversations*

To stimulate meaning-oriented conversations, invite a visual survey of the work to gather observations and discover ideas. Ask for "seeable" evidence that supports ideas, and use the following questions and prompts to encourage more looking and thinking about meaningful categorizes.

Look/See—Think/Feel Process

- Describe what you're looking at or seeing. What are you thinking/feeling? What's going on? What's happening?
- What's visible? *Prompts:* art elements, design elements, persons, places, things.
- What can you see from different distances and angles?

Personal Connections

- What does this remind you of? What ideas does [object] make you think of?
- Associate or relate the object to something known (previous experiences/knowledge).

Comparisons

- How is this [object] different or like [another object]?
- Compare and contrast. This [object] is like _____ because ____. This [object] is different from _____ because _____.

Sensations

- Associate smells, tastes, sounds, and tactile responses.
- Describe feelings/emotions.

Imagination, Interest, and Curiosity

- What are you seeing that catches your eye?
- What captures your imagination?
- What's curious? Interesting? Puzzling?

Unseen

- What is unseen, implied, or invisible? (e.g., mood, relationships, symbols, metaphors).

Point of View

- What is the viewer's point of view (POV)? Where are you looking from? What messages does the POV send about the [object] and artist's intentions?

Process. Materials, Tools

- What did the maker do to create this [object]?

Inspiration

- What might have motivated the maker?
- Prompt with categories: nature, light, beauty, event, people, place, thing.

Importance

- What seems most important?
- Prompt with signs of importance: repetition of colors, lines, etc.; emphasis, size; design or composition of the object.
- Why should anyone care about this? How does it enlighten understanding about humanity, places, things, and so on?

Conclusions/Themes

- What is this work mostly about?
- Give this [object] another title or caption that encapsulate the message.

Quick Reference 7.6: *Features of Meaningful Conversations*

To facilitate substantive conversations, coach participants to …

- Join in brief "icebreakers" that prime inquiry: Shake hands. Wear name tags. Share non-threatening information (cake or pie preference?).
- Not worry about saying something "wrong." *Note:* This builds trust, which stimulates the release of oxytocin, while distrust closes down responses (Glaser, 2014).
- Engage in *respectful* exchange of ideas and viewpoints to move thinking forward. Show respect through what you say and how (e.g., voice facial expressions).
- Co-create meaning by discovering and sharing ideas.
- Honor and support unfamiliar or odd viewpoints.
- Delay judgment.
- Empathize by considering viewpoints of others.
- Listen to *connect* versus reject. Meanings are what listeners hear, not what speakers say (Glaser, 2014).
- Improvise and play off each other's ideas.
- Support new ideas, tolerate conflict, and enjoy surprises.
- Feel free to add to the "agenda."
- Co-create conclusions, truths, and insights.
- Value relationships over being right or completing tasks.
- Enjoy shared success.

Tracking Conversations

Talking together, people can make sense of complex artworks. Tracking eases meaning construction by making it obvious how thinking unfolds. During tracking, guides connect visitor observations in real time, which can inspire continued searching until diverse ideas coalesce into strands of thought (Vue, 2009, Spring).

To facilitate the process of pulling together common threads of thought, guides must attend to what visitors' say while simultaneously connecting ideas. It takes practice, but tracking can motivate transformational conversations. *As participants debate and share ideas …*

1. Acknowledge agreements and disagreements: *"It seems that several people see___,"* or *"We now have a variety of opinions that include_____."*
2. Point out that repeats of similar observations add accuracy and can spark more and different views: *"Joe, Bob, and Iris all focused on the unusual viewpoint, so let's look at that some more."*
3. Connect ideas that reference someone else's idea: *"Reba said the figure looks sad because his head is tilted, but Bob thinks he's concentrating."*
4. Note shifts: *"Several of you first thought he was sad, but now you're saying he might be worried about falling."* Or *"You changed your mind and added another possibility."*

VIGNETTE: *PUBLIC ART CHAT*

Every museum holds hundreds or thousands of objects, each with a unique backstory. So many riches can tempt guides, docents, or interpreters to "wax encyclopedic" about fascinating facts. But that defeats the tour purpose of empowering guests to create personal meaning (French, 1995).

Instead, guides should inspire powerful moments of understanding by coaching guests to investigate comprehensible images, along with frustratingly incomprehensible ones. Guides do this by facilitating casual inquiry conversations that seek fresh perspectives and meaningful connections. Inquiry can also stir unease and anxiety, but some degree of dissonance "awakens the brain to look again, rethink, and reassemble itself" (Hein, 1998, p. 178). But as respectful discourse becomes increasingly difficult, museums are offering rare opportunities to engage in really good conversation (Baird, 2017).

Observation Cues

The following vignette begins fifteen minutes into a scheduled public event called "Art Chat." Art Chat is advertised as an open-ended conversation about an object or objects, facilitated by a docent. Visitors joining the tour understand the participatory format and know the goal is to create personal meaning anchored in seen and unseen aspects of artworks.

After welcoming guests, Hazel, the docent, offers name tags and folding stools, then escorts the group to a gallery. As you "observe" Hazel, take her point of view, but also take a visitor's perspective. Note how guests make personal connections. Pay attention to strategies Hazel uses to engage looking, thinking, and feeling. How and why does she . . .

- Recap the Creative Inquiry Process (CIP): review the collect phase, and coach guests to connect and conclude?
- Use open-ended *process-oriented* questions?
- Integrate important information about the artist and artistic processes (e.g., quotes and facts)?
- Validate speakers' ideas?
- Facilitate conversations that generate conclusions?

Vignette: Kandinsky's Improvisation No. 30

View art online at https://www.artic.edu/artworks/8991/improvisation-no-30-cannons?print=true.

Hazel's group of eight visitors—one using a walker and two in wheelchairs—has been responding to her question, "What are you seeing?" as they examine at Wassily Kandinsky's large, abstract painting.

"So far, you've collected details like curvy lines and bright colors—especially lots of reds and blues—and geometric shapes," she says. "What else are you seeing and *feeling*?"

Samantha rolls back and squints. "I'm seeing a crowd of frightened people on the lower left."

When Evan steps closer, others lean forward. Everyone stares in silence.

"What makes you say, 'frightened people'?" Hazel asks.

"The red blobs look like the mouth in Munch's *The Scream*."

Figure 7.1 Improvisation #30 (Cannons). Wassily Kandinsky, Imrpovisation #30 (Cannons), The Art Institute of Chicago, Creative Commons (CCO).

"I see that," Ava says. "They're huddled together as grayness engulfs them."

Thelma edges forward. "Maybe that's smoke. It looks like that leaning tower is about to topple. The brown rectangles on the far right could be a cannon going off. Up higher, the red, squarish thing looks like a falling building."

"It feels like things are coming apart," Robin adds. "It's a beautiful painting, but it's frightening, and overwhelming."

Hazel gestures toward the group. "What else are you sensing?"

"Disoriented," Evan says. "The sinuous lines appear to outline an explosion from the cannon Thelma spotted. The canon's wheels suggest Civil War–era artillery."

Charlotte points to an area above the cannon image. "I see piano keys!"

"It's interesting you said, 'piano keys,' Hazel says. "The artist was influenced by musical elements like rhythm. He also wrote about making colors 'sing with intensity.'"

"These buildings have the look of iconic architecture I saw in Moscow—brightly colored domes, grand spires, towers," Robin says. "But war plays on."

"What year was this painted?" Ava asks.

Hazel steps aside to read the museum label. "1913. Right before World War I broke out."

"I see the title is *Improvisation*," Evan says. "Which could relate to variations on events like war, or music or art or any creative work."

"Kandinsky's art, born of 'great bursts of creativity,' influenced most twentieth-century abstract art."

"That explains why the vaunted Art Institute of Chicago thinks it's important enough to hang in their gallery," Charlotte announces.

"Kandinsky also wrote about how art expresses emotions and 'spiritual vibrations' better than actual reality. This idea put him out front in the art world."

"An *avant-garde* guy?"

"More like *the* avant-garde guy. He's credited with creating the first piece of abstract art in 1913: *Black Lines*. He painted powerful, imagined, dreamlike images of 'what-ifs.'"

As the group moves around for different views, Samantha says, "The lines have aggressive energy. Amplified by surging blobs of color that feel primal and violent."

Evan smiles. "You sound like a museum curator!"

Chuckles lighten the moment.

Hazel leans in. "So, we've talked about smoke and artillery and buildings falling and lots of uncomfortable emotions triggered by shapes and colors. What didn't I mention?"

"It's shocking," Evan murmurs.

"Evan says it's 'shocking.' Think about his reaction and take a few minutes to consider takeaways from our conversation. What message does this painting communicate? What's the truth that's bigger than this artwork itself?" She pulls clipboards and pencils from a bag. "I have these if you think better in writing. Feel free to sketch a web or create a caption or headline." She holds up an example of a web. "Questions?" Hearing none, she steps away.

Two guests pair up and immediately begin writing. Several continue examining the art. After three minutes, Hazel asks guests to share whatever thoughts they have with others. As people talk in twos and threes, she circulates and hears:

"I'd call this *Dark Visions of the Future*."

"It's a fight against chaos. A never-ending battle."

"Artists are the only winners."

"Humans are innately violent. We can't control ourselves."

"It's about creating beauty from the horrific, like Picasso did with *Guernica*."

"Abstraction of reality can feel more real than reality."

"Robin nailed it: War plays on."

Debrief

Return to *Observation Cues* to reflect on Hazel's strategies.

- What evidence is there of inspiration or insight? When and how?
- How did she link to universal concepts and themes?
- What else could she have said and done to encourage meaningful conversations?

MUSEUM GUIDE TOOL KIT

See the appendix for *Concluding* strategies.

Conversation Strategies

Since human brains open up to fairness, sharing, sense of ownership, and cooperation (Glaser, 2014):

- Form a circle so everyone can hear and see.
- Stress that there are no right or wrong answers.
- Model openness with your words and behavior (gestures, facial expressions).
- Show enthusiasm: Make eye contact, smile, and share your passion.
- Build relationships through questions, humor, and warm-ups.
- Listen to connect, not reject. Focus on "we," not "me" (Glaser, 2014).

- Ask questions you *can't* answer.
- Admit when you don't know.
- Provoke interest by soliciting personal connections.
- Partner guests together to share ideas.

Troubleshooting

Note that conversations are derailed by ...

- Threats: hurtful comments, tone, exclusion, anger, and rejection.
- Distrust: Participants who put up a wall of caution and seem ready to appease, fight, or take flight.
- Too much telling and not enough asking.
- Interrupters.
- Emphasizing results over relationships.
- Trigger words that cause people to "drop out."

Strategies

Helpful strategies include . . .

1. Reframe, refocus, or redirect the conversation.
2. Ask the obvious: "What's going on? Please say that in a different way. What would help clarify this for you?"
3. Be transparent. Explain common fears, like saying something "wrong."
4. Lean on trust to change perception of reality.
5. Honor ideas: Paraphrase and then reframe to clarify.
6. Ask for evidence: "What makes you say that?"
7. Avoid trigger words. See *Adapting for Differences*.

ADVICE FROM MUSEUM GUIDES: *FACILITATING CONVERSATIONS*

> *"Conversation makes connections possible."* —Charles Cornett, interpreter, Wright Brothers National Memorial

Rate the importance of each recommendation from 1 (low) to 5 (high):

1. ___Learn to facilitate conversations by observing those who do it well. Gradually add conversation strategies to your repertoire.
2. ___Make a "go bag" of questions that produce "meaty" conversations.
3. ___Start by asking what conversation is. Expect answers like "one person talks while the others listen, then there's back-and-forth."
4. ___Explain that conversation propels investigation into connections and meanings.
5. ___Select artwork that captures attention or stops people in their tracks.
6. ___Capitalize on comments like "Is it real?" and "What is that?" that indicate curiosity.
7. ___To keep conversation natural, encourage guests to ask and answer each other's questions.
8. ___Active listening is key to conversational tours. Listen, paraphrase, and connect responses to ensure every voice is validated.
9. ___When guests start sounding like friends chatting on the porch, you're on the right track.
10. ___The best conversations are "visitor takeovers," where conversation moves organically from person to person.
11. ___The best conversation happens when guests become so enthralled the guide could disappear, and no one would notice.

ADAPTING FOR DIFFERENCES: *INCLUSIVE LANGUAGE*

Guides can become powerful mediators when they connect external and internal worlds, like Annie Sullivan did by finding the "hook" that transported Helen Keller into the world of communication. Inclusive language suggests all people can learn, given the right hook.

Both inclusive language and political correctness assume that hurtful words should not be said. "Inclusive" language also encourages open participation by honoring individual identities. The goal is to use language that creates an atmosphere of acceptance rather than isolation or segregation and that demonstrates empathy and respect.

To Ameliorate Racism

1. Avoid stereotypes that turn people into "other."
2. Explain that comparing humans with animals or colors is hurtful. Invite examination of figures to discover uniqueness that signals human emotions and thoughts.
3. Use common anti-racism tools in inquiry approaches that invite free exchange of ideas, diverse perspectives, and evidence sharing.
4. Integrate contextual information to deepen understanding (Heller, Michell, & Tobin, 2021).
5. When in doubt, ask about preferred labels, names, pronunciation, and so on.

Self-Assessment

To what extent do you use the following?

a. ___Gender-neutral terms like "flight attendant" instead of "stewardess"; "server" instead of "waitress;" "mail carrier" instead of "mailman." Note: Options for addressing groups are "everyone" or "folks" instead of "guys."
b. ___Respectful terms for race and ethnicity like "immigrant" and "person of color" instead of "alien" or "foreigner" or derogatory labels.
c. ___Religious-sensitive terms like "faith" instead of "religion."
d. ___Signage that accommodates multiple languages.
e. ___References to "mental health issues" instead of using labels like "retarded."
f. ___Descriptors like "polite" and "courteous" instead of "ladylike" and "gentlemanly."
g. ___Respectful age-related terms like the adjectives "older," "experienced," and "knowledgeable" versus "elderly" or "aged."
h. ___Use of "neighborhoods" coupled with directional terms like "north" and "southwest" to describe areas versus labels like "ghetto," "inner city," "disadvantaged."
i. ___References to a person *with* _____ to indicate importance of person over disability.
j. ___Respect for sexual orientation. Example: Refer to "dating" instead of "having a girlfriend or boyfriend."
k. ___Avoid condescending *mansplaining* and microaggressions: sarcastic descriptions of someone as "articulate" or "clean," or tone policing (e.g., saying, "calm down").
l. ___Rethink words and phrases that can offend like . . .
   - "bossy" (women)
   - "grandfathering"
   - "man" the booth
   - "uppity"

RECAP

This chapter focused on the what and why of generating conclusions during conversation tours and included a roundup of effective strategies that promote *meaningful* conversations. The section on

Advice from Museum Guides addressed recommendations for facilitating inquiry conversations, and *Adapting for Differences* offered a self-evaluation regarding "inclusive" language. For another self-check, return to *Learning Goals* at the chapter outset.

UP NEXT!

Chapter 8 tackles making good, better through critique, taking meaning-making up a notch.

REFERENCES

Baird, Kate. (2017). https://museumquestions.com/2017/02/13/how-can-museums-help-us -relearn-the-art-of-conversation/.

Brown, Claire. (2022, May 4). What is visible thinking in the museum? Thinking Museum Podcast. https://thinkingmuseum.com/2022/05/04/visible-thinking-in-the-museum/.

Cherry, K. (2020, July 19). What is cognitive bias? *Very Well Mind*. https://www.verywellmind.com/ what-is-a-cognitive-bias-2794963.

Cornett, Claudia. (2010). *Comprehension first: Inquiry into big ideas using important questions:* London: Routledge.

French, Kathy. (1995, Autumn). Transitions: The workhorse of a tour. *Docent Educator*, 5(1). https:// www.museum-ed.org/transitionsthe-workhorse-of-a-tour/.

Glaser, Judith. (2014). TED talk: Conversational Intelligence (C-IQ), Gates Foundation TED Talk. https://www.youtube.com/watch?v=6Nb_6DFjIAE.

Hein, George. (1998). *Learning in the museum*. London: Routledge.

Heller, Hannah, Michell Antonisse, and Amanda Tobin. (2021). In Tara Young. *Creating meaningful museum experiences for K–12 audiences: How to connect with teachers and engage students*. Lanham, MD: Rowman & Littlefield.

Kahneman, Daniel. (2013). *Thinking fast and slow*. New York: Farrar, Straus and Giroux.

Kaufman, Scott. (2011, November). Why inspiration matters. *Harvard Business Review*. https://hbr.org /2011/11/why-inspiration-matters.

Marinho, G., J. Peta, J. Pereira, and M. Marguilho. (2021). Stendhal syndrome: Can art make you ill? *European Psychiatry* 64(S1). doi:10.1192/j.eurpsy.2021.852.

Murawski, Mike. (2011, October 22). https://artmuseumteaching.com.

Newman, Cathy. (2022, May 20). How "Eureka" moments in science happen. *National Geographic*. https://education.nationalgeographic.org/resource/how-eureka-moments-science-happen/.

Pallas, Jason. (2021). Inspiration quotient. In Tara Young, (Ed.), *Creating meaningful museum experiences for K–12 audiences: How to connect with teachers and engage students*. Lanham, MD: Rowman & Littlefield.

Panofsky, Erwin. (1955). *Meaning in the visual arts: Papers in and on art history*. Garden City: Doubleday, 14.

Picasso Speaks. (1923, May). *The Arts*, 315–26.

Schapiro, Evan. (2022). A Framework for Understanding How People Can Draw Different Conclusions Based on the Same Information. University of Massachusetts. https://scholarworks.umb.edu /cgi/viewcontent.cgi?article=1400&context=cct_capstone.

Shermer, Michael. (2002). *Why people believe weird things*. Henry Holt & Company.

Thrash, T. M., and A. J. Elliot. (2003). Inspiration as a psychological construct. *Journal of Personality and Social Psychology*, 84(4), 871–89. https://doi.org/10.1037/0022-3514.84.4.871

Viola, Tullio. (n.d.). *Pierce and Iconology: Habitus, embodiment, and the analogy between philosophy and architecture*. https://doi.org/10.4000/ejpap.764.

VUE. (2009, Spring). Visual thinking strategies: Understanding the basics. *Visual Understanding in Education*. San Jose Museum of Art. https://sjmusart.org/sites/default/files/uploads/files/ Understanding%20Basics.pdf.

8

Tour Closing

CRITIQUE TO MAKE BETTER

Critique (v.): do careful analysis to identify positive and negative features and make improvements.

LEARNING GOALS

By the end of this chapter, you should be able to . . .

1. Give reasons to include critique in tours.
2. Compare the process of critiquing artwork to the Creative Inquiry Process (CIP).
3. Engage visitors in using critique to evaluate conclusions about objects.
4. Critique your own tours and implement improvements.
5. Improve tours by adding purpose-built transitions.
6. Consider planning and conducting guided tours to meet goals and purposes that reflect your museum and your own "style."

CRITIQUE: WHAT? WHY? HOW?

WORD BOX: 8.1

- *Describe*: tell or depict.
- *Analyze*: examine, inspect.
- *Interpret*: explain meaning.
- *Judge*: give informed opinion.
- *Evidence*: proof.

Critique is an oral or written process that includes describing, analyzing, interpreting, and evaluating evidence to reach judgments about works, products, or performances. If this sounds similar to the Creative Inquiry Process (CIP), that's because it is (Kennedy Center; Helpful Professor).

In the art world, critique refers to art criticism, but critique is used across fields and disciplines. The challenge in critique is to examine a work and judge the degree to which it achieved its intended goals. This chapter suggests ways to critique a product—conclusions produced by visitors, as well as performances of guides and docents.

Criteria for making judgments vary according to standards developed by experts in particular fields. Criteria for meaningful conclusions were outlined in chapter 7, and sources for standards for effective guided tours were outlined in chapter 5.

Art Critique

Although guides don't often engage guests in formal art critique, you'll recognize parallels between it and the Creative Inquiry Process (CIP).

Describe

Objectively report overall aspects of the work without words like *poor* or *good*.

- Cite information similar to that on a museum label.
- List prominent elements: color, line movement, light, use of space, etc.
- Point out technical aspects: tools, materials, methods.
- Name the subject matter: representational, abstract, and so on.
- Explain what's going on.

Analyze

Provide details about the work's composition (organization).

- Identify repeated elements, use of variety, balance, unity, etc.
- Identify points of emphasis (e.g., central figure).
- Point out relationships between figures, elements, parts, and pieces.

Interpret

Explain and give evidence about what the work makes you think about and how it makes you feel.

- Describe the work's expressive qualities (emotions/feelings).
- Relate the work to personal experiences or things: "It reminds me of_____."
- Explain what the overall work is about (meaning).

Judge or Evaluate

Present an *evidence-based* opinion of the work's effectiveness and shortcomings.

- What aspects are strong? Weak?
- How does the work compare to works more or less effective?
- How original (unique and different) is the work?
- What criteria should be used to judge this work?
- To what extent does the work fulfill a purpose or have meaning?

Broudy's critique method (1987), *Aesthetic Scanning*, starts with personal questions that are easier to answer:

1. Sensory properties: What do you see (colors, lines, etc.)?
2. Formal properties: How was it made and why?
3. Expressive properties: What's it about, and how does it make you feel?

Plus One

For an example of an actual art critique, see Feldman's Aesthetic Criticism: https://www.museum-ed.org/looking-at-art/.

To meaningfully use unexpected time with a group, consider a fast-paced critique, like that in Quick Reference 8.2. Give a copy to each group, explain directions, set time, and go!

Quick Reference 8.2: *Quick Critique Challenge*

Work in small groups to critique an object. Be flexible about time and process (e.g., do seven, stop, discuss, rest). Explain there are no wrong answers.
Get ready, get set, GO! Look/See—Think/Feel—Know!

1. Describe your immediate reaction.
2. Look purposefully to notice colors, lines, and shapes.
3. Name "things" you're seeing (e.g., a triangle, figure).
4. Describe how the work is arranged: use of patterns, repetition, variety, rhythms, emphasis.
5. Explain what's going on or happening.
6. Relate to self: "This reminds me of _____."
7. Associate: "This makes me think _____ and feel _____."
8. Describe materials, tools, and techniques used to make the object.
9. Describe the style (e.g., realistic?).
10. Compare/contrast with another object. Consider the look, how it's made, messages, and emotional impact.
11. Review observations and discoveries. Explain what you've learned about yourself, others, and/or the world.
12. Give the object a title, caption, or headline to encapsulate its meaning. Compare with the artist's title and share pros and cons.
13. You're done! Compare current thoughts and feelings with first reactions and note changes.

Adapted from Project MUSE, 1994; Rice & Yenawine, 2002; Stafne, 2013.

CRITIQUING CONCLUSIONS AND INTERPRETIVE STATEMENTS

Unless tours are limited to two or three stops, it's difficult to find more than a few minutes to critique conclusions. That doesn't mean critique isn't important and can't happen—in an abbreviated form.

Critiquing Conclusions

To facilitate the critique of conclusions:

1. Restate the goal/purpose: *Synthesize an overarching meaning (conclusion) communicated by the object.*
2. Review proposed conclusions, then . . .
   - Rate: Ask individuals to take a position on the degree to which each conclusion achieved the goal: 1–5 with 5 high.
   - Analyze: Focus on how conclusions convey universal messages:
     1) Consider coherence, unifying concepts, and the extent to which the conclusion is anchored in valid evidence.
     2) Consider clarity, use of words, what's missing. or could be added.

- Interpret: To what extent is the conclusion *significant* or *important*? Consider new perspectives, the original use of words, and universal messages (themes).
- Judge: Express an opinion about each conclusion's value. Which conclusions . . .
  1) Are based on solid evidence?
  2) Are the most clear and comprehensible?
  3) Expand thinking?
  4) Capture the overall message and/or emotional impact?
  5) Wrap important ideas into a coherent whole?
  6) Present an original or new perspective?
  7) Express significant meanings?
  8) Achieve the intended purpose or goal?

Critique Practice

To practice critique, use the following conclusions from earlier chapters. Refer to the chapters for images of objects and review the guiding strategies in the vignettes that produced these conclusions.

Chapter 1: *Tightrope Walker*:

- Art is an important form of communication.
- What's unseen can be more important than the seen.
- There's a dark background to life.

Chapter 2: *Wright Flyer and the Creative Process*:

- Creative thinking isn't magic.
- Insight isn't one thing: it's putting a lot of stuff together.

Chapter 3: *Fort Ancient*:

- All people share the same wants and needs.
- Survival depends on being inventive.

Chapter 4: *Toulouse Lautrec Artworks*:

- Honesty makes the best art.
- Inner beauty is more important than outer.

Chapter 5: *Lost and Found Sculpture*:

- Everyone feels lost or found sometimes.
- There's a thin line between the real world and dream worlds.

Steps and Pointers

1. Invite multiple perspectives when evaluating any work or product.
2. Refer to agreed-upon criteria for judging effectiveness. Note: *art* critique focuses on art elements and composition ideas (balance, rhythm, and so on).
3. To judge the degree to which the work achieved its purpose . . .

- Consider the whole work in light of its purpose to convey significant meanings.
- Use concrete nouns, verbs, adjectives, and adverbs to describe or express opinions and interpretations.
- Decide the extent to which conclusions or interpretations achieve the overall goal.

4. Listen to all opinions and supporting evidence. Ask each other questions: "What is the work trying to communicate?" "How do you know that?" "What would make the work more successful?" "What's working?"
5. Resist blanket statements: Give or ask for supporting evidence.
6. Survey to get a sense of agreement or disagreement.
7. Focus on positive aspects, but don't ignore flaws, especially conflicting evidence.
8. Be alert to "confirmation bias": the inclination to seek out and prefer ideas that support current beliefs and ignore contradictory information.
9. If individuals struggle with justifying their positions, ask how they reached the judgment or if they're reacting to another person's comments.
10. Play devil's advocate to stretch thinking.
11. Present aspects that work and that don't, and suggest revisions. As a rule of thumb, offer two positive comments and one suggestion for improvement.

Refining Critique

Take critique to the next level with review and additions to what has been said. During group critiques, track ideas and periodically ask, "What have you seen, thought, and heard so far that makes the most sense?" "What ideas make the most sense given what we are seeing?"

Invalid Conclusions

Humans are pattern seekers who look for meaning in a complex world. The problem is figuring out which patterns (connections) are truly meaningful, and which are bogus (Shermer, 2002). Furthermore, humans don't do well with uncertainty: People want fast answers, but those can produce invalid conclusions (Schapiro, 2022). In uncertain situations, people make quick connections, identify surface patterns, and form intuitive conclusions using mental shortcuts, called *heuristics* (Kahneman, 2013). These "rash" conclusions are less reliable than those subjected to slow, deliberate thinking. For example, news collected from clickable websites can lead to spurious conclusions about the integrity of our government and the state of our planet. Fortunately, most museums have credible objects, so guides don't have to worry about fake information.

Valid Conclusions (useful and meaningful)

If you grew up on a lake with many ducks, you might wrongly conclude that all swimming birds are ducks. But if coached to observe (collect details) about lake birds, you could be guided to identify likenesses and differences among swimming birds, like swans, geese, and mergansers versus ducks. Time spent comparing and contrasting things is a step toward *valid conclusions*. Reaching meaningful and useful conclusions also requires considering exceptions and more complex relationships.

CRITIQUE: GUIDE PERFORMANCE

Guides, docents, and interpreters are the public face of a museum. Guides enjoy opportunities to share their enthusiasm for specialized knowledge and facilitate collaborative investigations among visitors interested in art, history, science, nature, and more. As mediators of conversational tours, guides progressively acquire skills to coach visitors to create their own meanings and become lifelong museum enthusiasts.

Chapter 5 offered a self-evaluation that outlines research-based competencies for "effective" guides (Schep & Kintz, 2017; Bajrami et al., 2022). The following tool represents additional perspectives from multiple museums, including the Dallas Museum of Art (Butler, 2009) and the Smithsonian. This tool also embeds major aspects of Creative Inquiry Process (CIP) into planning, leading, and critiquing guide performance.

Consider your comfort level at this point in planning and executing tour phases. Think about overall goals to engage guests in creating meaning—learning and experiencing enjoyment or pleasure—and justify your judgments using knowledge about how and why to engage visitors in CIP. Keep in mind that guides gain insights from successful tours as well as failures.

Assess-Plan-Implement-Evaluate is a reliable pedagogical cycle that engages educators in invaluable critique that continually refreshes perspectives. After an objective self-evaluation (critique), prioritize needs and devise a doable improvement plan using ideas from this and previous chapters and appendices.

Roles of Museum Guides in Creating Meaning

Use the rating scale: 1=low comfort to 5=high comfort.

Planning

1. ___Research content, including information about the artist/maker, object, or artifact (e.g., timelines, quotes).
2. ___Plan theme-based tours with an introduction, development, and closing, along with transitions.
3. ___Develop and use a Guide Tool Kit of strategies to engage museum visitors in conversations and multisensory activities to facilitate meaning-making. Include transitions.
4. ___Create tour transitions.

Introduction (beginning)

1. ___Create a relaxed context for the tour.
2. ___Orient visitors to museum spaces.
3. ___Introduce yourself: *Who* and *what* you are, *what* you do, and *where* the group is.
4. ___Preview tour goals and processes: *What* visitors will see and do (inquiry process/conversation) and *why*, and *when* the tour will end. Mention tour themes (encapsulated in the tour title) and key concepts (e.g., inquiry).

Development (middle)

1. ___Emphasize that the goal is to create meaning or understanding using the Creative Inquiry Process (CIP), which involves connecting to interests and personal discovery.
2. ___Coach visitors to work together during inquiry conversations.
3. ___Keep the group together by sustaining interest and showing enthusiasm.
4. ___Coach/prompt visitors to use purposeful/strategic looking to collect information.
5. ___ Ask open-ended, process-oriented questions to engage CIP.
6. ___Coach visitors to connect ideas and form and share "big concept" conclusions.
7. ___Build on visitor responses and interests to develop themes.
8. ___Weave in relevant content to expedite inquiry.
9. ___Use transitions to create continuity between stops.
10. ___Give positive descriptive feedback to encourage participation.
11. ___Adapt tours for needs and interests of diverse visitors.
12. ___Track visitors' ideas to encourage connections that support conclusions about universal concepts (themes) "greater than the object itself."

CLOSING (END)

Wrap up.

1. ___Offer communication options to express conclusions rooted in thoughts and feelings, anchored in objects. *Examples:* writing, drama, storytelling, movement, writing, and visual art.
2. ___Ask about big ideas, insights, and highlights: "What was most interesting, important, or surprising?"
3. ___Manage the group by keeping it together through sustained interest.
4. ___Solicit feedback: What questions or confusions do you have? What worked? What suggestions for improvement do you have?
5. ___Escort group to the lobby or exit area.
6. ___Encourage repeat visits.
7. ___Thank guests for their interest and participation.

After the Tour (assess)

- Audio-tape yourself to collect more feedback.
- Invite a colleague to observe and provide feedback.
- Review visitor suggestions: What worked? What needs improvement?
- Reflect on your performance by identifying strengths and needs: What went well, and why? What could you do better? How?

Strategies for Improvement

- Practice with a coach.
- Observe other guides or docents.
- Co-guide with another docent.
- Conduct additional research or study (e.g., guiding books, videos, etc.).

References: Andelelkovic, 2022; Brown, 2022; Butler, 2009; Cornett, 2012 and 2015; Greene, 2001; National Docent Symposium Council, 2017; Schep & Kintz, 2017; Vatsky, 2023.

TRANSITIONING TO TRANSITIONS

Imagine an enjoyable trip to learn about your heritage. You have a goal, and you have expectations about points on a map. A tour is a trip, but instead of points on a map, visitors stop to investigate objects, and guides coach them to make connections between objects and their lives, other objects, people, and life. At each stop on a trip or tour, you take stock of what you've discovered, determine what you still want to know, and anticipate connections ahead. Anticipation propels interest in moving forward, which is what tour transitions do, too.

Authors use transitions at the ends of chapters to pull readers through a story or work; transitions within tours do likewise. Objects offer unique ideas that can ground conclusions, but without transitions, individual stops are disassociated experiences. Transitions tie together thoughts and feelings of guests and give tours a sense of continuity. Once guides start using effective transitions, they see their value (French, 1995).

Purposes and Forms

Transitions have different purposes that include connecting now and next: where we started, where we are, and where we are going. And effective guides never lose sight of the importance of curiosity and interest in any transition that reviews or previews. Given these parameters, transitions take many forms, from enticing questions to concise sentences to prompts that encourage guests to consider new angles themes.

Introductory Transitions

Introductory transitions capture attention and provoke interest in inquiry, preparing guests to collect and connect ideas. For example, the transition, "This house was built in what was one of the richest small towns in America. It provides a window into how people thought and lived *before* the Civil War and what happened that created the *after*." This is an "advanced organizer"—a transition 1) directs attention to the tour's theme, and 2) forecasts that visitors will enter "another time," inside a house with artifacts that are clues to a bigger story, not simply "isolated facts and interesting trivia" (French, 1995).

Next Stop Transitions

Thoughtful transitions create anticipation: "When you look out the Palladian window, you'll see where 'dependencies' stood, which gives a sense of daily life for enslaved people owned by the Verdier family." This kind of transition offers guests an opportunity to bring personal experiences into the tour and make connections that support understanding.

Quick Reference 8.3: *Transitions: Purposes and Forms*

Note purposes of the following transition statements, questions, summaries, and directives.

1. *Introduce themes*: "During the tour you'll see objects that reveal what the Verdier family believed and how they lived and thought."
2. *Capture attention*: "Two objects in the next room have curious functions."
3. *Emphasize key concepts*: "Rice, indigo, and cotton are labor-intensive crops that fueled the slave trade and made plantation owners rich."
4. *Trigger imagination*: "Most antebellum town houses had ballrooms, where plantation families and friends gathered to dance and match-make. That's our next stop."
5. *Link concepts*: "As we move to the next room, think about the consequences of human greed."
6. *Sustain interest* (hint at reasons for the next stop): "As you ascend the staircase, notice the elaborate Vitruvian scrollwork and what it suggests."
7. *Invite personal connections*: "Think about how this parlor is similar or different from rooms in your home."
8. *Suggest contrasts*: "Unlike members of the Verdier family, enslaved Africans lived and worked in dependencies adjacent to the house."
9. *Set the stage for surprise*: "In the next room, you'll see what's behind the beautiful wallpaper and elaborate molding."
10. *Help visitors to "live" the experience*: Envision being Caroline, standing at this window, hearing the booming cannons."
11. *Ask "So what?" and "Why should I care?"*: "So, why would this community want to preserve this house?"
12. *Extend comments*: "Since you noticed the rope molding, let's go inside and see more, then figure out why there's so much."

References: French, 1995; National Docent Handbook, 2017; Vatsky, 2023.

Transitions to Make Meaning

Transitions turn a series of disconnected stops into unified investigations of objects where visitors gain different perspectives on multifaceted themes. By linking concepts in individual works, transitions lift the focus to universal themes.

Creating and Employing Transitions

To create worthwhile transitions, objects need to illustrate aspects of tour themes (e.g., greed, selfishness, hope). When objects are connected to themes, it's easier to devise interesting transitions and thread together meaning.

To plan coherent tours, either . . .

1. Choose a theme in advance and find objects that highlight theme points, *or . . .*
2. Survey the museum's collection *first* and scan for possible themes. See chapter 7 and Quick Reference 4.4 for Theme Examples.
3. Next: Pull out variations on the theme by answering the question, "What is _____about?" in the context of the object. *Examples:* Greed is doing anything to retain power and possessions. Greed is thinking of yourself first. Greedy people lack empathy.

   To start using transitions . . .

4. Reflect on presentation factors: voice projection, eye contact, facial expressions, body language, use of pauses, and so on.
5. Decide when, where, and what transitions you'll use given time constraints.

CLOSURE: FINAL-FIVE WRAP-UP

In the tour closing, guides can tie up loose ends and reinforce big points about how creating meaning in objects is learning for its own sake (VUE, 2009). It's helpful for visitors to understand that just as no one can ever step in the same river twice, no two investigations of the same work will turn out the same. Objects look different because people change. Visitors need to know that objects can be revisited, with each encounter revealing something new. Other wrap-up strategies include the following (NDSC Handbook 2, 2017):

Skip Summaries

If ideas were linked throughout the tour, summarizing is redundant.

Ask Questions

Invite visitors to review highlights, special moments, and thoughts. Ask . . .

- What did you enjoy?
- What was your favorite object?
- What object would you like to own? Why?
- What will you remember most?
- What was a highlight?
- What would you tell a friend?
- Which of the group's conclusions made the most sense?

   If there's time, follow answers with "Tell me more," or "What makes you say that?"

Solicit Feedback

Ask questions or use sentence starters (this can also be done in writing):

- "What worked?" and "What suggestions do you have?"
- "What surprised you about the experience?" or "Something that surprised me most about today was_____."

- "What activities helped you understand?"
- "What did you enjoy?" or "The part I enjoyed most was _____."
- "What will you remember most about this experience?" or "I'll never forget _____."
- "What will you tell others about the tour?"

Encourage Repeat Visits

- As you escort visitors to the exit, point out intriguing objects to investigate another time.
- Invite visitors to return with family and friends and guide their groups.
- Advertise free events, coming attractions, upcoming installations, special behind-the-scenes tours, and so on.
- Spotlight the museum's website and suggest downloading the app.

Gracefully End the Tour

- Compliment: Comment on how visitors probed objects and carefully listened to one another.
- Invite reflection: Suggest thinking about the inquiry process and meaning-making.
- Close with a quote or provocative question that might remind visitors of the tour.

TOUR VIGNETTE

The York Bailey Museum is located in Penn Center, a National Historic Landmark set among live oaks, dripping with Spanish moss. This peaceful place has a chilling history. For centuries, thousands of enslaved Africans planted and harvested crops on this South Carolina island, enriching plantation owners who exported indigo and coveted "long staple" cotton. The fifty-acre campus now symbolizes how former "Gullah Geechee" slaves became a proud, self-sufficient people.

Observation Cues

No two tours are the same. Each tour's format, emphases, and strategies need to be adjusted to meet unique museum goals and strengths of guides and visitors. And some tours require more storytelling than others.

In this vignette, notice the docent's personal style and depth of knowledge. Think about . . .

1. Her main goals.
2. How her enthusiasm and passion affect the audience.
3. Her use of pregnant pauses.
4. Strategies she uses to engage visitors and change minds.

Vignette: Bringing Light to "Firsts"

"Good morning. I'm Marie, your docent for this tour. I do interpretive education."

"What do you mean by 'interpretive'?" Cecilia asks.

"History has done us a disservice. A lot of things happened here that people don't know about." She stretches her arms. "You're in the York W. Bailey Museum, and you are on sacred ground—the site of the first school in America for emancipated slaves, started in 1862." She indicates a photograph above a glass case.

The group moves to examine a worn doctor's bag and stethoscope.

"York W. Bailey was a student here at Penn School. He went to Howard University and returned to St. Helena as our own home-grown doctor where he practiced for fifty years."

"He looks dignified," Merl says.

"Why do you say that?"

"His posture, how he holds his head, the look of his hands."

Creating Meaning in Museums

"He was a gentleman," Marie says. "And St. Helena Island's first Black medical doctor. Another Penn student, Sam Doyle, painted Dr. Y.B.'s portrait. Sam's art is featured in our current exhibit." (View at https://www.gibbesmuseum.org/news/artist-spotlight-sam-doyle-american-1906-1985 /1983-03-01_500/.)

"I've seen his art at the Red Piano 2 gallery. Didn't he paint on roof tin?" Kay asks.

"Yes. And Sam became famous enough to shake Nancy Reagan's hand. He chronicled our unique history, especially our 'firsts,' from emancipation on."

"Are you a 'beenya'?" Chuck asks.

"Born and educated here. I was in the last class at St. Helena before integration in 1970. Are you a 'comeyah'?"

"Lived here twenty years."

"That makes you a 'beenya,'" she announces.

Harry harrumphs. "If Doyle witnessed emancipation, he lived a long life!"

"It's not that simple. Sam was a spiritual man and an imaginative visual storyteller. You'll see in the exhibit. Let's go look at a photo that takes us back in time."

She waits while the group examines a photo of Penn School.

"I'll give you three dates: 1861, when the Civil War started; 1862, when the Gullah Geechee people were emancipated, became land owners, and started being educated at this school. And 1863?" She waits.

"Lincoln signed the Emancipation Proclamation?" Merl asks.

"I thought the people here were already emancipated," Cecilia says.

"Exactly. The year 1863 was when enslaved people in states that had seceded were freed. We were emancipated when the Union arrived in 1861. We are a different kind of people."

"Was this island occupied by slave owners until 1861?" Merl asks.

"Yes sir. But when the White population heard Union cannons firing on Confederate forts, they skedaddled, abandoning the land along with ten thousand enslaved people. The United States urged former slaves to support the federal government, fight for freedom, pay taxes, and learn to read and write. Which they did. But they needed food, clothing, shelter, education, and medicine. To transition emancipated people to self-sufficiency, a plan was formed called the 'Port Royal Experiment.' Aboli-tionist Laura Towne traveled south and founded Penn School in 1862. With General Saxon's permis-sion, Towne, Ellen Murray, and Charlotte Forten helped free people learn to be free. They started at a kitchen table and ended up with a progressive curriculum based on theories of Tuskegee, Booker T. Washington, and W.E.B. Dubois. Kids had academics in the morning and industrial arts in the after-noon, and they worked off their tuition."

"What kind of work did they do?"

"Work needed to run the school," she says. "We became free by abandonment. Planters' land was foreclosed on and sold for a dollar and twenty-five cents an acre. But emancipated people didn't have nothing until the government started paying them one dollar to pick four hundred pounds of cotton."

"And they managed to buy land?" Cecilia asks.

"By combing resources! Families purchased acres and acres, making us the first Black land own-ers in America. They made the land productive and built financial independence far earlier than other enslaved African Americans. There was never a sharecropper system here. And no connecting bridge until 1927. We became self-reliant people saved by isolation. We had a utopia."

"Way back, Blacks owned land here?" a teenager asks.

"I'd do anything for the land," Marie says. "If my ancestors could pick four hundred pounds of cot-ton, I can too. We fight like crazy for our land. Land is power, one of the greatest things someone can have. We are the land. The land feeds us, clothes us, keeps us warm, and keeps us cool. Developers coming in don't understand: they see land; we see life."

Figure 8.1 Penn School Experiment. The Penn School in the York Bailey Museum: First Official School for the newly emancipated Gullah Geechee People on St. Helena Island, S.C. 1862. Courtesy York Bailey Museum.

"What happened to Penn School?" a man asks.

"It was a shining success. I'm living proof. It stayed open until 1948. It was the only school in South Carolina where students could get a high school diploma. After *Brown v. Board of Education*, students here were entitled to go to Beaufort public schools."

"Did you?"

"I was at a St. Helena public school. We got used books from the depository that already had eight names."

"What about today?"

"St. Helen's population is 11,753, and fifty-five percent are Black land owners. Dr. Gibbs herself is the proud owner of forty-five acres of land owned by our family. I am the land, the land is me. That's my life."

The group follows her to the art gallery.

"Growing up, I knew Sam Doyle." She points to his photograph. "I knew nothing about his art. He was giving us these pieces, but we didn't know the greatness we had in our own community."

"How long did he live?"

"He died in 1985. Everything he found was his canvas. That's my favorite piece—the old refrigerator door."

"That's so creative!" Kaye squeals.

"He was going to junkyards, pulling out pieces of cars and looking for treasures in his own backyard."

Merl walks over to a painting. "He painted this on a scrap of wood." (Note: View artwork online at https://high.org/collection/lincoln-in-frogmore/.)

"I like the vivid colors and the bold brushstrokes," Kaye says. "But what's going on?"

Figure 8.2   Lincoln in Frogmore. Courtesy High Museum, Atlanta.

"Where is Frogmore?" the teen asks.

"Right here," Marie says.

"Did Abraham Lincoln visit?"

"President Lincoln holds major *symbolic* importance. Sam called him the great emancipator. Many believe he made a secret appearance to enslaved people early in the Civil War and promised the Island would be theirs if they supported the Union."

"So, this art is an imagined event?"

"Sam drew on ancestral lore and integrated elements of faith, myth, and spirituality into his paintings. He painted the 'spirit of the person.'"

"The bright colors and Lincoln's upward-pointing hand make it feel uplifting," Cecilia says.

"But those heads on the ground are disconcerting," Kaye says. "Is this about emancipation or atrocities?"

"Some things are more about stepping out on faith than evidence from seen things."

The group assembles around the painting.

"Sam's paintings embody the soul of St. Helena and the richness of Gullah culture. They are testament to the Island's transformation. His art captures memories, tells stories of change, and reminds us of the importance of preserving community and history. His work inspires us to connect with our roots, embrace our narratives, and express our creative spirits. Take a few minutes to look around, and I'll meet you back by the Penn School photo."

"He painted about anything and everybody," Chuck says reading a wall label. "First midwife, first doctor, first school, first undertaker, first senator—that's Robert Smalls."

Marie speaks from the doorway. "Dr. King came here five times. Sam painted him, too." She turns and the group follows her.

"Penn Center is the hub of this community. When there's a problem, the community joins forces. We show up. We stand up. The Gullah Geechee people and Penn Center are synonymous: *without them is not us; without us is not them.* Because education was suppressed for so long, it's our job to bring knowledge to people. A lot of people don't know that Black people could only go to seventh grade for a long time. They did everything *not* to educate us."

"Reconstruction failed," Merl says.

"But *we* didn't. We were not accepted. We were trying to fit in, but where do you fit in when everything is suppression, barriers, and roadblocks? If history was taught the correct way, how different today would be."

"I like how you don't dwell on what people did *to* you, but how the Gullah Geechee people helped themselves," Chuck says.

"Thank you. What other thoughts and questions do you have?"

"What else should we see?"

"Don't miss the sweetgrass baskets. They have their own story. Stay as long as you like. I'll be here." She holds out a basket. "Take a paper strip with words from the Gullah language, which wasn't allowed in school for a long time. Try to figure out the meaning and check back with me."

The paper strips have short phrases and sentences:

- "You yent."
- "See um da."
- "Da pot da boil."
- "Yeddie so."
- "Res you mout."

Debrief

Think about . . .

1. What struck you about the tour?
2. What was the mood, and how did Marie create it?
3. Where do you pick up distinct tour parts in this vignette: Introduction, Development, Closing, Transitions?
4. What evidence shows that visitors were engaged and made sense?
5. How does Marie's tour differ from other vignettes?
6. What does Marie's tour suggest about ways and reasons to integrate information?
7. What conclusions (big ideas/truths) can you draw from the tour's content?

Note: This vignette was based on information from Dr. Marie Gibbs, docent and program coordinator for Penn Center. See https://www.penncenter.com, and *A World within Worlds: The Visionary Art of Sam Doyle*, Penn Center, Inc.

MUSEUM GUIDE TOOL KIT

Refer to the Tool Kit in Appendix A for these and other critique strategies:

- Fortunately or Unfortunately
- Debate
- Take a Stand
- Vote with Your Feet

ADVICE FROM MUSEUM GUIDES: *PLANNING AND INTRODUCTION*

"The best part is the light-bulb moment." —Terry Hanes, docent, Cincinnati Art Museum

Tour Planning

1. ___Don't be afraid not to know.
2. ___Connect all aspects of the tour to a common thread (big idea/theme). (See Quick Reference 4.4.)
3. ___Plan a clear beginning, middle, and end for each stop and a wrap-up for the entire tour.
4. ___Plan the tour in "chunks." If something isn't working, you can easily add or remove parts.
5. ___ Have a "Go Bag" of open questions. See Quick Reference 2.2 and 2.3.

Tour: IDC

1. ___Go with the flow. Follow guests' interests.
2. ___Focus on coaching visitors to make connections.
3. ___Invite questions and pause for emphasis and time to think.
4. ___Tell stories about objects that make them more accessible.
5. ___Share anecdotes about artists to make content feel more approachable.
6. ___Use artist quotes to humanize artists and the creative process.
7. ___Share relevant art/artist information to clarify and extend key points and boost interest.
8. ___Engage visitors in investigations so they can *discover* insight.
9. ___Integrate facts/information that have the power to engage visitors in further inquiry.
10. ___Ask yourself whether the information promotes dialogue or might shut down insights.
11. ___Encourage comparisons: "How is __like/different from ___?"
12. ___Invite guests to associate colors with emotions/feelings by taking two minutes to visualize and share emotions.
13. ___Check out organization websites. *Examples:* National Docent Symposium and American Alliance of Museums that sponsor regular conferences.

ADAPTING FOR DIFFERENT AUDIENCES: *BIAS-FREE COMMUNICATION*

Guides should *avoid* . . .

- Stereotyping: using words and images that suggest members of a group are all the same. *Examples:* Describing a Mexican child as "clean" implies the youngster is an exception to a generalization about a group. Avoid adjectives and qualifiers that do likewise, as in "industrious Black man."
- Mentioning irrelevant identity traits: *Example:* Don't discuss someone's gender, race, religion, or sexual preference unless this information is pertinent to understand a situation or solve a problem.
- Negative language: words that have unfavorable gender, racial or ethnic connotations. *Example:* 1) Calling someone a "sissy" or using vulgar terms that refer to female body parts, 2) Referring to someone as "culturally deprived," which implies there are "superior" cultures, or using "non-White," implying that "White" is the standard or majority, which it is *not* worldwide.
- Symbolic use of color words: *Example:* Calling someone "yellow" implies cowardice.
- Patronizing language and tokenism: demeaning women or racial, ethnic, and religious groups. *Note:* Tokenism is making symbolic gestures to deceive, as in photos staged to show diversity within a workforce.
- Images that fail to fairly represent all groups: *Example:* Not including women in a photo for an article about top American CEOs.
- Using misogynistic, racial, religious, and ethnic clichés: This is stereotyping, which fails to acknowledge an individual's full life. *Example:* Asking a Catholic couple how many children they have during a conversation overture.

For More Information

- American Alliance of Museums: https://www.aam-us.org/wp-content/uploads/2017/11/lgbtq _welcome_guide.pdf.
- American Psychological Associations (APA): https://apastyle.apa.org/style-grammar-guidelines /bias-free-language/general-principles.
- Anti-Defamation League (ADL) https://www.adl.org/resources/tools-and-strategies/guidelines -achieving-bias-free-communication.
- Microsoft Ignite https://learn.microsoft.com/en-us/style-guide/bias-free-communication.

RECAP

This chapter addressed the sixth *C* in the Creative Inquiry Process: critique. *Critique* was outlined for artworks and other creative products, including conclusions reached during tours and guide performances. The section on *Advice from Museum Guides* suggested more strategies for phases of tours, and *Adapting for Differences* recommended ways to recognize and avoid bias. To self-evaluate, return to *Learning Goals*.

UP NEXT!

Our world would have trouble communicating without the arts, so the next chapter suggests strategies for using the arts as communication tools during museum tours.

REFERENCES

Bajrami, Dunja Demirović, Nikola Vuksanovic, Marko Petrovic, and Tatyana Tretyakova. (2022, June). Competencies of a museum guide as predictors of visitors' learning outcomes: A case from Canada, *Journal of Museum Education* 47(2): 251–62. DOI: 10.1080/10598650.2022.2062542.

Brown, Claire. (2022, May 4). What is visible thinking in the museum? Thinking Museum Podcast. https://thinkingmuseum.com/2022/05/04/visible-thinking-in-the-museum/.

French, Kathy. (1995, Autumn). Transitions … The workhorse of a tour. *Docent Educator,* 5(1). https:// www.museum-ed.org/transitionsthe-workhorse-of-a-tour/.

Helpful Professor. https://helpfulprofessor.com/critique-examples/.

Kahneman, Daniel. (2013). *Thinking fast and slow*. New York: Farrar, Straus and Giroux.

Kennedy Center. https://www.kennedy-center.org/education/resources-for-educators/classroom -resources/articles-and-how-tos/articles/educators/critique--feedback/teaching-students-to -critique/.

National Docent Symposium Council. (2017). *The docent handbook 2.* www.nationaldocents.org.

Project MUSE, Harvard Project Zero. (1994). The Generic Game. Cambridge, MA: Harvard University.

Rice, Danielle, and Philip Yenawine. (2002). A conversation on object-centered learning in art museums. *Curator: The Museum Journal* 45(4), 289–301.

Schep, Mark and Pauline Kintz eds. (2017). *Guiding as a profession: The museum guide in art and history museum.* https://www.lkca.nl/wp-content/uploads/2020/02/guiding-is-a-profession.pdf.

Schapiro, Evan. (2022). A framework for understanding how people can draw different conclusions based on the same information. University of Massachusetts. https://scholarworks.umb.edu/cgi/ viewcontent.cgi?article=1400&context=cct_capstone.

Smithsonian Institution. https://museumonmainstreet.org/sites/default/files/tips%20for %20museum%20docents%20and%20tour%20guides.pdf.

Stafne, Marcos. (2013, April 19). Working with visual thinking strategies, AHTRWeekly. http://arthist oryteachingresources.org/2013/04/844/.

Vatsky, Sharon. (2023). *Interactive museum tours: A guide to in-person and virtual experiences*. Lanham, MD: Rowman & Littlefield.

9

Communication Options to Show You Know

Communicate (v.): receive, process, and express thoughts (ideas) and/or feelings (emotions).

LEARNING GOALS

By the end of this chapter, should be able to ...

1. Explain basic goals and processes of communication.
2. Describe what's included in arts communication and why.
3. Explain why and how to use arts communication during tours.
4. Add arts-specific strategies to a personal Museum Guide Tool Kit.
5. Describe ways to adapt tours for ages and stages.
6. List questions about using the arts as guide tools.

THEORY INTO PRACTICE (TIP): CREATIVE INQUIRY PROCESS (CIP)

This chapter addresses the final phase of creating meaning during tours. Before delving into communications options that "make thinking visible," the following CIP review invites you to put theory into practice. Think like a guide or docent who aims to motivate visitors to participate in casual inquiry conversations. Respond to each C by adding strategies to the sentence starter.

Context

Inquiry conversations thrive in welcoming, respectful contexts where participants trust one another and feel comfortable taking risks. Open "atmospheres" feature guests listening to connect with one another and museum objects. *To facilitate this environment, guides can ...*

Challenge

Participants need to understand that the tour goal is to make sense by observing and talking about interesting, curious, and important ideas. They need to know you'll be asking open-ended questions to promote meaningful conversation. *To present the challenge of creating meaning, guides can ...*

Collect

To address the meaning-making challenge, guests need to gather information by purposefully observing and sharing ideas. *To facilitate collecting ideas, guides can ...*

Connect

Making sense of collected information requires divergent (zoom out) and convergent (zoom in) thinking, forging relationships with past experiences, and considering implied meanings. Meaningful connections are found by thinking about what's *between and beyond* what's seen. *To help participants connect disconnected concepts, guides can ...*

Conclude

Concluding involves convergent thinking to identify potential themes and big ideas that could create understandings. By alternating between zooming in and out, participants synthesize (pull together) overarching meanings derived from connected ideas. The result is a conclusion that can rise to insight—an *aha! To help visitors generate conclusion statements, guides can ...*

Critique

With tentative conclusions in hand, participants need to reflect and evaluate. The goal is to select and revise unifying statements that express messages greater than the object itself. *To facilitate critique, guides can ...*

Communicate

Once a group settles on "best" overall conclusions, the next step is making conclusions public (as in publish). Conclusions may be shared through word-based (oral or written) forms or through art forms like sketching, or music, dance, or drama (e.g., tableau). The goal is to exhibit understanding(s) using the language arts and the fine and performing arts as communication vehicles. Note: *Communicate* restarts the Creative Inquiry Process because it presents the challenge to *create* and share meaningful ideas. *Knowing this, guides should ...*

References: Cornett, 2015; Csikszentmihalyi, 1990; Dewey, 1899; Glaser, 2014; Greene, 2010; Jung, 2014; Osborn, 1963; Root-Bernstein & Root-Bernstein, 1999; Rubin, 2023; Torrance, 1973; Treffinger, Isaksen, & Dorval, 2005; Vue, 2009; Wallas, 1926.

THE ARTS AS COMMUNICATION TOOLS: WHAT? WHY? HOW?

WORD BOX 9.1

To understand and convey thoughts and emotions, people use ...

- *Language Arts*: listening, speaking, reading, writing.
- *Literary Arts*: artful oral and written words.
- *Visual arts*: images created with art elements.
- *Drama*: pretending using body, gestures, and voice.
- *Dance*: body shapes and movement.
- *Music*: organized sound.

Communication happens when people receive, process (understand), and express thoughts (ideas) and emotions (feelings). The most common communication tools are the *language arts*: listening, reading, speaking, and listening. But until the turn of the twentieth century, competent communication, or "literacy," referred to the ability to sign your name. Today, literacy requires skill in multiple communication forms to effectively convey and understand messages. The language arts remain key vehicles, but we now live in a multimedia (arts-rich), technology-driven world. To meet contemporary life demands, we've gone back to the future to embrace humanity's first communication forms: visual art, drama, dance, and music.

Thousands of years before inventing the "written word," humans were painting images on cave walls (visual art), beating out messages on drums (music), and using facial expressions, gestures, and movement (dance and drama) to transmit ideas and emotions. Twenty-first-century humans do likewise. As a National Endowment for the Arts publication *American Canvas* explains, the arts are "fundamentally communication vehicles" (Larson, 1997).

In schools, workplaces, and everyday life, the fine and performing arts are now expanding meaning-making possibilities. In educational institutions, the arts now stand alongside the language arts as essential teaching and learning tools that give "voice" across curricular areas. When words come up short in expressing thoughts and emotions, music, visual art, drama, and dance substitute for or amplify words, adding sound, movement, and images that enhance messages, giving new meaning to the axiom, "a picture is worth a thousand words."

The language arts continue to play leading roles during museum tours, but the original arts are now recognized as important multimodal communication forms with unique motivational force to represent ideas and feelings about objects. During tours, visitors . . .

- *pretend* (drama) to walk into paintings and describe imagined images, sounds, and smells.
- *assume poses* (dance) related to sculptures and participate in conservations about how movement extends thinking.
- *sketch* (visual art) important, curious, and interesting aspects of artworks and artifacts.
- respond "in role" (drama) by offering "one-liners" as the artist or figure in a work might.
- *write songs or poems* (literary arts) about core emotions and messages.
- collaborate to shape *tableaux* (drama) that depict pivotal moments.
- speak the words of artists—using the *music* of their voices (volume, rate, tone, pitch, pause, and emphasis) to convey interpreted thoughts and feelings.

In these examples, participants aren't simply taking meaning; they're *making* meaning. Instead of low-level responses (recalling, naming, echoing, or matching), they're creating and expressing *original* thoughts and emotions.

Transforming ideas and emotions into other forms is significant for understanding, and "nonverbal" arts broaden possibilities for doing that. Music, visual art, drama, and dance are equally and uniquely suited to accomplishing communication's purposes and yield more diverse results than the language arts alone.

Differentiating for diverse museum audiences requires adjusting the "what" (goals/outcomes), "where" (place), and "how" (instruction) for unique "who's" (people). Arts-based teaching and learning makes the *what* richer, the *where* more aesthetic, and the *how* more engaging. And for those who speak little or no English or face other barriers to full engagement in life, the arts are "languages" that free potential and boost motivation to learn (Deasy, 2008).

As humanity's first communication tools, the arts were used to transmit and elevate ideas and emotions. Researchers are currently investigating the unique communication powers of art forms. For example, a 2023 study of body movements and touch sensations found that visual art stirred emotions essential to an aesthetic experience (Nummenmaa & Hari). By engaging bodily response, visual art triggered movement associated with dance, which conveys emotions and thoughts. The point is, while the fine and performing arts remain treasured repositories of culture, their instrumental purposes have been rediscovered. Using the combined force of the arts and the language arts, guests can be coached to grapple with the profound and determine for themselves what's important.

The arts have joined the inner circle of teaching and learning to become the fourth *R* of communication. As invaluable tools in all educational settings, including museums, the arts extend the message with visual images and music, and bring words to life through dance and drama (Cornett, 2015). The arts motivate meaning-making, bridge understanding, and give life to learning.

Arts Integration in Museums

Arts integration, or "infusion," is about creating meaning across disciplines using all art forms, including the literary arts. When museum educators integrate the arts as communication tools, they can *transform* learning about artistic and historical objects. The unique hands-on, minds-on motivation force of the arts is well-suited to engaging imagination and propelling creative inquiry.

SHOW YOU KNOW! ARTS INTEGRATION

Arts options can be incorporated during any tour phase: the voice of Aristide Burrant fills a gallery as visitors enter a Toulouse Lautrec exhibit; during a tour stop, guests take the pose of a woman in a lithograph to understand that she's ice-skating, and middle schoolers compose a rap to wrap up a tour about creative thinking used by the Wright brothers:

CIP Rap
This museum place/ inspired us/ to take more risks/ and join the race.
To solve more problems/ ask what-ifs/ take on challenge/ imagine it!
Collect, Collect, Collect (2X)
Gather data/ ideas and facts/ quantity first/ stacks and stacks.
Zoom in–zoom out/ add evidence / find details/ look for sense.
Connect, Connect, Connect (2X)
Combine and sort/ experiment/ seek the new/ and diff-er-ent.
Take time out/ incubate/ free your brain/ to create.
Then, *Conclude, Conclude, Conclude (2X)*
Think big ideas/Realize/ Important stuff/ Synthesize.
When a light goes on/ in your mind/ the great *aha/* is an insight find!
So that's Collect, Connect, Conclude.
Collect, Connect, Conclude!
Critique is next/ evaluate/ revise the thing/ then communicate.
Share your work/ dance or sing/ read a poem/ or paint some-thing!

Arts Response Options

Museum educator Mike Murawksi argues for "doing" creative thinking, not just "viewing" creative works during tours (2012). The following strategies actively engage participants in creative thinking using the language arts and the fine and performing arts to make invisible thoughts and emotions visible by "doing," not just "viewing."

All Purpose Strategies

- *Partner:* Turn and talk to stretch thinking.
- *Half and Half:* Half the group performs for the other half. The audience then gives descriptive feedback. Reverse roles and repeat.
- *Pick a Strip:* Print questions or arts response options, cut apart, and have small groups choose. See options below.
- *Quote Cards:* Print artist quotes on cards, hand out, and ask each cardholder to read aloud. Discuss what the quote suggests about the work itself.

Creating Meaning in Museums

Drama (pretend)

Use facial expressions, voice, body shapes and movement to show imagined ideas and emotions. Make thinking visible: *"Show how this artwork makes you feel or think, using your imagination, face, body, and/or voice."*

1. *Pantomime:* Show an emotion or movement suggested by the object using face and/or body. Invite the audience to describe "telling" details.
2. *Tableau:* Work with three to five people to create a "frozen picture" about an important idea in the work (theme, emotion). *Extension:* Ask each participant to "say something" in role.
3. *One Liner:* Take the role of someone or something in the work and say something. Sentence starters: "I'm thinking . . ." or "A question I have is . . ."
4. *Imagine and Describe: Example:* Walk into the painting and explain where you are, how it feels, and what you think.
5. *Talking Portrait:* "If this art could talk, what would it say?"
6. *Pretend to be . . .*
   - a news anchor and report on this work.
   - the creator and tell three things about your work.
   - a thief and explain what you're seeing, thinking, and feeling.

Dance (move)

Use body shape, energy, space, and time to convey thoughts and emotions.

1. Become part of the work and show shapes, angles, and lines with your body. *Example:* Jackson Pollock's *Number 1A*, 1948: https://www.moma.org/collection/works/78699.
2. Create a body shape to show the emotional message of the object (Weisberg, 2011).
3. Work with a group to create a frozen shape with different levels about a work's theme. On a count of eight move out of the shape and freeze.
4. *Freeze/Move/Freeze:* Choose three parts of the art and create a frozen shape for each. Start with a frozen shape, then move on a count to the next shape. Vary levels among participants. *Variation:* Create a 3-part group dance that reflects the object's meaning. If the object has a story, freeze in a beginning shape, move to count to show middle of the story, and then freeze in an ending shape.
5. Take a pose. *Example:* "Take a pose as if you are the tightrope walker. Hold for a count of three and relax. Describe how the pose made you think and feel." *Other options*: Half the group poses while other half observes and describes what they see. Then reverse roles.

Music (sound)

Use voice or another instrument to express ideas and emotions using sounds, featuring rhythm, beat, tempo, texture, harmony, varied dynamics, and melody.

1. Find background music that conveys the mood of the work.
2. Create a rhythm/beat based on aspects of the art or object.
3. *Sound Concert:* Brainstorm sounds for parts of a work. When a "conductor" points to an area, make that sound. Or create a sound symphony by using repetition. Suggest volume using gestures (hands). *Variation:* Use found or made instruments (anything that can produce sound by striking, blowing, etc.).
4. *Vocal instrument:* Choose words (verbs, adjectives, adverbs, etc.) that represent the art and say/sing them as phrases, using different volumes, rates, pitch, etc.
5. Write lyrics to a familiar tune that focus on meanings in an object. *Example:* Advertising jingle: *Like a good tightroper, he teases patrons below.*

Example CIP Song: Army Cadence

Creating meaning is the goal,
And the arts "soothe the soul,"
Bring us joy and motivate,
Help us to communicate . . .

Sing out! Integrate!
Sing out! Let's create!
Sing out! Drama, Dance, Music, Art
Drama, Dance, Music, Art
Have a thought? Sing a song!
What you sing, can't be wrong.
Hands-on makes ideas concrete—
Paint or move or keep a beat.
Refrain
Learn in such abnormal ways,
Peers will think you're in a daze.
Soon they'll finally realize,
To learn, we must externalize!
So, use the arts to show you know,
Transform ideas and let them grow.
Show unseen thoughts deep inside,
Surprising insights that satisfy.
Refrain

Visual Art

Use color, line, shape, texture, and composition design to show ideas and feelings (PBS Learning Media).

1. Magnify: Examine the work, then sketch an enlargement of one detail or part.
2. Abstract: Squint to blur the work, then use any media to create an abstract work of colors and shapes.
3. Collage: Tear pieces from magazines or other materials to create a collage that shows the mood, message, or emotions in the work.
4. Inspired Art: Use an idea from the object to create your own art.
5. Brushstrokes: Create an original work using similar "gestures" to those in the work. *Example inspiration:* Jackson Pollock's drip paintings.
6. Storytelling: Use the work to create a story with a beginning, middle, and end.

Research and Technology

1. Do online research about the artist's style, place of origin, and time period. Check YouTube videos.
2. Use the image-search function to find related objects.
3. Visit museum sites to find art and artist information to use as response springboards. *Example:* View Sully's portrait of Elias Dayton and then examine a twenty-dollar bill (Andrew Jackson) and note similarities. Repeat for the one-dollar bill and Stuart's portrait of a woman.
4. Take photos of favorite objects and artworks, create captions, and post on a blog.
5. Create a video tour of five to ten works and post on YouTube or TikTok with commentary.

6. After art investigation, tweet thoughts and questions using a hashtag and/or the museum's Twitter account. Choose a theme: places, people, animals, POC artists, women artists.
7. Curate an Instagram exhibition by posting important, interesting, and curious objects. Use a hashtag or the museum's account.

Literary Arts

Use words to express thoughts and feelings through speaking and writing (narrative, expository, persuasive, etc.). See Quick References 9.2–9.4 for writing forms, poem patterns, and performance options.

1. Choose a poem structure (haiku, cinquain, or limerick) to write about the object's theme. *Example:* Onomatopoeia Poem: Search the object for sounds that can be captured with words (e.g., *gasp, crash, buzz, hiss*). Write words on cards and group to create a poem, like this one about the *Tightrope Walker*: Oohs Ahhs, Gasps, Clap Clap Clap, Hooray!"
2. Write a thank-you note to the artist or creator about what you learned.
3. Create an ad to sell the object to a specific audience.
4. Write a news blurb as if the object just arrived at the museum.
5. Create a word web or map of important things you see in the work.
6. Write an introduction about the artist, suitable for an audience.
7. Create a title, headline, or captions that pull together the work's meaning.

Quick Reference 9.2: *Writing Forms*

Use these A–Z writing forms to show meanings. To combine with drama, take the viewpoint of the artist, someone or something in the work, or a bystander (Philadelphia Museum of Art).

- Acceptance speech
- Advertisement
- Advice column ("Dear Abby")
- Announcement
- Apology
- Award
- Biography
- Blog entry
- Bumper sticker
- Certificate
- Chant
- Cheer
- Complaint
- Compliment
- Editorial
- Email
- Epilogue
- Epitaph
- Exaggeration
- Excuse

- Explanation
- Fable
- Greeting card
- Headline
- Horoscope
- Invitation
- Journal entry
- Letter (business or friendly)
- Lie
- Magic spell
- Narrative (story)
- Nominating speech
- Note
- Obituary
- Ode
- Poem (see Quick Reference 9.3)
- Postcard
- Poster
- Ransom note
- Report

- Résumé
- Slogan
- Telegram
- Text message
- Thank you
- Title
- Tongue twister
- Tribute

- Tweet
- Wanted poster
- Warning
- Weather forecast
- Wikipedia entry
- Will
- Wish

Quick Reference 9.3: *Poem Patterns*

Different poem structures are creative ways to express key ideas. Examples are based on Shinn's artwork, *Tightrope Walker*.

Tips: First co-create an example poem about important ideas, images, and/or feelings. Experiment with repetition, rhyme, alliteration, rhyme, imagery, onomatopoeia, and metaphor.

Repeat Poems: Start with a stem and keep adding lines.

- I wish: *I wish I was brave enough to try tightrope walking.*
- Colors: *Red is the color of the fear of falling.*
- Five senses: *Courage sounds like a low humming/Looks like bright light/Tastes like copper. Smells like sweat/Feels strong like steel.*

If/So or If/Then: *If I were in the audience/I wouldn't even breathe/If he falls, he'll die/And it won't be worth the tease.*

Five-Line: Each line focuses on a: (1) thing, (2) person, (3) special place, (4) feeling, (5) sound or movement: *Tightrope/Performer/Circus/Exhilarated/Frozen.*

Riddle: Three clues, general to specific: *Breathless. Weirdly excited. Ticket holders.*

Lie: Each line is untrue: *Example first line: Circus performers are robots.*

Preposition Poem: *Within the theater/On a thin rope/Above an expectant audience.*

Concrete or Shape: Write words to look like the topic (e.g., adjectives on a line).

Couplet or Triplet: Lines rhyme: *He tentatively glances down/Hearing not a sound.*

Quartet: Four-line poem with chosen rhyme patterns (aabb, abab, abcb, abca): *He accepted the challenge of his life/Never thinking he could fall/But feeling the knife of chance/He worried he'd lose it all. Note:* A *clerihew* is a four-line biographical poem.

Limerick: Humorous five-lined verse (aabba pattern). *There once was a circus guy/Who loved taking chances up high/Until he stopped on the rope/Looked down at the folks/And thought, "Oh no, I'm going to die!"*

Syllable/Word Count:

- *Haiku:* Japanese nature verse with seventeen syllables distributed 5–7–5, in three unrhymed lines.
- *Lune:* Three lines with 3–5–3 words per line: *People like to watch others/Do things they won't try/And let time pass them by.*
- *Tanka:* Five lines with the syllable pattern: 5–7–5–7–7.
- *Cinquain:* No rhyme five-line poem. Words per line: 2–4–6–8–2 (subject, adjectives, action, feeling or observation, adjective/synonym).

- *Diamante:* Seven-line poem (diamond-shaped): 1 noun, 2 adjectives, 3 -ing words, 4 word phrases or nouns, 3 -ing words, 2 adjectives, 1 antonym. *Variation:* Change topic on line three to an antonym.

Found Poems: After looking at object, cut words or phrases from magazines or newspapers and arrange until the words sound like a poem (no rhyme needed).

Question and Answer: *Example pattern:* Christina Rossetti's Q = Who has seen the wind? A = Neither you nor I.

Tongue Twisters: Alliterative phrases: *Teasing, tiptoeing tightroper.*

Quick Reference 9.4: *Poem Performance Options*

- *Choral or Unison*: All together.
- *Cumulative*: One speaker begins, then more voices join.
- *Antiphonal*: Groups go back and forth using different voices.
- *Refrain*: Chorus speaks repeated lines.
- *Character Roles*: Create imagined voices.
- *Narrative Pantomime*: Perform as suggested as narrator reads aloud.
- *Sign Language*: Perform by signing.
- *Background Music*: Play music as poem is read.
- *Reader-Responder*: Reader reads a line; responder improvises response.
- *Reader's Theater*: Write poem in script form.
- *Use Props*: Add musical instruments, puppets, etc.
- *Sound Effects*: Substitute sounds for select words.
- *Movement*: Dance or mime as poem is read aloud.
- *Recite*: Do oral interpretation by varying volume, pitch, tone, rate, and emphasis.
- *Call and Response*: Audience echoes leader's oral interpretation line by line.
- *Canon or Round*: Read with different groups starting at different times.
- *Ostinatos*: Chant sounds at chosen times. *Example:* Ooh-ahh or "clapping" (audience).

TOUR VIGNETTE: *PICTURE BOOKS*

In this final vignette, Catori uses the literary and visual art of a picture book to spark conversation about museum artwork.

Observation Cues

Notice strategies Catori uses to . . .

- Get attention.
- Clarify goals and challenges.
- Validate student comments.
- Engage students in big ideas.
- Provoke interest and curiosity.
- Direct purposeful looking to collect ideas.

Figure 9.1 Using Picture Books. Source: Molly Flasche.

- Coach students to anchor comments in evidence.
- Cause students to connect to personal experiences.
- Coach for interpretations and draw conclusions.

Vignette: The Art of Picture Books

A group of second graders sits on the gallery floor, legs twisted like pretzels. A Toulouse Lautrec painting hangs on the wall—an image of a horse he painted as an adolescent.

"Hi, everyone. I'm Catori, and I brought this book to share." She holds up *Matthew's Dream* by Leo Lionni. "If you know this book, give me a big smile."

The face of one girl catches her eye. "Okay, Jill, I have a special challenge for you: Discover something you didn't notice before in the book."

Jill nods.

"I'll check back with you. Before I read aloud, please take a look at the cover. Describe what's going on."

"Two mice are looking at the sun," Marco says.

"What makes you say 'sun'?"

"The yellow circle in the sky?"

"Everyone, show me a circle with your body," she says.

Some students use hands and fingers; others use their arms.

"Wow! Big and little circles. Great variety!" Catori says.

"But there are two circles," Cobb says, making two circles with his fingers.

"Good spy," Catori says.

"And I've never seen a sun with fat rays."

"Are you saying this doesn't look real?"

"A lot's not real," Thomas says. "Mice don't walk around on two legs!"

"What looks real?"

"The colors are like real rainbows."

"Where else have you seen colors like this?"

"Paint boxes."

"Art museums!"

"The painting behind you."

Catori twists. "Another good spy. I'm glad you saw that, because today's challenge is to compare this picture book with that art."

"Artists are dreamers," Sal says.

"What makes you say that?"

"Artists use imagination, which is like dreaming. And the title has 'dream' in it. I compared, like you said."

"Goodness! This group is on a roll. Keep your discoveries coming." Catori flips to the title page, holds the bottom of the book in her left hand, and runs her right fingertips under the title as she reads aloud *Matthew's Dream* by Leo Lionni.

"I now see three suns!" Donna says.

"Show me," Catori says. They name colors as she points. After they do, Catori turns the page. "Let's read the art before I read the words. What are you seeing on this page that surprises you?"

During the next fifteen minutes, Catori coaches students to describe and connect ideas in the art to their lives. They talk more about dreams and what's real and not real. They make discoveries about where art comes from and how it affects people. Near the end, she asks, "What's making Matthew change?"

"The artwork in the museum inspired him," Marco says. "And he got a girlfriend!"

After the giggling subsides, Catori asks, "What else?"

Following seconds of silence, Jill says, "He didn't think his attic looked so dreary."

"I think he's going to become an artist or a musician," Sal says.

"What makes you say that?"

"He hears music, but he'll probably be an artist 'cause we're sitting in an art museum."

"Let's hear the ending," Cobb says.

Catori smiles. "Sounds like you want to know the whole story!"

Heads nod repeatedly, so she starts reading. When she gets to the last page, she dramatically pauses before the final words, "My dream."

The kids clap, Catori takes a sitting bow, and then points to the artwork. "Let's talk about what this art and this picture book have in common."

They have a spirited conversation, and Catori shares information about how Toulouse Lautrec merged art and real life. Here's a sampling of student conclusions:

1. Art can change your thinking and life.
2. You should follow your dreams.
3. Things don't have to be real to be important.
4. You can make art from anything.
5. Going to museums helps you see with new eyes.

As for Jill, she discovered, "The more you look, the more you see, and the more you see, the more you know."

Debrief

1. What stood out about Catori's "tour"?
2. What indicates that second graders can create deep meaning?
3. How did using a picture book help students make sense of a museum painting?

4. What other arts communication forms could Catori offer for students to show or perform thoughts and feelings?
5. Return to the *Cues* before the vignette to further investigate Catori's strategies.

For a treat, watch this five-minute video that's a "whistle stop" tour of fifty museum-themed books for kids: https://www.thebearandthefox.com/50-great-museum-books-kids/.

MUSEUM GUIDE TOOL KIT: EPR

Since this chapter focuses on alternative forms of communication, here are some ways to get attention using *nonverbal* responses.

Every Person Responds (EPR)

To promote participation, ask guests to use these cues to respond to prompts like "If you spotted (e.g., an unusual shape) . . ."

1. *Give me a big smile.*
2. *Thumbs-up (or) down:* Give a thumbs-up, thumbs-down, or a flat palm to show you're unsure. This also works to show that you agree/disagree/are unsure.
3. *Put your finger on . . .* chin, nose, ear . . .
4. *Put up the number of fingers that show . . .* how many different ways Washi paper is used in this gallery.
5. *Crook your index finger,* if you have a question.
6. *Step in* (form circle or line) . . . if you can describe what's missing, something not yet mentioned, the three ways to make sculpture, etc.
7. *Fist to five:* Raise the number of fingers that shows your level of understanding (fist = none to five fingers = a lot).
8. *Choice cards:* Make cards with back/front choices. *Examples:* yes/no; true/false; negative/positive; or any other two categories. Ask a question, then everyone chooses. On a signal, answers are simultaneously revealed.
9. *Place your hand on your head* (or another place) . . . if you can hear me, see something curious, etc.
10. *Think, pair, share:* Think of an answer, share with a partner. Number partners "one" and "two" and randomly debrief pairs.
11. *Sign language* (Quick Reference 10.1): Teach signs for "yes," "no," "maybe," etc., for guests to response to prompts or questions. *Example:* Do you know what ROYGBIV stands for?"

ADVICE FROM MUSEUM GUIDES

"I want them to enjoy themselves." —Janine Kinnison, museum guide, Dayton Art Institute

My final piece of advice is that there is no one right way to do a museum tour. I'm obviously a big fan of tours that feature conversational investigations into the meanings of a few selected objects, but some guides do more questioning while others use more storytelling and information giving. And I know of museums where docents are empowered to leave artwork selection up to visitors, and ones where prescribed tours are written by on-staff museum educators. I've also participated in delightful co-guided tours, and ones where there's a different docent at each stop.

Flexibility is vital. At any moment, guests may change their minds and self-guide, decide to do a quick walk through a gallery, and then return to rejoin the tour. It's wise to "work with people where they are" (curator Andera Causey).

For more advice on stepping up visitor motivation to learn, check out https://arthistoryteachingr esources.org/lessons/how-to-visit-an-art-museum-a-guide-for-students/.

ADAPTING FOR DIFFERENT AUDIENCES: *AGES AND STAGES*

Adjust for Ages and Development Stages

All students need ...

- a reason to learn.
- to feel important.
- to feel safe.
- to touch.
- to be the center of the universe.
- simplicity and enthusiasm to stay engaged (Evans-Palmer, 2013).

Also see website for Universal Design for Learning (UDL).

Ages 5 to 7

- Limit tours to thirty to forty-five minutes and focus on fewer objects.
- Forecast large rooms with special lighting and sound distortion.
- Assess reactions to noise and lighting, and adapt: Face those with hearing loss; have children face away from distracting activity.
- Sit together in front of objects. Use proximity to boost attention.
- Follow interests: Offer choice about objects to talk about.
- Encourage personal connections: *"How is this like something you've seen or done?"*
- Emphasize themes: *"You'll see things people make for daily use in different countries."*
- Challenge: *"Find something that no one else noticed."*
- Sustain interest: *"Try to find a curious shape in each painting."*
- Invite imagining: *"Pretend to be the person in this painting and finish this sentence: 'I'm thinking ... (or feeling) ...'"*
- Use vocabulary cards with art elements: color, line, shape, texture, and so on. See Quick Reference 5.2.

Ages 8 to 11

Capitalize on interest in exploring why and how things are made and what's real and not real. Coach to ...

- Observe and describe similarities and differences in objects.
- Examine how objects reflect specific time periods, cultures, and places (clothing, architecture).
- Explore cultures by comparing and contrasting clothing, housing, tools, and rituals.
- Investigate tools and techniques used to create art forms.
- Compare textures and types of clay, paper, shells, etc., by passing around samples.
- Introduce science concepts like physics of light and color, and time.

Ages 12 to 14

Museum visits are viewed as freedom from school. It's normal for students to chat among themselves, hold hands, and lean on each other. Respect growing independence and offer more choice.

To maintain group cohesiveness, appeal to burgeoning interest in meaningful experiences:

- Explain the theme's importance in understanding self, others, and the world.
- Explain benefits of using creative inquiry to decode meanings.
- Include facts about how the brain connects ideas.
- Set rules for the tour and conversation—respect everyone's perspective, talk one at a time, piggyback on comments, ask questions.
- Forecast that questions can have many answers.
- Invite everyone to share unique discoveries.
- Offer a "pass" option to give students control over whether to respond.

Ages 15+

High schoolers giggle, use slang, and can seem rude. But they're usually open to new ideas and experiences. Treat them with respect and use a combination of humor and clear, sophisticated language. A relaxed attitude narrows the gap between you and late-adolescent audiences (Evans-Palmer, 2013). Limit the group to ten to twelve at a time to encourage participation.

Tour Beginning

Ask about . . .

- Personal interests and goals for the tour.
- Expectations about what they'll do and see.

Tour Development

1. Explain that conversation builds knowledge by creating a collective experience where everyone learns from one another (Evans-Palmer, 2013).
2. Assume everyone has prior knowledge.
3. Offer choice of objects to investigate and options to demonstrate understanding.
4. Allow choice of partners for activities.
5. Connect their insights and ideas to tour goals/themes.
6. Link to subject areas and personal experiences.
7. Solicit opinions and interpretations.
8. Respect offbeat viewpoints.
9. Coach students to compare and contrast works, find hidden relationships, and note curiosities.
10. Ask questions that call for conclusions supported by evidence. Ask, "What makes you say that?" following open-ended questions like . . .
    - What would make something important enough to be in a museum?
    - What makes this work important?
    - If you could own an object, which would you choose?
    - What emotions or mood does this work provoke?
    - How does this object relate to life today?
11. Pose challenges that promote conversation and insight
    - Find an object that intrigues or surprises you.
    - Choose two paintings with opposite moods or messages.
    - Find an object that makes you wonder about its origin.
12. Encourage students to "ask questions, explore phenomena, construct their own theories, and express understandings in ways meaningful to them" (Evans-Palmer, 2013, p. 372).

Avoid . . .

- Lectures.
- Talking down to students.
- Giving too much information.
- Dwelling on one object.

References: Cornett, 2015; Evans-Palmer, 2013; National Docent Symposium Handbook 2.

RECAP

This chapter outlined the whats, whys, and hows of communication and emphasized expanding communication options by offering arts vehicles to make and show meaning. The vignette featured an art-based children's picture book used to encourage conversation about meanings in visual art. The *Guide Tool Kit* offered "every person response" options and attention-getters, and *Advice from Museum Guides* recommended staying open to different tour protocols. *Adapting for Differences* outlined age and stage guidelines.

NEXT UP!

Wondering about troubleshooting or have more questions? Check out the next chapter, which tackles difficult issues, like nudity.

REFERENCES

Cornett, Claudia. (2015). *Creating meaning through literature and the arts.* Boston: Pearson.

Deasy, Richard. (2008, March). Why the arts deserve center stage: Committing to creative learning for students that will restore America's role as a leader in nurturing innovation. *School Administrator.* American Association of School Administrators.

Evans-Palmer, Teri. (2013). Raising Docent Confidence in Engaging Students on School Tours. *Journal of Museum Education* 38(3): 364–78. DOI: 10.1179/1059865013Z.00000000037.

Murawski, Mike. (2012, April 26). Doing, not just viewing: Working towards a more participatory practice. Spotlight on practice. Teaching tools. *Art Museum Teaching.* https://artmuseumteaching.com/?s=doing+not+just+viewing.

National Docent Symposium Council. (2017). *The Docent Handbook 2.* www.nationaldocents.org.

Nummenmaa, Lauri, & Riitta Hari. (2023). Bodily feelings and aesthetic experience of art. *Cognition and Emotion,* vol. 37, no 3, 515–28. DOI: 10.1080/02699931.2023.2183180.

PBS, *Visual Arts Toolkit Responding Guide:* https://wosu.pbslearningmedia.org/resource/responding_guide/visual-arts-toolkit/.

Philadelphia Museum of Art. (n.d.). Looking to write, writing to look. https://philamuseum.org/learn/educational-resources.

Weisberg, Shelly. (2011, Summer). Moving museum experiences. *Journal of Museum Education* 36(2).

10

Troubleshooting and FAQs

TROUBLESHOOTING (V.): INVESTIGATING AND SOLVING PROBLEMS

Guides, docents, and interpreters have to be problem-solvers, which requires the creative thinking outlined in CIP. The following advice falls under "collecting and connecting ideas" to devise informed solutions. Of course, no strategy works with all guests all the time, and most need to be adapted. For specific museum site issues, ask questions during training and seek guidance from veteran colleagues. And consider the advice from Molly Flasche at the Columbus Museum of Art, who says, "When all else fails, I laugh!"

I learned a lot from interviewing seasoned guides for this chapter that drills down on troubleshooting and frequently asked questions (FAQs).

PREVENTION PREVENTS PROBLEMS

Cell Phone

Inform visitors about museum policies for using cell phones for photography. Request that phones be muted. If emergency texts are received, suggest the person step away to deal with the problem.

Group Management

As a part of the tour introduction, explain "museum etiquette": stay an arm's length from works, only take non-flash photography, respect others by listening and participating, stay with the group, and so on.

Teacher Takeovers

Upon group arrival, clarify the roles of teachers, chaperones, and caregivers to *prevent* problems. Explain they can help . . .

- Keep the group together.
- Maintain student focus and attention. See Museum Guide Tool Kit, chapter 9.
- Limit cell phone use to photos and note taking.
- Enforce museum rules.
- Occasionally model participation in the conversation.

Wanderers

To keep the group together and focused ...

- Explain up front that the group needs stay together and participate in sharing ideas about objects.
- Circulate, using proximity to bring stragglers along.
- Ask what interests visitors most.
- Check in: Ask "How are things are going so far? How's the pace, my volume, and so on?"
- No amount of personal attention, eye contact, sharing intriguing facts, or asking about personal connections will stop some adults from wandering. Don't take it personally.

Audience Participation

Visitors are reluctant to participate in inquiry conversations and other activities for various reasons; they may expect a lecture, feel uncertain about the unfamiliar setting or working with strangers, lack confidence about background knowledge, or have hearing, seeing, or other sensory issues. The follow strategies may help.

1. Limit the tour to three to five total works with a common thread/theme. Less is more.
2. Never skip introducing yourself, what you do, and the conversational nature of the tour.
3. Create a welcoming context using personal greetings and name tags, and ask about interests and concerns.
4. Emphasize that participation is a choice, but different perspectives increase everyone's understanding. Offer the "pass" option.
5. Explain that conversation involves asking questions and sharing connections and interpretations.
6. Form a half circle to create an environment physically conducive to meaningful conversation. Try to have guests on the same level (all sit or stand) (Murawski, 2013).
7. Invite "initial impressions" and general "thoughts."
8. Start with easy questions that invite looking at what's seen (colors, shapes, lines). Progressively ask more interpretive questions that call for personal connections and exploring unseen relationships.
9. Share examples of open-ended questions.
10. Emphasize that there are no wrong answers or questions. Be tolerant with visitors who expect "right" answers.
11. Follow visitor interests when possible.
12. Occasionally use "Turn and talk to each other."
13. Confirm that everyone understands by paraphrasing and clarifying.

Difficult Visitors

When someone challenges facts, respectfully acknowledge concerns and explain that your information comes from the museum, usually curators. If you might be incorrect or inaccurate, acknowledge that and explain you'll follow up after the tour. Don't hesitate to say, *"I don't know."*

Off Comments

When guests say something inaccurate or inappropriate:

- Try to determine what's behind the remark. Ask, *"What makes you say (or think) that?"*
- Consider what the comment suggests about the person's thinking.
- Clarify by asking, *"Are you saying ... ?"* and paraphrase the guest's answer.
- Attempt to validate part of an inaccurate comment, then gently offer accurate facts. *Example:* "You're correct that the artist loved the circus, but he was not *in* any circus acts."

- If possible, repeat different perspectives to boost creative inquiry by everyone.
- Paraphrase inappropriate comments to soften the remark. *Example:* If someone calls dancers in Toulouse Lautrec's artwork "whores," explain that many dancers were poor women driven to prostitution to pay rent. Bias fades when people are given unexpected, reasonable viewpoints.

Racist, Sexist, or Demeaning Remark

A short exchange during a tour probably won't alter hard-core opinions. But don't let a hurtful comment be the last word. At least say, *"That's not been my experience,"* and move to another question or piece of artwork. (Troubleshooting Tips: https://artsmia.github.io/tour-toolkit/reflection/.)

Monopolizers

Nonstop talkers are often smart individuals with a lot of information who enjoy attention. But don't allow visitor takeovers to annoy other guests and derail the tour.

- Disrupt long-winded monologues by refocusing on the work: Invite. *"Describe what you're seeing that makes you say that,"* or ask, *"What do others think about Bob's idea?"*
- Say, *"Doug has more to say, but let's hear other perspectives."* Or say, *"Shelley has shared many ideas, but what do others think?"*

Nonresponsive Guests

Without positive nonverbal signals from guests, be thoughtful about calling on them.

- Give brief, relevant information and invite questions and responses.
- Ask, "What does this remind you of?"
- Return to easy questions: *"What is going on?" "What's happening?" "What's the story?"*
- Encourage wider participation. Ask, *"Who has a different idea?"*
- Ask, *"Who wants to say something who hasn't spoken?"*
- Scaffold with starter sentences to encourage broader response. *Example:* "One interesting (or confusing thing) about this piece is _____."
- Ask questions in a different way or prime thinking with example responses.

Repeaters

Repetition is a common learning strategy. Visitors may repeat to help process thinking, and repetition often decreases as people become more comfortable with inquiry conversations.

When visitors repeat, thank them for the comment, and *perhaps* mention that the idea was already expressed by saying, "So you noticed that, too." Then ask, "What else can you find?"

Sensitive Topics

When topics like religion and science come up, stick with facts: religion answers *why* questions about the meaning of life, while science focuses on *what, where, when,* and *how* questions using direct and indirect observations.

Abstract Skeptics

When objects provoke negative reactions . . .

- Explain that artists often intend to convey emotions and ask about feelings the work evokes.
- Suggest thinking about popular inspirations for art, like nature and beauty.
- Invite exploring commonalities between abstract works and music—both focus on intangibles. Suggest that sounds communicate images, thoughts, and emotions through pattern, rhythm, beat, variety, mood, and so on.

Troubleshooting and FAQs

- Invite conversation about techniques, materials, and tools used to create the object.
- Offer information about the context: Historical and political events often motivate artists to explore styles.

You Don't Understand

Paraphrase what you think the person said: *"Are you saying that___? Or say, "Tell me more."* Apologize if you can't manage to understand.

Nothing's Working

- If you're stuck, move to another work.
- Invite visitors to choose a different work to talk about.
- Ask for personal connections to works.
- Engage the five senses: *"What do you see, hear, etc.?"*
- Ask for evidence: *"What makes you think/say that?"*
- Track remarks and link them to one another: *"Sarah said ____, and Liza thinks ____, and now Barry has brought up a whole new idea."*

General references: National Docent Symposium Handbook 2, 2017; Vatsky, 2023; Vue, 2009.

Quick Reference 10.1: *Sign Language*

Use these signs with groups. See demonstrations: https://www.lifeprint.com; YouTube: https://www.youtube.com/watch?v=QevF4xh5kgg.

1. *Welcome/hello:* wave or salute.
2. *What?:* palm up/lean forward frown.
3. *Repeat* or *again:* V hands one bend.
4. *You, he, she, it:* point index finger.
5. *You all:* look about and point around.
6. *Yes:* fist nod like head.
7. *No:* two finger tap thumb.
8. *Please:* V hand on chest and circle.
9. *Help:* thumbs up, hand on top of other palm.
10. *Thank you:* V hand from chin and out.
11. *You're welcome:* circle fingers, palm out.
12. *Nice:* slide palms across each other.
13. *Good:* touch palm to chin and drop hand.
14. *Understand:* baby O hand near head and flick.
15. *Like:* Pull string from chest with thumb and middle finger.
16. *Maybe:* like weighing options.
17. *See:* V fingers with middle on cheekbones.
18. *Sorry:* fist, thumb out, circles chest.
19. *Group together:* make claw hands and rotate.
20. *Sit down:* bend right two fingers on left hand.
21. *Think:* pointer finger up and touch head.
22. *Thank you:* flat right hand to chin and curve to chest.
23. *Wait:* wiggle finger like you're waiting.
24. *Walk:* flatten palms and walk them.
25. *Question:* curl index finger and wiggle.

FAQS: THE NUDE IN THE ROOM

Guides don't need to apologize for art, including nudes or partially clothed figures in paintings or sculptures. Curator Merilee Mostov suggests thinking about underlying triggers for discomfort, to "learn a thing or two about ourselves, our friends and family, and our communities" (2014). Here's more advice . . .

Be Proactive

Inform visitors that the collection includes nudes that might be seen in passing or are a part of a tour. If needed, offer further explanation, or possibly modify the tour.

Show Respect

Be sensitive to reactions and questions. Some people view nudity in art as pornographic.

Expect the Unexpected

When nude images surprise visitors, guides can choose to ignore gasps or giggles, move on quickly, or provide education.

Build Understanding

Nudity means different things in different cultures. Share historical, cultural, and religious information to help guests understand why artists create nudes. To expand thinking, explain that art "shines a light on difficult issues, such as nudity and sexuality, challenge[ing] us . . . to notice things we may or may not want to think or talk about" (Mostov, 2014, May 2).

Nudity 101

Depending on the group's age and stage, the following information may help guests understand why the museum includes nudity in the collection. *Explain that . . .*

- *Art is a form of communication*: Explain that it's normal to feel uncomfortable about encountering unusual images. Seeing an unclothed body can be embarrassing because it's surprising, but museums show artworks and objects from diverse cultures to stretch thinking about the world's people.
- *Naked is not the same as nude*: Explain that unclothed figures in art are called *nudes*. While "naked" refers to someone defenseless and deprived of clothes, "nude," suggests a proud and confident body (Kenneth Clark, *The Nude*, 1956).
- *Museums display works that can be confusing*: Art often depicts difficult concepts like violence, war, sickness, death, and sex. What a figure wears or doesn't wear can be equally difficult to understand.
- *It's natural to wonder why artists create nudes*: One reason artists create nudes is that everyone has a body, and artists want to depict the fullness of humanity. To glimpse how artists view the challenge of painting nudes, put on a mitten and try to describe a hand.
- *Capturing human figures is difficult*: Artists like challenges! Human figures have been studied for millennia, and communicating complex feelings and thoughts by painting or sculpting the colors and textures of skin and veins; the shapes of muscles and the skeletal structure; with appropriate body proportions and postures is a definite challenge. To depict humans, artists make careful sketches of muscles, bones, and limbs, and their art celebrates how body parts combine to create individuals.

- *Cultural views about the human body differ*: Nudes or partial nudes are sometimes created to express that human bodies are beautiful. The early Greeks revered the human body, and Western Europeans were influenced by ancient Greek art. In contrast, African art can include partially nude figures because of climate. Chinese artists concentrate more on nature than the human body.
- *Real life and accuracy are portrayed by some artists*:: In ancient Greece, men exercised nude, so that's how artists represented athletes. Taking a bath requires nudity, and nursing a baby requires removing clothing. In the Roman legend about Romulus and Remus being raised by a mother wolf, it wouldn't make sense to clothe the boys.
- *Clothes reflect time periods, places, and cultures*: Nudes are timeless. They remind us that without clothes, anyone could belong to almost any time or place or culture.
- *Religious views are sometimes depicted*: Art based on the Christian Bible sometimes depicts an undressed baby Jesus to show he's fully human and also divine.
- Information for adults and young adults can include the themes of sex and fertility
  a. In African sculpture, the female body is often a symbol of agrarian fertility.
  b. Hindu art may show sexual unions of males and females as metaphors for the union a follower seeks with God.
  c. In the early twentieth century, Picasso shocked the art world by painting Les Demoiselles d'Avignon, which distorted the female form. Painted abstractions of nudes were thought to be "rebellious" through the twentieth century.

References: Clark, 1956; Mostov, 2014; Shoemaker, 1993; the John and Mable Ringling Museum of Art: https://www.ringling.org/sites/default/files/basic_page_download/Nudity_FamilyGuide-web .pdf.

FAQS: BEHIND THE SCENES AT MUSEUMS

Museums preserve, protect, and share important artworks, objects, and artifacts. But the mission of museums is to use the collection and museum spaces to educate people, enrich lives and communities, and bolster democracy. From curating and archiving to conservation and art handling, it's people who are the backbone of museums.

The following are examples of museum job descriptions, but responsibilities, titles, and qualifications vary based on the museum's size, focus, and needs.

Museum Director

Museum directors lead the institution. They oversee financial operations, facilitate strategic planning, set the vision, cultivate relationships with donors and stakeholders, and represent the museum within the community. *Qualifications:* Advanced degree in arts administration, museum studies, or relevant field; extensive management experience; strong leadership and strategic planning skills.

Curators

Curators hold a high position in museum hierarchies. As guardians of collections, they are responsible for researching, acquiring, and interpreting artifacts and artworks. They curate exhibitions; collaborate with artists, historians, and collectors; and play key roles in shaping the museum's narrative by the selection and presentation of items. While demands on a curator depend on the museum, lead curators usually plan and organize exhibits, seek funding, promote their ideas in board meetings, initiate community involvement, and review items in their area of expertise. *Qualifications:* Master's degree or Ph.D. in art history, museum studies, or related field; extensive knowledge about collection areas; research experience.

Registrar

Registrars manage the collection, meticulously documenting and cataloging acquisitions, loans, and movements of objects. They ensure proper handling, storage, and display, adhering to best practices in collection management. Working out of the public eye, registrars must be experts in database software.

Dayton Art Institute registrar Sally Kurtz explains that she strives "to treat someone's gift as if it is equal to every other piece [and the] most precious thing in the world." She also explained that registrars who arrange transportation for objects sometimes enjoy a special perk—accompanying objects going to interesting destinations as a courier. *Qualifications:* Bachelor's or master's degree in museum studies, library science, or related field; experience in collections management; attention to detail.

Archivist

Archivists organize and preserve historical documents and photographs. They catalog and digitize materials, manage archives, and provide resources for scholarly and public investigations. Archivists must have a strong detail orientation. *Qualifications:* Master's degree in library science, archival studies, or related field; experience in archival management; knowledge of preservation techniques.

Conservator

Conservators are preservation experts who assess, clean, repair, and restore artworks and artifacts using techniques that ensure an object's longevity and integrity. This work involves balancing scientific analysis with artistic sensitivity. Conservation specialists conduct extensive study to understand and implement preventive measures, including techniques to control environment and climate, to conduct pest management, to store and package items, and to encase artifacts. *Qualifications:* Master's degree in conservation or related field; specialized training in conservation techniques; strong scientific and artistic skills.

Exhibit Designer

Designers give life to the museum's most treasured items by creating exciting exhibits They consider aesthetics and visitor experience in layouts and displays, and they collaborate with curators to oversee installations, working closely with curators, the marketing team, and other directors to plan future exhibitions. *Qualifications:* Bachelor's degree or master's degree in design, art, architecture, theater, set design, or related field; proficiency in design software and spatial planning.

Education Coordinator

Education coordinators design and implement programs for diverse audiences. This includes developing tours, lectures, workshops, classes, and multimodal activities that appeal to individuals and groups. Museum educators also train guides, conduct tours, and publish information on the website to expand educational opportunities. Some educators conduct research for the museum and write materials for exhibits. The job requires a passion for history, culture, and learning. *Qualifications:* Bachelor's degree or higher in education, museum studies, history, art, or relevant field, along with strong communication skills and experience in program development.

Guide, Docent, and Interpreter

This job entails leading tours that feature storytelling, stir insightful conversations, and integrate relevant information about the historical context and artistic content of objects. Guides are expected to facilitate interactive experiences that make objects accessible and engaging for diverse audiences. As the public face of a museum, guides need to be flexible and possess an enthusiasm for learning and customer service. A great guide can transform an ordinary museum experience into an extraordinary one. *Qualifications:* Varied, but often a bachelor's or master's degree in education, the arts, history, or related field. Strong communication and presentation skills are necessary, and museums often provide additional training.

Development Officer

Development officers secure funds and other support for museum activities. They cultivate relationships with donors, apply for grants, and develop fundraising strategies to sustain programs and growth. *Qualifications:* Bachelor's or master's degree in fundraising, nonprofit management, or related field; experience in fundraising; excellent communication and networking skills.

Marketing Coordinator

Marketing coordinators devise and implement strategies to promote the museum using advertising, social media, and public relations. They design campaigns that highlight exhibitions, events, and educational offerings. *Qualifications:* Bachelor's degree in marketing, communications, or related field; experience in marketing; creativity and strong communication skills.

Museum Technician

Technicians provide essential support for museum operations, from assisting with installations and maintenance to managing inventory. *Qualifications:* Bachelor's degree in museum studies or related field; technical skills in handling and caring for artifacts; attention to detail.

Security Guard

Museum heists make intriguing plots for films, but thefts at museums are rare. When guards aren't writing bestselling books, they're responsible for preserving the museum building and its collection, and being "present" to gently remind visitors of rules and give directions. *Qualifications:* Experience with security, employment in law enforcement or the armed forces; solid communication skills.

For more information on additional museum jobs, refer to Tara Young's 2019 book, *So You Want to Work in a Museum?* American Alliance of Museums.

REFERENCES

Clark, Kenneth. (1956). *The nude. A study of ideal art.* New York: Pantheon.

Mostov, Merilee. (2014, May 2). Encounters with nudity. Columbus Museum of Art. https://www.columbusmuseum.org/blog/2014/05/02/encounters-nudity/.

Murawski, Michael. (2013, December, 13). Reflecting on the learning power of conversation in museums. https://artmuseumteaching.com/2013/12/17/power-of-conversation/.

National Docent Symposium Council. (2017). *The Docent Handbook 2.* www.nationaldocents.org.

Shoemaker, Maria. The naked truth: Or how to respond to the tell-tale giggle. *Docent Educator* 2(3) (Spring 1993): 16–17.

Stafford, Tom. (2012, June 18). BBC Future. https://www.bbc.com/future/article/20170512-what-causes-that-feeling-of-being-watched.

The John and Mable Ringling Museum of Art: https://www.ringling.org/sites/default/files/basic_page_download/Nudity_FamilyGuide-web.pdf.

Vatsky, Sharon. (2023). *Interactive museum tours: A guide to in-person and virtual experiences.* Lanham, MD: Rowman & Littlefield.

VUE. (2009, Spring). Visual thinking strategies: Understanding the basics. *Visual Understanding in Education.* San Jose Museum of Art. https://sjmusart.org/sites/default/files/uploads/files/Understanding%20Basics.pdf.

Epilogue

Epilogue (n.): closing statement to tie up loose ends.

Snoopy in Charles Schulz's comic strip once commented that sometimes it's just too early to learn. But it's never too late or too early to become a museum guide, docent, or interpreter.

According to Michael Roediger, president and CEO of Dayton Art Institute (DAI), "Museum guides are an important part of the museum's overall education department and programs," and DAI guides are quick to articulate benefits of working with guests and visitors. Most talk about intrinsic rewards of learning about art and how guiding tours is "fun." Guides also enjoy creating memorable guest experiences and feeling appreciated (Norma Landis, Rick Hoffman), while others enjoy helping their community (Wayne Witherell).

As for me, I agree that it's never too late to learn: I learn something new from every tour! But it's "passing on light" that's most rewarding. At this point, I hope you feel empowered to do that by encouraging visitors to participate in conversations that help each person create their own sense of art, objects and artifacts. When that happens, you'll witness moments when people of all ages experience the joy of discovery—all because *you* tapped the human capacity to create insight and shaped the environment to make it happen.

You've reached the end of this book, but that doesn't mean you're done. Here are additional ways to continue learning about Creative Inquiry Process (CIP) and expanding the role of making meaning during museum conversations:

1. Join or form a group that wants to dig deeper into CIP's role in museum experiences and life.
2. Consult online research about guide work at museums like the National Gallery in Washington, D.C.
3. Watch YouTube videos that relate to guide and docent work, like those featuring all sorts of artists creating all sorts of art forms.
4. Start a blog or newsletter to share ideas and FAQs for guiding.
5. Suggest a monthly lunch to have meaningful conversations with colleagues.
6. Participate in docent-sponsored projects at the museum that engage the community (e.g., monthly Art Chats on untold stories about works and creatives—like the history-changing tale of Wilbur Wright getting attacked by a young man who became a mass murderer.
7. Volunteer to mentor, which is rewarding.
8. Invite newbies to observe your tours because shadowing is essential.
9. Continue to observe other guides to acquire new strategies and remind yourself that no two tours are the same.
10. Ask for five minutes to Turn and Talk about new guiding ideas at regular training sessions.
11. Start a DOG (docent or guide) book club, and discuss a chapter a month. Start with this book!
12. Have a Museum Meet-Up: Invite interpreters, docents, and guides from nearby museums to discuss common questions, new strategies, books, etc.
13. Propose a new event, like the Columbus Museum of Art's "Ten on the Dot": docent-led ten-minute conversations.

14. Bring in speakers (e.g., docent directors or guides from other museums) to talk about topics like troubleshooting.
15. Attend a conference sponsored by the National Docent Symposium or the American Alliance of Museums: https://www.aam-us.org.
16. Create new and different ways to promote creating meaning in your museum that bolster the joy of discovery and keep visitors coming back!

To celebrate how much you've learned about creating meaning in museums, follow these directions: Raise your right hand and give yourself a pat on the back, repeating, "Pat, pat, pat on the back, back, back for a job well done!"

Feel free to contact me with questions and ideas!

Claudia E. Cornett, PhD
Professor Emerita, Wittenberg University
ccornett@wittenberg.edu

Appendix A

STRATEGIES AND SCAFFOLDS FOR USING CREATIVE INQUIRY TO MAKE MEANING

Appendix (n.): a collection of supplementary materials at the end of work.

Purpose: Engage museum visitors in conversations that use the Creative Inquiry Process (CIP) to make sense of artworks, objects, and historic and cultural artifacts.

Adaptations: Most strategies *can* be formatted for written response or used in pairs or small groups. See *Adapting for Differences* in chapters 1–9.

Note: *QR* is short for "Quick References" in chapters.

MULTIPURPOSE

1. **Warm-ups**: Break the ice by asking visitors for a preference, like "cake or pie," "cat or dog."
2. **Pass Option** (transfers choice and control): Announce that anyone can "pass" on any question or activity.
3. **Pair Share** or **Turn and Talk**: To increase comfort, ask participants to share ideas with a partner or small group. Debrief the whole group.
4. **Partner Paraphrase**: To debrief small groups, invite participants to share something *heard* that needs to be shared with the whole group.
5. **EPR**: "Every Person Responds" is an alternative to hand-raising. *Example:* "Thumbs up if you have an idea about . . ." Other suggestions include: fold arms, touch chin, cross your legs. See Museum Guide Tool Kit, chapter 9.
6. **Step In**: Form a circle. Say, "If you (*see something curious*) about this object, step in (or hop, or slide, etc.)." Vary by changing categories (*interesting, unique*).
7. **Descriptive Feedback**: To encourage participation, reinforce contributions by *describing* what was said or done instead of using judgmental praise. *Example:* "That's a new idea," instead of "Very good idea."
8. **Open Questions**: Ask "fat" questions that have multiple answers (versus closed "yes/no" or one-word answers). *Examples:* "What might the artist be saying in this sculpture?" Vary with "So, what?" "What next?" "What if?" "Why not?" "What might?" or "How might?" "What do you see?" "Smell?"
9. **All-Purpose Response**: Ask, "What makes you say that?" Or say, "Show me where you see that."
10. **Piggybacking**: Encourage adding to another viewpoint. *Example:* "What can you add to Liam's idea about contrasting colors being important?"
11. **Cloze**: Using Gestalt psychology, nudge guests to fill in gaps: Pause or leave blanks in sentences (oral or written). *Example:* "RoyGBiv is an _____ for red, orange, yellow, green, _____, indigo, violet."

TOUR INTRODUCTION

~Context: Chapter 3~

n. circumstances surroundings an event, statement, or idea.

1. **Get Comfortable**: Create a "risk-free" climate. Be welcoming. Meet and greet people personally. Give your name. Make eye contact. Smile. Offer name tags.
2. **Explain Yourself**: Describe what guides do and why (e.g., ask open questions, give prompts, and integrate key information to help visitors learn and enjoy).
3. **Museum Etiquette**: Explain that the goal is preserving objects and keeping guests safe. *Example guidelines:* Stay an arm's length away from objects. Alert visitors to security guards charged with protecting people and the collection.
4. **Inventory** (assess): Say, "Raise your hand if . . . first-timer? Visited other museums? Have special interests? Needs? Folding stools?" Ask, "What else should I know about you?" Inquire about expectations and connect inquiry, discovery, and conversation to enjoyment.
5. **KWL**: Assess by asking, "What do you *know*? *Want to know*?" During the tour wrap-up, ask "What did you *learn*?" (Ogle, 1998).
6. **Orient** (offer map): Point out restrooms and elevators. Give three museum facts and invite guests to look at building architecture. Ask: "What do you notice?"
7. **Advanced Organizers**: Tell the theme/title. Give a heads-up about the conversational format and using the Creative Inquiry Process (CIP) to *collect* and *connect* ideas to figure out objects.
8. **Share a 7 Cs Cue Card**: See chapter QR 1.3 and 2.1.
9. **Look/See-Think/Feel-Know**: Use this shorthand to explain how to figure out meanings of objects.
10. **Sign Language**: Teach a couple of signs you'll use during the tour. *Examples:* Think, Thank You, Very Good (see QR 10.1).

~Challenge: Chapter 4~

n. Present a question, problem, interest, or curiosity to investigate.

1. **Share Goals**: Understand and enjoy investigative conversations about objects. Emphasize there is no one or "right" interpretation.
2. **Forecast**: Invite participants to share insights, surprises, and questions during the tour. Cue that you'll ask them to revisit what stood out or will be remembered during the closing.
3. **Share the Creative Inquiry Process (CIP)**: Context-Challenge-Collect-Connect-Conclude, *then* Critique-Communicate. Periodically ask how CIP changes thinking/feeling.
4. **Use Synonyms**: *Make sense=understand, interpret, appreciate, conclude, learn. Themes=universal truths, insights, big ideas, maxims, sayings, wisdom.*

TOUR DEVELOPMENT

~Collect: Chapter 5~

v. Gather, assemble, or pile up ideas, information, or things.

1. **Scan/Survey**: Invite guests to scan whole work. Debrief after thirty seconds with: "What did you see?" or "What's going on?" or "What's happening?" See QR 2.2 and 2.3 (Questions & Responses).

2. **Splatter Vision**: Suggest a slow scan to identify what stands out: "Squint like a policeman searching for movement." *Debrief:* "What catches your eye?"

3. **Strategic/Purposeful Looking**: Observe for thirty-plus seconds to notice ___." Prompt with categories: "What's interesting or curious?" or "What details, ideas, or emotions stand out?" or prompt to examine art elements (QR 5.2).

4. **Looking/Seeing—Thinking/Feeling—Know!**
   - What are you seeing (observing or noticing)? List, name, describe . . .
   - What's going on (action, story)? Explain what's happening.
   - What are you wondering (imagining, guessing, suspecting, feeling)? *Variations:* Ask about senses: hear, smell, taste, etc.

5. **Looking/Seeing/Describing**: Explain *seeing* versus *knowing* by noting that children draw what they "know" (stick people with huge heads) versus what they see. Suggest looking to really *see*. Follow with "Describe what you actually see." *Prompts:* art elements, composition design (QR 5.2). *Variation:* Ask for adjectives and adverbs to expand nouns and verbs (e.g., red roof—"What kind of red?").

6. **Look 40, List 5**: Look purposefully for forty seconds to see five things. Repeat to find more.

7. **You see/I see**: First person shares an observation; second person says, "You see __, and I see ___." Keep going until everyone adds something. Allow "pass" if someone stalls, but come back with a second chance or ask, "What did someone else say that you want to repeat?"

8. **Points of View (POVs)**: Try near/close and far. Use cardboard tubes, make fist telescopes, or shape finger frames to observe. Look from above/below, focus on different sections (parts versus whole). Experiment with magnifying glasses. Squint. Squat down and look up. Look through colored lenses. Debrief: "What makes it interesting or unique? What did you discover?" Use Turn and Talk to discuss effects of changing viewpoints.

9. **Half and Half**: Form groups with each looking at half the work: Left, right, top-bottom, quadrants, etc. Debrief about discoveries using Turn and Talk. Share highlights with the whole group and ask about likenesses and differences: "They found _____, but we found _____."

10. **Walk into the Painting**: Smell, taste, touch, hear, then take the role of _____ and create a one-liner: "I smelled ____, and heard_____," and so on. Role options: tourist, job seeker, etc.

11. **Journalist**: Take the role of reporter and describe the work objectively. *Example:* A large chandelier hangs over a ghostlike figure, paused on a thin white line. One foot points down on the rope/wire. In the background (below) is a dark scene of what appears to be an audience.

12. **Find Five Flip**: Study the object for one minute to remember as much as possible. On signal, flip around and list five things with partner. Repeat to discover more. *Variation:* Create light competition with teams writing down and sharing what they saw. *Prompts:* colors, shapes, figures, places, things.

13. **Look, Sketch, Web**: Use clipboards. Take five minutes to look at an object and sketch or web. *Suggestion:* Focus on a small area or part or a few art elements (color, line, shape). *Variation:* Free-write or list.

14. **Short and Silent**: Everyone looks for thirty seconds and puts up a finger for each detail. *Debrief:* On signal, everyone displays number of found details using fingers.

15. **Round About**: Make a circle. Go around with each person saying a word (noun, verb, or adjective) about the object. Go fast. Offer "pass and come back" option.

16. **Speed Viewing**: Stare at an area of a work until leader signals "change." Then look at another area. Do this for one minute, then debrief using "Round About."

17. **Shifty-Eyed**: Variation on "Speed Viewing," but the leader says, "Change focus to" (colors, shapes, lines, or textures). Do a partner debrief.

18. **Scavenger Hunt**: Challenge to find five meaningful categories or connections in multiple works. *Example:* Interesting, Curious, Important, Unique, Reminds me of . . .

19. **Puzzle Pieces]**(National Portrait Gallery: https://www.npg.si.edu/): Take photo of object, print, and cut into pieces, each showing something significant. Give each group one piece to study. Then ask each group to describe what's seen and explain how the piece relates to the whole. Finally, work together to assemble the puzzle on the floor. Debrief about importance of parts to whole messages.

20. **Coached Categories**: Suggest participants look purposefully to notice colors, shapes, lines, details in foreground, background, etc. For categories, see QR 5.2.

21. **Conversation Cards**: Use tour theme to write *what-ifs* and other open questions on cards. Have each group draw a card and discuss. If needed, offer choice to draw another card. Examples: "What question would you like to ask Wilbur Wright?" "What's one word that describes how you feel about flying airplanes?" "What do you do when you get stuck?" "What's a key ingredient in a partnership?" "What/who makes you laugh? Why?"

~Connect: Chapter 6~

v. Bring together, link, categorize, sort, or group ideas.

1. **C-C-C Round Up**:
   • Collecting: looking/seeing—thinking/feeling—listening—say/list/tell/describe.
   • Connecting: sorting observations into meaningful categories, finding associations and relationships (visible and invisible).
   • Concluding: synthesizing (pulling together) important connections, insights/understanding. *Key questions:* What's this about? What's the message?
2. **Look/See, Hear/Listen, Think/Feel, Know/Wonder**: Use as shorthand for key communication processes.
3. **Five POVs**: Coach investigation of objects by suggesting different points of view or roles (adapted from Harvard's Project Zero):
   • *Pleasure seeker*: "How does this work make you feel?" "What makes it beautiful? "How much do you like it? Why?"
   • *Storyteller*: "What's happening?" "What's going on?" "What happened first, second . . ."
   • *Problem Solver*: "What's the problem? What's puzzling? Curious? Intriguing?"
   • *Explainer*: "What's this about? How do you know? How did this happen? Why?"
   • *Transformer*: "What are ways you could communicate your thoughts and feelings about this object?"
   Follow with asking for examples or evidence: "What do you see that makes you say that?"
4. **Vantage Points**: Ask, "What do you . . ."
   • See/notice (hear, smell, taste, touch)?
   • Think/feel?
   • Know/understand?
   • Care about?
5. **Multisensory Inventory**: Survey the object using all senses and emotions, then sort into groups.
6. **ME Connections**: Link to prior experiences and known information by asking, "What does this make you think of?" "What's familiar?"
7. **Metaphors and Analogies**: Experiment with associations between objects and music, persons, places, things, animals, etc. *Example:* "How is this painting like a glass of ice water?" "If this painting was a song/genre of music, it would be . . ."
8. **Closed versus Open Sorts**: A *closed sort*s start with a category and then continues with finding ideas that fit (connections). Categories include art elements and interesting, curious, and

surprising elements. (See QR 5.2.) *Open sorts* begin with observing to *discover* patterns or catego-ries, followed by *determining* how to group ideas.

9. **Squeeze** (closed sort): Look at a work and invite brainstorming in a category. *Example:* "What are all the *colors* you see?"
10. **ICI**: Observe for "interesting, curious, and important" details. Partner to share one of each.
11. **Pick 2 for 2**: Offer categories to look for in an object and invite add-ons. *Examples:* mood, curiosi-ties, confusions, uniqueness, interestingness, objects, places, figures, body parts, nature, emo-tions, art elements. Individuals pick two and search for two minutes. Group or partner to debrief.
12. **Two from Twenty**: Look at an object for twenty seconds, then share two adjectives that describe how it looks or feels.
13. **Before and After Poem** (Baird, 2017): Write down three to five words that describe immediate reactions to a work. Then do purposeful looking, share thoughts, and make connections. Finally, write down three to five words that express thoughts and feelings. Example from "Lost and Found": *Before:* dumb, weird, silly. *After:* interesting, helpful, deep.
14. **Metaphoric Thinking**: Ask, "What does this object make you think of?" "What experiences can you associate with the work?" Starters: "This reminds me of ____ because ____."
15. **Associations and Relationships Frames**: "This seems related to _____ because_____." "I asso-ciate ____ with _____ because_____."
16. **Thinking Frames**: Use a cause-effect frame to respond: "I felt _____ because _____," "I heard _____ because _____," and so on. *Variation:* Use compare-contrast or problem-solution.
17. **Concept Cards**: Make a card deck with art elements (color, line, shape, texture, etc.) and design principles (see QR 5.2). Invite participants to draw a card and focus on the category as they observe. *Variation:* Emotion cards: sad, happy, funny, worrisome, beautiful, disconcerting, uneasy, scary, joyful, surprising.
18. **Emotion Seek**: Find a painting or section of an object that makes you feel happy, sad, confused, light, uncertain, and so on. Explain what the artist did to evoke that emotion.
19. **Before and After**: Ask what happened right before a "scene" in an artwork and "what's next?" *Key questions:* "What's the story?" or "What's happening?"
20. **Space X**: Ask, "What takes up most space in a work?" "What's repeated?" "Missing?" "What could this mean?"
21. **Mood**: Ask, "How does this art make you feel?" "What's the atmosphere?" "What's creating the emotions/mood?" *Alternative:* "Show the mood with your face and/or body shape."
22. **Mystery Meanings**: Ask what's hidden in the work (unseen or implied), such as relationships among figures. Ask, "If you could read between, what would you say is going on?"
23. **Fast or Fun Facts**: Share three to five relevant facts (not gossip) at key points in conversation: *Example:* "Fact number one is . . ." Then ask how the information changes thinking about the object. *Variation:* Put facts on individual cards or separate strips and invite participants to read aloud on request or as they see fit.
24. **Museum Label**: Also called a didactic (something that informs). See QR 7.7.
25. **Visible/Invisible (Seen/Unseen)**: Use frames to scaffold responses: "The most important things I *see* are _____, and important *unseen* things are _____."
26. **Their Own Words** (quotes): Read a quote from the artist or creator and ask what it says about the object or thinking behind the object.
27. **Multisensory Response**: Invite participants to pick one of the five senses to show thoughts and emotions (about a work) with face, body posture, movement, sketching.
28. **Hot Seat**: Make art cards with categories: art elements, emotions, composition aspects. Sit in circle with IT in the center, eyes closed. IT throws a knotted sock that's caught and tossed around the circle. When IT calls, "Stop," whoever holds the sock is on the Hot Seat. IT then chooses a card, reads the category, and says, "Go." Hot Seat passes sock to left. While sock is passed

around the circle, Hot Seat tries to list five things in the category. If Hot Seat fails to do so before sock comes back, Hot Seat becomes IT. *Variation:* Choose categories relevant to the exploration of specific objects (e.g., historic artifacts).

CLOSING/WRAP-UP

~Conclude: Chapter 7~

v. Experience an aha! *or create an interpretation, big idea, insight, or meaning after collecting and connecting information.*

1. **Brain Recess**: (incubation): Breathe in deeply for count of ten, hold for five, then exhale slowly to let the brain process possibilities. *Other examples:* Take a lap around the gallery.
2. **Brain Gym**: Show "two-way" drawing (e.g., old/young woman from internet) to give short experience with discovering hidden images.
3. **Crowd Sourcing**: Ask visitors to finish the adage "Two heads are better than ____." Then explain that when more people work to pull together interpretations and conclusions, better results are achieved more quickly.
4. **Big Ideas**: Squeeze objects for "big ideas" or themes by asking, "What's this about?" Accept ideas without judgment. Use fast pace. Probe with "Which ideas make the most sense?" Coach to turn big idea/theme into sentence: *Example:* "What does this painting say about light? Loneliness? Work?" *Example:* Light or white suggests hope in the face of "dark" facts of life in the background.
5. **What else?**: Stretch ideas by asking what hasn't been mentioned. *Example:* "Where is the light (white) coming from?" "What is being illuminated? Why?" (referring to the theme of light).
6. **EPC**: "How is this object 'exciting, puzzling, or connected' to you? Why?"
7. **SSW**: "How does this object 'surprise, stump, cause wonder'?" or "What emotions are you left with from this object (e.g., sad, angry, awed)?" Follow with, "What makes you say that?"
8. **Cover Up**: Imagine that part of the object is concealed to check if a conclusion remains solid, or ask, "What if there was no chandelier in the painting?"
9. **Close Your Eyes**: "Think about the object. What do you see? Think? Feel?"
10. **One-Liner**: "Become the object and tell what you are about."
11. **Different Hats (POVs)**: Assign different roles to look at and respond to objects: Big Picture, Analyst, Marketer, Thief, Real Estate Agent, Devil's Advocate, etc.
12. **Conversation Strategies**: See Museum Guide Tool Kit, chapter 7.
13. **Speed Conversation**: Give two to three minutes to circulate and talk with different people about the object's message.
14. **Inside-Out Brain**: Create a web to show connections about the object. See Appendix C for example of *Tightrope Walker. Example of "legs":* emotions, big ideas, what stands out, intangibles, etc.
15. **Sticky Notes**: Offer cards or notes for visitors to write down a big idea, theme, conclusion, or provide the starter: "An important or interesting thing I learned was ____."
16. **Sentence Frames**: Scaffold by offering frames to respond: "What I've seen and heard makes me think or feel ____ because ____." "The big idea seems to be _____ because ___." "I used to think/feel, but now I think/feel ____ and wonder ____." "The thing that's puzzling is _____."
17. **Forced Combinations**: To spark out-of-box thinking, ask questions that call for links between works or other items. *Example:* "How is the piece of art like a box of cereal?" Invite comparisons with previous objects: "How is this like _____? Different from ____?"

18. **Walk into the Art**: "Pretend to step into a work and explain what's going on, how you feel, and why." Ask, "What is being there about?"
19. **Empathy Roles**: Invite role-taking (POV) to "see with fresh eyes." *Example:* "Become a person, place, or thing in the art, or someone interacting with the object. Decide what you are thinking and feeling and why." Invite one-liners (with partner or whole group.) *Example:* "Humans can't stop being connected." *Variation:* "Pair up and talk to each other while in the role." "I see . . . smell . . . feel . . . wonder . . ."
20. **Title It**: "Give the object a title that captures what it's about. Explain choices." *Variation:* Choose two or three titles to critique based on which makes the most sense.
21. **Headlines or Captions**: After conversations, get to the point, but capture the heart with a object headline or caption. *Examples:* "Alone on the Wire." "Balanced between Life and Death." "An Oops and He's Out." "The Thin White Line." "No Wrong Steps Allowed." Pair/Share and then share with group.
22. **Talk Back**: "What would you ask or say to the artist, owner of the (historic) house, etc.?"
23. **Look-See/Think-Feel/Know-Wonder**: Think aloud to model each phrase, then invite practice with partners. Fold blank paper into a trifold and write each phrase across top and record ideas. Or offer sentence frames: "I see ___." "I think this is mostly about ___ because _____" (refer to evidence in work). "It makes me feel _____." "I now know _____." Finally, invite wondering: "What if . . ." "I wonder why . . ."
24. **Speaker/Responder**: Partner to share conclusions. Speaker shares with partner, then responds honestly. *Example:* Speaker: "The message is that everyone is both lost and found." Responder: "Yes, I've been lost many times, and it helps to ask for directions."
25. ***Aha!* Light-Bulb Moments**: Take a quick walk around to survey a gallery (one to two minutes). Ask, "What's the big idea of this gallery?" or "What stands out?" Explain that *aha!* (insight) results from incubation. Ask for "big ideas" or "special moments" during the tour. "How has creative inquiry changed your thinking about understanding art?" "What are the takeaways related to the theme of . . . ?"

~Critique: Chapter 8~

v. Analyze/give for a decision or judgement.

1. **Transitions**: See chapter 8 and QR 8.3.
2. **Nominations**: Ask for nominations of titles or headlines that best capture thoughts about the object's importance/meaning. *Variation:* Vote on top two. Or rank.
3. **Fortunately or Unfortunately**: Each person looks at the painting and says either "Fortunately . . ." or "Unfortunately . . ." (*Focus:* diverse POVs.) *Variation:* Divide group in half and assign "Fortunately" or "Unfortunately." Go back and forth between groups for sentence completion. *Variation:* Ask participants to complete: "The best thing about this work is . . ." and "The worst thing about this work is . . ."
4. **Debate**: Divide into two teams. Look carefully at the object. Then think and discuss "What works? What doesn't? Why/why not?" Next, assign pro (works) or con (doesn't work) viewpoints. Give one to two minutes for each side to present. Switch and repeat. Kick it up a notch: Challenge participants to use art elements to discuss what works and doesn't work and then report. Finally, ask, "Is this 'good' art? Why or why not?" "How is it important?" "Why would/ should it be in this museum?" "Is it beautiful? Why or why not?"
5. **Take a Stand**: Each person chooses an "interesting" or "important" artwork and explains their choice. *Variation:* Move to spots on an imaginary line to show agree-/disagree-with statements

or concepts about artwork. *Example:* "This artwork is confusing or puzzling." Follow with asking, "Why?" Other categories: curious, uncomfortable, beautiful, unsettling.

6. **Vote with Your Feet**: Invite participants to choose two "favorite" artworks and stand in front of one. Participants then look purposely for thirty seconds to prepare to explain choice. Categories for choices: original, unique, emotional, surprising.

7. **Little Thing/Big Difference** (What if . . .): Zero in on details and consider effects. "What if the tightrope walker had on baggy pants? A cowboy hat? Carried a bag? Wore different-colored shoes?"

8. **Wrap- or Circle-Up**: To wrap up tour, ask participants to tell 1) a highlight of the tour—anything that stood out or will be remembered (e.g., emotions, big ideas); 2) what they would tell a friend about the tour; 3) light-bulb moments, *ahas*, or discoveries about yourself, others, the world.

9. **Themes to Conclusions**: To stretch short themes into statements or conclusions, see chapter 7.

TOUR CLOSING

~Communicate: Chapter 9~

Express or receive thoughts and/or emotions by looking, reading, listening, writing, speaking, making, singing, dancing, pretending, and so on.

1. **Say Something**: After the tour, invite participants to "Say Something" learned, heard, or felt that stood out. Also called "Tell One Thing" (TOT).

2. **One-Liners**: Take a role (something or someone inside or outside the work) and say a sentence or phrase in that role. *Example:* "I am ____, and I think/feel ____ because _____."

3. **Show Me**: Ask participants to "show with your face or posture (body shape) how this art feels (or a figure in the art)." Follow with asking for one-liners that begin with "I feel _____ because _____," or variations.

4. **Fast Facts**: Invite participants to use frames: "I learned . . . ," "I felt . . . ," *or* "Something I thought was important or interesting is ____ because ___."

5. **Make Thinking Visible**: Sketch, mind map, or web the artwork or experience.

6. **Show You Know**: Think aloud, sketch, or pantomime the work's message or key aspects/moments.

7. **Pass and Pretend**: Coach participants to use pantomime (no words). Pass around a scarf to designate who is IT. IT then mimes something in the artwork (e.g., emotion, action, person), and audience describes what they're seeing until a conclusion is reached. *Example:* "I see ____, so _____" ("pointed toe, so this could be the tightrope walker").

8. **Freeze**: Take pose of figure and show emotions in the moment.

9. **On the Scene**: Give a two-sentence report about the tour like you're a television reporter.

10. **Write On!**: See QR 9.2 for an alphabetized list of writing forms, from ads to warnings.

11. **Poem Patterns**: See QR 9.3 and 9.4 for over a dozen structures and performance ideas.

12. **Creative Questions**: Brainstorm a list of questions that relate to the object, and start with: "What if . . ." "How might . . ." "Suppose that . . ." "It would be different if . . ."

13. **SCAMPER**: Invite participants to substitute, combine, adapt/add to, modify (minimize or maximize), put to new use, eliminate, and/or reverse concepts in an object. Example: "What could be made larger in this piece and how would that change things?"

References: Brown, 2023, 1/19 and 2022, 5/04; Cornett, 2015 and 2010; Murawski, 2012, 2013, and 2016; Project Zero; Tishman, 2017; VUE, 2009; Yenawine, 2013.

Videos: artful thinking; https://www.youtube.com/watch?v=jI34WTEI0Yw.

Appendix B1

TOUR OUTLINE: INVESTIGATING ART IN PICTURE BOOKS

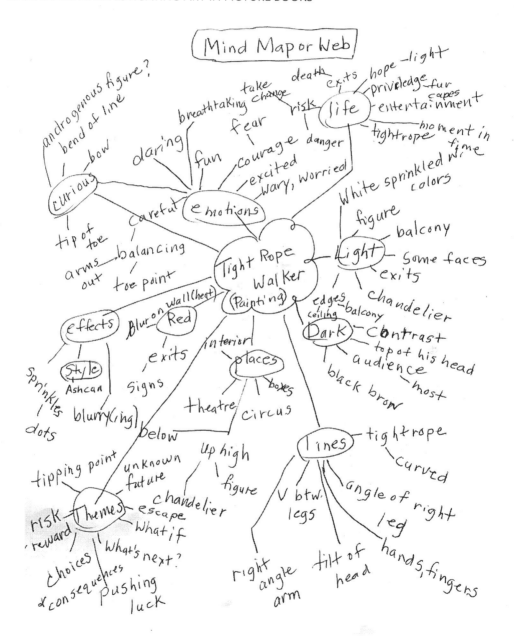

(Based on outline from Molly Flasche, Columbus Museum of Art)

Big Idea: Use picture books to initiate thinking and have conversations about artworks.

Audience: Students, grades 2 through 5.

Time: 50 minutes.

Rationale: Why use picture books?

Picture books provide rich visual learning experiences that lay groundwork for decoding patterns in images (colors, lines, shapes) used to understand artworks and print materials. Making sense of illustrations in picture books is a perfect bridge for looking at art in museums because both require creative thinking: collecting and connecting ideas and concluding what's most important and why. This parallels the reading process, which targets comprehension of word meanings in varying contexts.

Tour Outcomes: During the tour students will . . .

1. Observe and find details and patterns in artworks.
2. Listen and talk about discoveries in picture book art.
3. Connect personal experiences and prior knowledge.
4. Participate in conversations about common features between artworks and picture book art.
5. Make interpretations about meanings in art.

Links to Artworks:

Each picture book is a *bridge* to artworks. Four bridges for this tour are:

1. Looking purposefully to discover details in context.
2. Using different points of view.
3. Determining what is important.
4. Fostering imaginative thinking about what-ifs.

Note: Creating meaning is central to all tours and involves engaging students with open questions and encouraging reflection to determine significant messages in art.

Before the Tour:

1. Practice reading aloud as you hold the book so viewers can see the art.
2. Review strategies for stimulating conversation. See Quick Reference 7.5.

Beginning:

- Sit in a circle around the artwork.
- Ask students to look at art on book cover and describe what's going on.
- Read the title and names of the author and illustrator.
- Ask what picture books and art museums have in common.
- Challenge students to connect discoveries in the picture book to artwork.
- Read aloud the book, integrating questions that engage students in purposeful looking, connecting to personal experiences, and making meaning. Pause for comments.
- Incorporate bridges in the conversation as you read.

Development: Link or bridge to artwork.

Use "bridges" appropriate for connecting the book to the artwork.

- Use questions and prompts for conversations that stimulate investigation.
- Connect to prior knowledge, interests, and experiences, and let students shape the conversation.
- Choose collect-connect-conclude strategies to promote meaning-making.
- Select another work of art.

Closing: Invite students to . . .

- Tell about an artwork they liked and why.
- Pick an artwork to talk about with a friend.
- Tell something that surprised them about picture books and artwork.
- Finish this sentence: "An important idea I discovered was _____."

Connect these picture books and artworks using these four bridges:

1. Looking purposely to see details in context:
   Look Book
2. Imaginative thinking: thinking about what-ifs:
   Not a Box
   Not a Stick
   The Perfect Square
   The Squiggle
3. Point of view or multiple perspectives:
   Duck! Rabbit!
   Round Trip
   Seven Blind Mice
   Yo Yes
   They Saw a Cat
4. Interpreting or determining important messages:
   Ish
   A Ball for Daisy
   Square
   Matthew's Dream

Appendix B2

Tour Theme: *From Seen to Unseen to Understand*
Tour Length: 20–30 minutes
Audience: Adults/Young Adults
Art Stop: Gallery 204:
Museum Label: Everett Shinn (1876–1953), American, TIGHTROPE WALKER, 1924, Oil on canvas, 23½" x 18". Museum purchase with funds from James F. Dicke Family/E. Jeanette Myers Fund, 1998.7.
Description: In this interactive tour, visitors will be invited to *collect* details, engage in conversation to *connect* ideas, and create personal interpretations that lead to insights and a sense of enjoyment.

Goals: Participants will make sense of art using the Creative Inquiry Process (CIP):

1. *Collect* information (**look/see/think/feel/know** using all senses.
2. *Connect* by sorting ideas and finding relationships **(think)**.
3. Share *conclusions*: interpretations about the seen and unseen in art **(know)**.
4. *Critique* using criteria: supported by evidence, importance, beauty (pleasing).

Materials: Map, iPad photos, Art Elements, Fact Cards, Shinn book photos: *The Docks, Disappointments of the Ashcan* (Bellows); *Hippodrome, Conductor's Pit.*

INTRODUCTION

Folding stools. Map.
Meet and Greet: Names. Museum history (1927); rotunda (1997): daytonartinstitute.org/about/museum-history. Offer map. Explain my role.
Assess: First-timers? Interests/needs? (Forecast how they'll be addressed.) Offer stools. Remind to stay arm's length from art, silence phones, no flash photos.
Tour title/theme: *From Seen to Unseen to Understand.*
Advanced Organizer: The FOCUS painting is in American Gallery #204. Once we arrive, you'll have time to survey the gallery and get oriented. When everyone seems ready to start, I'll raise my hand.

Questions?

DEVELOPMENT STRATEGIES

Creative Process Focus Thinking: *Challenge, Collect, Connect, Conclude*

Challenge

Ask, "Have you ever wondered why a piece of art is considered important?" Prompt for thoughts. Relate "understanding" to "liking" art.

Explain goal is work together to understand art using the same thinking used to read books. As with books, it takes time to get a sense of the whole artwork (versus glancing at first page of book). Ask, "How is time involved in understanding music?"

Explain *truths* or *big ideas* are often hidden, so it takes purposeful looking to uncover *seen* and *unseen* meanings or interpretations. This is a conversational tour based on the "two heads" method, which can be fun. The first step is to observe like a detective. Concentrate on clues, not answers. And keep in mind there aren't any right answers.

Collect Information

Purposeful looking with ironwork, then proceed to gallery. After survey, debrief and focus on Shinn painting:

- One to three minutes: Look up and down, side to side, part to whole. Inventory the whole composition (background, mid, foreground).
- Coach: Squint to see what stands out. Try different distances: Step back. Move in closer. Make fist telescope. Use other senses to collect: sounds, smells, touch, taste.
- Describe what you're seeing. Offer frame: "I see . . ." *or*, "Choose ideas and turn and talk . . ."
- Encourage piggybacking on ideas of others.
- Ask, "What in the painting stands out? Why?" *Prompts:* See Elements and Principles (colors, shapes, lines, emphasis, space, foreground/background, pattern, repetition, etc.).
- Ask, "What else?" Keep looking: *The more you look, the more you see, and the more you see, the more you know* (receive/perceive).
- Option: Use Count F's poster or a two-way drawing to practice purposeful looking.

Connect

Group/sort ideas (think): Ask about . . .

- ICI: Interesting? Curious? Important?
- Narrative: What seems to be going on? What's the story?
- Try different perspectives (POVs). Viewer? Audience? Figure?
- What emotions does the painting express or trigger?

Conclude

(Look-See-Think/Feel-Know)

- Design elements: Repetition? Variety? Use of space? Emphasis? (focal point).
- Implied? Think about hidden (unseen). Background: What relationships are suggested? (e.g., between audience and figure).
- Feelings/reactions (to what?).
- What does it seem to be about?

Notes

Repeat Theme

From Seen and Unseen: Visible and Invisible (or hidden)

- Focus on white (the absence of color; not in color family). Spectrum acronym: ROYGBIV.
- What does the emphasis on white make you think? Feel? Other prominent colors? (contrast, thoughts, emotions).
- Look again: What are you noticing about line? ("tight"? rope) What is going on? *Prompts:* tension, toe, arms, head, etc.

- Symbols: (colors: white), shapes, lines, objects (tightrope?); other symbols?
- Metaphors: ___ looks like ____. This reminds me of _____. *Sentence Frames:* The white figure looks like _____. The chandelier is _____. The arched exit reminds me of ___. Walking a tightrope is like ____.

FEELINGS, THOUGHTS, RELATIONSHIPS, QUESTIONS AND PROMPTS

- Viewpoint: Who is the viewer? (eye-level with figure). What does the artist do to make you think that? What's the effect on you?
- Sensations or emotions: What words describe how the figure appears to feel? How does this painting make you feel? What emotions do you associate with this painting?
- Mood: What does the artist do to suggest mood? *Frame:* The mood of this painting is ____.
- One-liner: Take POV of audience member or figure. Complete this sentence: "I'm thinking ___, and I'm feeling _____."

Transition

So far, you have talked about what is seen and what's implied (unseen), like the mood, relationships, and possible meanings. *It's hard to like what you don't understand, but the goal is to understand the painting, not like it.*

- Information about the artist and his intentions can be a window into understanding (meaning, big ideas about humanity and life). I don't have quotes from Shinn about this painting, but I have some facts. Instead of telling … let's do Reader's Theater. **Artist Information**: https://americanart.si.edu/artist/everett-shinn-4430.

TOUR CLOSING

Key points: To understand this painting, we first **collected** information, described what is *seen* and **connected** ideas into categories, like *unseen* or implied relationships and mood. Information about the art and artist was then shared.

Q: How does content information affect your thoughts about this painting? (e.g., dark and light, subject matter, composition, symbols).

~What's seems most important?

~What might this work have to say about people, life, or the world? Think about overall thoughts and feelings and finish the sentence: "The overall message of this painting is____."

~Think of a title or headline (Turn and Talk). Ideas: daredevil, death-defying, death, ghostly, life as a balancing act; "Ghostly figure risks life as audience watches." Talk with partner or group. Invite sharing.

Wrap-Up

"Together we went from **LOOKING** to **SEEING** to **THINKING/FEELING** about the **UNSEEN** (e.g., implied mood and emotions). The goal was to **KNOW**: to understand what the art is about. The Creative Inquiry Process (CIP) was used to make sense. Instead of reading words, phrases, and sentences, we used the 'alphabet' of art (elements and principles) to arrive at understanding."

"Questions? TOT? What would you tell a friend about this experience? Next month's object is _____. Please come back!"

Strategy Options: See Museum Guide Tool Kit.

Index

Note: Page references for figures and Quick References are italicized.

connections/ing; creative inquiry process (CIP), thinking/backbone of tour; visual art elements

Causey, Adera, 11, 25, 79, 136

challenge: clear goals and expectations, 47–48; example strategies, 53–57, 64; overview, 125; role in understanding/CIP, 12, 23, 32, 47; what, why, how, 45, 64. *See also* expectations; forecasting/frontloading and previewing; goals

chaperones, roles of, 12

cheat card, 75

choice and control, visitor: rationale and strategies, 31, 33, 70. *See also* empowering visitors and guests; motivation to learn

Cincinnati Art Museum, 11, 23, 38, 42, 59, 74, 122

CIP thinking. *See* creative inquiry process (CIP)

climate/atmosphere, tour, 30. *See also* context; creative inquiry process (CIP)

cloze strategy: examples and rationale, 21, 23, 52

clues: to making sense, 53, 56. *See also* collecting to make meaning; creative inquiry process (CIP)

coaching, 12, 17, 28, 114. *See also* creative inquiry process (CIP); guiding strategies/best practices; introduction, development, closing (IDC); Museum Guide Tool Kit; tours, guided

collect-connect-conclude, 4, 12, 98. *See also* creative inquiry process (CIP), key phases/ thinking processes

collecting to make meaning: collection categories, 63, 68, 80; defined, 63–70; examples, 19, 22, 80; five senses, 64–65; overview, 125; reasons, 64; strategies to collect, 63, 80; time during tour, 65; vignette, 71–74. *See also* categories; creative inquiry process (CIP), key phases/thinking processes; details; looking; observation

Columbus Museum of Art, 16

comfort: defined, 31; make the unfamiliar familiar, 9; types and roles of, 5, 9, 22, 31; welcome and include, 27. *See also* welcoming strategies

communicate/communication: arts as first communication, 127; defined, 125; examples, 20–21, 23; fourth R, 128; history of, 127; invisible and visible thoughts and feelings, 66; literacy, 126; name versus explain, 69; phase of CIP, 125–26; processes, 126;

receive and express ideas/thoughts and feelings/emotions, 63–68, 126; research and technology, 130–31; research on arts-based, 127–28; show you know, 20–21. *See also* *Adapting for Differences*, inclusive language; language arts; show you know/make thinking visible

conclude, 93

concluding as making sense: connecting, role of, 98; defined, 93, 97; during conversations, 99, 102; overview in CIP, 126; speculate, role of, 98; summary of process, 98. *See also* conversation(s), meaningful, features of; creative inquiry process (CIP), thinking/backbone of tour; insight; inspiration; interpretations; questions/questioning strategies

conclusion(s): as important meanings/core content, 94; coaching for, 23, 93–95; creating, 57, 64, 94–95,102; criteria for judging, 111–12; defined, 93, 96; examples, 96, 104, 112; grounded, valid, 98; key questions, 94–95, 99; rash vs. valid features, 72, 92, 113; strategy round up/ meaning-oriented questions, 98–99; student conclusions, 135. *See also* anchoring with facts/evidence; critique; inference(s), versus interpretations/conclusions; interpretations; meaning, unseen and seen; Museum Guide Tool Kit; show you know/make thinking visible; signs and symbols; theme(s); understand(ing); universal meaning, as messages and truths

confirmation bias, 113

connecting to create meaning: examining and connecting details in art/artifacts, 86, 102; examples, 35; house museum tour, 87–90; summary/round up, 64, 82, 126; what, why, how, 79–92. *See also* associations and relationship; categories; creative inquiry process (CIP); vignettes of tours

connections/ing: brain research, 80; knew to known (prior knowledge/experience), 32, 81, 94; meaningful, 80–84; objects to self, others, world, 81; personal, 72, 76, 81, 89; strategies/questions, 82–84. *See also* categories

content and process: sources, 38; tours, 4, 5, 38

context: context for/setting stage, 29, 64; defined, 29; overview, 125; rationale for relaxed atmosphere, 29–30, 64, 87; visitor orientation, 30. *See also* comfort; creative inquiry process (CIP); tour introduction/beginning; vignettes of tours

conversation(s): casual, 48, 102; collaborative, 8, 17, 71; comfort, role of, 1; curiosity and interest, roles of, 1, 48–50, 100; defined, 30; facilitating meaningful, 1, 10, 12, 17, 28, 32, *99–105* ; inquiry-based, 22, *100*; meaningful, features of, *101*; stoppers, 34; threading strategy, 34; tracking strategy, 101–2, 114; troubleshooting, 105; types and goals, 1, 8, 17, 93, 102. *See also* creative inquiry process (CIP); empathy; engagement; inquiry; tour introduction/beginning

conversational tours: benefits, 75; examples, 5; guidelines for facilitating, 91, 104–5. *See also* conversation(s); guiding strategies/best practices; Museum Guide Tool Kit; vignettes of tours

creative/creativity: as meaning making/problem solving thinking, 22, 48; definition and nature of thinking, 1, 15, 21–22; history, 21; traits, 15; truths and myths, 22

creative inquiry process (CIP): as creating meaning, 94; as instinct, 17; CIP raps, 128, 130; dissonance and unease, 102; importance of, 16, 93; key phases/thinking processes, 16, 64; overview of what, why, how, 5, 15–28, 64, 94, 125–26; role in tour IDC, 29; thinking/backbone of tour, 21; ways to engage and coach, 2, 16; writing example, 28. *See also* challenge; collect-connect-conclude; communicate/communication; context; critique; experimenting; inquiry; Museum Guide Tool Kit; observation; understand(ing); vignettes of tours

creating meaning: brain/thinking processes, 66. *See also* creative inquiry process (CIP), thinking/backbone of tour; make meaning versus take meaning

critique: coaching for, 23; critiquing conclusions, 111; definition, 109; practice with tour conclusions, 112; purposes, 109; *Quick Critique Challenge* strategy, *111*; thinking processes, 109; tracking strategy, 113; types, examples, 110–11; using CIPs, 109; what, why, how to, 109, 112–13

curiosity: benefits, 48–49; cons, 50; defined, 49; hooks, 48, 53, 58–59; versus interest, 49–50; what, why, how, 47–50. *See also* engagement; motivation to learn

Dayton Art Institute, 7, 59, 71, 91, 93, 136, 147, 151

debriefing: after tour, 69; to boost conversation, 69. *See also* anchoring with facts/evidence; questions/questioning strategies

describe: definition, 110; examples, 110

descriptive feedback: benefits, 48; examples, 23, 114–15, 117; solicited from visitors, 118; versus praise, 23

details: CIP rap, 128; connecting to make sense, 79; important (salient), 6, 33, 79, 113, 160; isolated, 79; seeing and coaching, 18, 88, 102; visible, 79. *See also* creative inquiry process (CIP), key phases/thinking processes; visual art elements; visual information

disability(ies) etiquette. *See Adapting for Differences*

discomfort with the unknown: core feature, 47. *See also* conversation(s); creative inquiry process (CIP); investigation

discovery process: benefits, 47; curiosity and interest, effects of, 49; defined, 4, 21, 25, 32. *See also* creative inquiry process (CIP); investigation

diversity, types of. *See Adapting for Differences*

docent: defined, 2

dopamine, 48

emotions, feelings and sensations, roles in creating meaning, 100

empathy, 75, 99, 101. *See also* museum guide

empowering visitors and guests: rationale for, 16, 31; strategies, 32; zone of proximal development, 32. *See also* guiding strategies/best practices; motivation to learn; Museum Guide Tool Kit; scaffolding strategy

engagement: comfort and enjoyment (fun), 32; in CIP, 5; long and short term, 49; multisensory, 24; versus entertainment, 10; visitor, 3

enthusiasm: etymology of, 33; examples, 21, 33, 42, 44, 104, 113, 137, 148. *See also* guiding strategies/best practices; museum guide; tour introduction/beginning

Estep, Janet, 65

eureka. *See insight*

evaluate. *See assess(ment); judge/evaluate*

every person responds (EPR): purpose and strategies, 136, 153. *See also* vignettes of tours

evidence: defined, 109; importance of, 110. *See also* anchoring with facts/evidence; conclusion(s); critique; facts

expectations: role in tour success, 32, 47

experimenting: during creative inquiry, 12, 18–19, 64, 67, 96, 128, 132, 155–56; types of, 92

exploratory behavior, 49. *See also* creative inquiry process (CIP); curiosity; interest; motivation to learn

facts: drip feed, 75; examples, 26, 102–3; fishing for, 23; five facts, 38; relevant information, 18, 52, 56, 87–90, 119; storytelling with, 118–22. *See also* information dump

feedback, roles and examples, 119. *See also* descriptive feedback

Flasche, Molly, 59, 134, 141

flow state: definition and examples, 19

folding stools, 6, 102

forecasting/frontloading and previewing: benefits, 33, 48; goals and tour process, 48. *See also* expectations

form versus content, 94

fun: importance of, 5, 17, 32, 34, 80

fun facts strategy, 17, 23

gender neutral. *See Adapting for Differences*, inclusive language

generalizations. *See* conclusion(s)

gestalt, 48

go bag, 75, 105. *See also* Museum Guide Tool Kit

goals: example performance goals (learning objectives), 1, 15, 29, 63, 79, 93, 109, 125; learning and enjoyment, 12, 17; overall tour, 9, 33. *See* also expectations; forecasting/ frontloading and previewing

guide: defined, 2; dispositions and practices, 45, *101*; self-assessment, 106, 114–15; unique styles, 118. *See also* docent; interpreters, museum; museum guide

guided tours: overview, 65; structure, 65. *See also* goals; introduction, development, closing (IDC); Museum Guide Tool Kit; tours, guided, three-part structures/phases

guiding strategies/best practices, 4; coaching CIP, 22–23; every person responds (EPR), examples, 136; how to identify, 17; ice breakers, examples, 101; key questions, 22–23; look to see, think, feel and know, 100; meet and greet, 4, 42; pair share, examples, 69, 104, 136, 153, 159; paraphrasing, examples, 12, 15, 25, 27, 69, 91, 105, 143, 144; purposes and examples, 17; storyteller/telling, examples, 118–22;

wait time, examples, 25, 27, 70, 75. *See also* context; creative inquiry process (CIP); critique; introduction, development, closing (IDC); looking; Museum Guide Tool Kit; questions/questioning strategies; sentence starters/frames; show you know/ make thinking visible; strategic looking; tours, guided; tour introduction/beginning; vignettes of tours

Gullah Geechee: history, 121; language, 122

Hall, Pam, 35

Hanes, Terry, 11, 122

Hoffman, Rick, 151

humor: source and nature of, 34, 57; types and benefits, 34; uses, 37, 43, 96, 104, 138. *See also* aha! to ha-ha

imagine: defined, 47; possibilities, 19, 22, 47

importance/significance: determining, 65, 94, 100, 112

incubate: how to, 99; in creative process, 20; in insight, 96

inference(s), versus interpretations/ conclusions, 98

information dump, 10, 26

inquiry: defined, 4, 15; examples, 9; purposes, 9. *See also* conversation(s), collaborative; creative inquiry process (CIP)

insight: art attack, 97; defined, 4, 96; eureka, origins and moments, 65, 96; examples, 21; experiments on chimps, 96; fun, 5; inspiration for, 93, 95–97; light bulb moment, 96; sudden understanding, 65; surprise, awe and wonder, 5, 97. *See also* concluding as making sense; inspiration; understand(ing)

inspiration: coaching dispositions and thinking, 97, 100; process, 96–97, 107. *See also* conclusion(s); insight

interest: defined, 47; importance, 23, 28, 45, 48–49, 80, 116. *See also* curiosity

interpret: defined, 110, 112

interpretations: in critique, 109–10; in forming conclusions, 99; versus inferences, 93, 16. *See also* conclusion(s); theme(s); understand(ing)

interpreters, museum, 2, 18, 26, 118

introduction, development, closing (IDC): definition and examples: 5, 18–21, 29, 38, 40, 123; strategies in guide tool kit, 153–60.

paraphrasing strategy, 25

patterns. *See* categories

Penn Center, National Historic Landmark, 118

personal knowledge/connections: and artifacts, 86; importance of, 5, 23, 32; in generating conclusions, 100. *See also* creative inquiry process (CIP)

picture book: example art tour, 133–35; tour plan, 161–62

planning. *See* tours, guided, planning CIP tours; tours, guided, planning template

poem patterns, example, 74

point of view (POV), perspective: alternative/different views, 70–71, 104; examples, 12, 54, 100; strategies to stretch, 70–71, 92. *See also* looking; visual informationpost tour, 115

problem solving process. *See* creative inquiry process (CIP)

progress checks, 43. *See also Adapting for Differences*, read the room assessment

purposeful looking, 6

puzzle, figure out, problem solve, 4, 48, 80. *See also* creative inquiry process (CIP)

questions/questioning strategies: important, 23–24; meaning-oriented, 19, 22–24, 51–57, 59, 70, 82–83, 90, 98–99, 114; open versus closed, 17, 24; process-oriented, examples, 82, 114; what to avoid, 25; what, why, how, 24–25. *See also* vignettes of tours

quotes, artist, 24, 52, 56, 57

racism, ameliorating tools, 106

rapport, 33

reason(ing), role in concluding. *See* concluding as making sense

recap, strategy, 104

relationships. *See* categories

respect(ful). *See Adapting for Differences*; guiding strategies/best practices

responding to answers: active listening, 25; asking follow ups, 25; paraphrasing, 25; pass option, 25; piggybacking, 25, 52, 134

Rindsberg, Helen, 74

risk-taking: curiosity and interest, roles of, 49; defined, 30; preparing for, 29–30; role in CIP, 29, 42. *See also* comfort; conversation(s); guiding strategies/best practices; tour introduction/beginning

Rock and Roll Hall of Fame, 3; mission, 3

roving docent, 59

rules and etiquette, museum, 35

scaffolding strategy, 15, 23, 94

scavenger hunts as problems, 26

seeing isn't knowing, 80

sentence starters/frames: examples, 59, 69, 70, 83, 95, 98, 125, 143, 157–58. *See also* gestalt; Museum Guide Tool Kit, curiosity hooks

show you know/make thinking visible: arts response options, 128–33; captions, headlines, titles, 57, 99; examples, 104, 128–33; songs and poems, 20, 128, 130

sign language, 144, 41, 136

significance or importance, determining, 50, 101

signs and symbols, 83

sorts. *See* categories

spatter vision, 71. *See also* point of view (POV) perspective

speculate: defined, 95, 98

stereotyping and bias examples, 123; sources of information, 124

Stock, Linda, 42

strategic looking: coaching, 69, 72; defined, 66; motivation for, 80; process and timing, 65; purposeful, 66; purposes, 63–64, 66; strategies, 67–69, 72; tips for, 70. *See also* looking

strategy(ies): defined, 17; repertoire, 10. *See also* guiding strategies/best practices; Museum Guide Tool Kit

surface versus deep thinking/meaning, 65

synthesize: defined, 93; to create conclusions, 95; versus summarize, 95

tell one thing (TOT) strategy, 23

text: defined, 93. *See also* communicate/communication

theme(s): as big ideas, 61, 94; as big picture truths, 94, 104; as steppingstones to conclusions, 94–95; deep meanings, 50, 57; defined, 50, 61, 93; identifying, 50, 57; in artforms, examples, 94; in tours, examples, 50–51, 73, 5, 10, 87–90, 96, 104, 119; overarching and unifying, 94; topics/concepts versus statements, 50, 93, 96; universal messages/important ideas, 50, 22, 36, 93. *See also* conclusion(s); interpretations; understand(ing); universal meaning(s); vignettes of tours

think aloud strategy, 99

thinking: about thinking, 15; back and forth, 17; deep and surface, 16. *See also* creative inquiry process (CIP)

thinking frames: cause-effect, 84; compare-contrast, 83; defined, 83; problem-solution, 84; sequence, 84; similes, metaphors, 84; thinking, 91. *See also* sentence starters/frames

thoughts and feelings, 63

tour closing: ending tour, 117–18; wrap up, *4, 114–17,* 158–60. *See also* introduction, development, closing (IDC); vignettes of tours

tour development: effective, 114; strategies, 138, 154–58. *See also* introduction, development, closing (IDC); vignettes of tours

tour introduction/beginning: advice from guides, 42; effective, 114; first five minutes, 32–33, 42–43, 138, 154, 163; strategy checklist, *33*. *See also* introduction, development, closing (IDC); vignettes of tours

tours, guided: defined, 15, 115; example plans, 38–40, *161–65* ; goals, 114; live guides, values of, 3, 81; planning CIP tours, 114; planning template, 40–41, 29, *39,* 52; pre-tour gathering information, 41, 114; pre-tour packets, 41; steps to plan theme-based, 117; three-part structures/phases (IDC), 5, 18–21, 38–39, 114–15, 123; transformative, 10, 81. *See also* goals; theme(s); vignettes of tours; web/webbing

transforming ideas and feelings: examples using art forms, 127; importance, 127

transitions: as strategies, 17, 114, 117; introductory, 116; next stop, 116, 199; planned, *41*; purposes and forms, *115*; theme-based, 117; timing and presentation, 117; to make meaning, 116

troubleshooting: conversation strategies, 105; group management, 141–43; Nudity 101, 145–46; overview, 141–46; sensitive topics, 143; sign language, 144. *See also Adapting for Differences; Advice from Museum Guides;* Museum Guide Tool Kit, curiosity hooks; tour introduction/beginning

understand(ing): big ideas, 9, 50, 158, 164; comprehension, 80, 161; constructing meaning, 17, 81, 127; defined, 4; examples, importance of, 4, 32; insight, 9; nature of and types, 9; thinking beyond ourselves, 35, 50, 90, 97, 114, 126; underpinnings, 9, 80–81; unifying parts and wholes, 81, 95,

156. *See also* aha! moment; creative inquiry process (CIP); conclusion(s); connections/ing; expectations; interpretations; understand(ing); theme(s)

universal meaning(s): as messages and truths, 23, 94–95, 98, 100–101, 112, 138, 161, 126; coaching for, 55, 94–95, 99; importance, 94, 50. *See also* conclusion(s); theme(s)

validating ideas, 50, 102, 113. *See also* anchoring with facts/evidence; critique

viewfinders, 71

vignettes of tours: 1905 Wright Flyer (Charles/history), 18–21; Alison Saar (Miguel/sculpture), 72–74; art of picture books (Catori/picture books), 133–35; creative inquiry into art (Nick/art), 5–8; defined, 4; Fort Ancient (Pam/outdoor), 35–38; JMV House Museum (Brantley), 85–90; Kandinsky Public Art Chat (Hazel), 102–4; Toulouse Lautrec (Clara/art), 52–57; York Bailey Museum, Penn Center (Marie/history), 118–22. *See also* introduction, development, closing (IDC); tours, guided

visible and invisible thinking/ideas, 6, 104; as clues to meaning, 65; brain research, 64; collecting, key processes, 63, 66; surface level, 65; types/categories, 67, 81. *See also* strategic looking

visitors and guests: as curious companions, 75; takeovers, 105

visual art elements: composition/design, 68; defined, *68*

visual information: brain processing, 77; categories for collecting, 67; sources, 67. *See also* visible and invisible thinking/ideas, surface level

web/webbing: categories for, 29, *39,* 52, 63; defined, 39; examples, *52. See also* tours, guided, planning CIP tours; tours, guided, planning template

welcoming strategies: comfort with self, 34; face and body language, 33; guide behavior, 34; humor, 34, 37; what you say, 34. *See also* fun; humor

what if thinking, 64

Witherell, Wayne, 151

word boxes, 2, 4, 28

Wright Brothers National Memorial Museum, 18

About the Author

Claudia E. Cornett has been a docent for over twenty years, and she is currently a museum guide and history interpreter at two museums.

After earning a PhD in curriculum and instruction and community education from Miami University, she joined the faculty of Wittenberg University and taught courses on communication and arts integration for over two decades. Two of her previous textbooks are *Creating Meaning through Literature and the Arts* and *Comprehension First: Inquiry into Big Ideas Using Important Questions*. During a wide-ranging consulting career, Claudia has presented hundreds of keynotes and professional development programs for school districts and arts organizations throughout the United States and Europe, and in Canada and Mexico.

Her interest in applying creative approaches to museum guide work is rooted in a commitment to helping people create personal meaning and experience the joy of insight.